THOSE
TURBULENT
SONS OF
FREEDOM

ETHAN ALLEN'S
GREEN MOUNTAIN BOYS AND
THE AMERICAN REVOLUTION

CHRISTOPHER S. WREN

Simon & Schuster
NEW YORK   LONDON   TORONTO   SYDNEY   NEW DELHI

Simon & Schuster
1230 Avenue of the Americas
New York, NY 10020

Copyright © 2018 by Christopher S. Wren

Endpapers from *The American Military Pocket Atlas*, 1776. Printed for R. Sayer
and J. Bennet, map and print-sellers, London.

First Simon & Schuster hardcover edition May 2018

SIMON & SCHUSTER and colophon are registered trademarks
of Simon & Schuster, Inc.

For information about special discounts for bulk purchases, please contact
Simon & Schuster Special Sales at 1-866-506-1949
or business@simonandschuster.com.

The Simon & Schuster Speakers Bureau can bring authors to your
live event. For more information or to book an event, contact the
Simon & Schuster Speakers Bureau at 1-866-248-3049
or visit our website at www.simonspeakers.com.

Interior design by Paul Dippolito

Manufactured in the United States of America

1   3   5   7   9   10   8   6   4   2

Library of Congress Cataloging-in-Publication Data

Names: Wren, Christopher S. (Christopher Sale), 1936-
Title: Those turbulent sons of freedom : Ethan Allen's Green Mountain boys
and the American Revolution / Christopher S. Wren.
Description: New York : Simon & Schuster, 2018. | Includes bibliographical
references and index.
Identifiers: LCCN 2017053023 (print) | LCCN 2017056325 (ebook) |
ISBN 9781439110119 (ebook) | ISBN 9781416599555 (hardback) |
ISBN 9781416599562 (trade paperback)
Subjects: LCSH: Allen, Ethan, 1738-1789. | Vermont--History--To 1791. |
Vermont--Militia. | Ticonderoga (N.Y.)--History--Revolution, 1775-1783. |
United States--History--Revolution, 1775-1783--Regimental histories. |
BISAC: HISTORY / United States / Revolutionary Period (1775-1800). |
HISTORY / United States / State & Local / New England (CT, MA, ME, NH, RI,
VT). | BIOGRAPHY & AUTOBIOGRAPHY / Historical.
Classification: LCC E263.V5 (ebook) | LCC E263.V5 W74 2018 (print) |
DDC 973.3/443--dc23
LC record available at https://lccn.loc.gov/2017053023

ISBN 978-1-4165-9955-5
ISBN 978-1-4391-1011-9 (ebook)

-CONTENTS-

-PREFACE-

They called themselves Green Mountain Boys and George Washington did not trust them. He wanted their leader detained for interrogation. The other colonies balked at letting them join the United States of America. Britain plotted to exploit their discontent and cajole them back under the Crown.

Some of the harshest combat in the American Revolution fell to the homesteaders who settled New England's northern frontier. Defending shaky titles to the land they cleared, they made their own rules to create an independent republic called Vermont.

Insubordination flowed through the blood of these Green Mountain Boys and their kin. Driven by self-interest more than patriotism, they waged their own wars for independence, first against the neighboring colony of New York, which laid claim to their homes, and then against King George III in an insurgency across a boundless expanse of wilderness.

Their disrespect of authority became a signature American trait that continues to manifest itself today. Choosing officers who led by example rather than rank, those turbulent sons of freedom, as one of Washington's toughest generals called them, excelled as light infantry rangers with tomahawks as well as muskets, which the best could fire as rapidly as three rounds per minute.

The skirmish they started in this insignificant corner of the world, from London's perspective, would become a thread to unravel the tapestry of the ascendant British Empire, which had grown adept at ruling over restive subjects as far afield as India, French-speaking Canada, the Caribbean, and countless islands acquired in European wars and kept in thrall by redcoats and the Royal Navy. Missionaries were sent forth to propagate the gospel according to the Church of England.

But this uprising in North America was launched by Yankee cousins at a distance who shared the same language, habits, and customs, even as they fussed about unequal trade and taxation without representation (unlike the loyal emigrants of Newfoundland and Nova Scotia). They offered Britain a wealth of valuable raw resources from ship masts to potash and animal pelts, not to mention a dumping ground for convicts and other undesirables exiled to America.

The hapless General Johnny Burgoyne was undone by what he called "the most active and most rebellious race" in Vermont who would frustrate his plan to impose law and order on an unruly backwater of the British Empire. Vermont differed from not just England but also the American colonies, and couldn't hold a candle to civilized cities like Philadelphia and New York.

So here is what happened in this wild and neglected corner of the American Revolution, as told through a strapping trio of Green Mountain Boys with outlaw bounties on their heads—Ethan Allen, his second cousin Seth Warner, and their companion Justus Sherwood. Allen, a charismatic rogue, would lose command of his Green Mountain Boys, botch an invasion of Montreal, and be shipped overseas in chains for a public hanging. His cool-headed cousin, Seth Warner, would forge the raucous Green Mountain Boys into a disciplined force whose hit-and-run tactics honed in strategic retreats helped save a broken, diseased American army from annihilation. And their friend Justus Sherwood, who opted for law and order over anarchy, would become their worst enemy as a master spy for Britain.

Hindsight assures us that the American Revolution would succeed, but those who fought on both sides could not foretell the outcome. This is their story too.

THOSE
TURBULENT
SONS *OF*
FREEDOM

ONE

A Land Rush North

I t was the lure of cheap land that drew pioneers like Ethan Allen, Seth Warner, and Justus Sherwood to leave Connecticut in one of the first great migrations in colonial New England. The virgin wilderness of the New Hampshire Grants, as Vermont was once called, attracted farmers from across Connecticut, Massachusetts, and New York, where their fathers' fields had become unaffordable or parceled among too many sons.

Some were religious separatists rejecting the Calvinist dogmas and taxes imposed by established Protestant churches to follow the "new light" of a spiritual Great Awakening across New England. These pilgrim settlers brought their children and households on horseback through the woods from Massachusetts, following native trails too narrow for a cart.

What limited their numbers were the hardships of daily life on the northern frontier. Winters ran wicked cold, with blinding blizzards and avalanches of ice. Bloodsucking gnats and mosquitoes infested the humid summers. Rattlesnakes coiled among the rocks. Wolves stalked the shadows. Hacking a plot from such dense forest demanded backbreaking toil from dawn to dusk. And a screaming catamount, the fiercest predator, could vault a split-rail fence and destroy a homesteader's livestock and livelihood in seconds.

Misfits in colonial society, whether hell-raisers, fugitives, or down on their luck like Ethan Allen, found an outlet for their frustrations in the vast backcountry of the Grants, so named for several million acres that New Hampshire's colonial governor, Benning Wentworth, granted for settlement between 1749 and 1764. The Crown encouraged governors like Wentworth to attract immigrants by offering them land to clear and cultivate. Land in eighteenth-century America was wealth for the taking. In a colonial society without banks or negotiable credit, property was the route to social status in an ostensibly classless society. Speculators vied to buy and flip grants for profit. Where fortunes could be made, rascals and mischief followed.

The hierarchy of self-interest extended upward to Governor Wentworth, who grew rich on the commissions and fees he charged and the five hundred prime acres he reserved for himself in each township he created. He would charter and sell off nearly three million acres in 135 such townships, from the Connecticut River to Lake Champlain, until he ran out of land. The first he named after himself, Bennington.

Once the sun dropped below the rim of surrounding hills, Wentworth's paper townships plunged into pitch-blackness lit only by moonlight, the firefly flicker of campfires, and glowing cabin hearths.

The journey was best undertaken in late winter, when the trammeled snow stayed frozen enough to make travel easier, before the ice thawed into a springtime morass of mud.

Families who could afford them rode sleighs or pushed sleds up the frozen Connecticut River or Lake Champlain. They herded cattle and sheep through the valleys and foothills, passing up marginal tracts in expectation of better land ahead. Wives and children walked if there was no room in the oxcarts or sledges stuffed with farm and household implements.

The more intrepid sallied forth to claim and clear their land, building a hovel habitable enough for their families to join them after the next winter. The earliest homes in the New Hampshire Grants looked nothing like the tidy farms left behind in Connecticut or Massachusetts. Logs were felled and notched to frame a cabin. More logs, split and hewed, made a floor. Bark covered the roof. Sticks plastered with clay became walls. Axes and augers were used to build a table, benches, and bedsteads. A large rock flanked by smaller stones formed the fireplace. The huts filled with smoke and leaked with rain, and were occupied before they were habitable. In winter, hefty logs would be fed into the fire and kept ablaze, not just for warmth but also to keep away predators. Homesteaders slept on their unburned woodpiles, swaddled in animal pelts.

When the French and Indian War spilled into New England, its militias marched north to fight for the English king, hacking a road through the forests to Lake Champlain. The peace that followed France's surrender of Quebec in 1760 opened up the New Hampshire Grants as prime real estate. Veterans coming home from the war raved about fertile topsoil and trees so thick that it was hard to ride a horse among them. In the decade that followed Britain's treaty with France in 1763, the Grants swelled with nearly eighteen thousand new immigrants, including the children conceived during the long nights.

Ethan Allen was almost thirty-one years old when he fled to the New Hampshire Grants around 1769, trailing failures, beset by lawsuits, and in a boring marriage. He had been born in northwestern Connecticut on January 10, 1738, but when he was two, his father moved the family to Cornwall, a settlement that he helped start. Farmers toiled six days a week on the stony soil, coaxing out crops between pine stumps. Their wives spun clothes at home from local flax or wool. Families came together on Sunday to worship in an unheated meetinghouse, where Joseph Allen, a Church of England adherent, arranged for a preacher.

He wanted Ethan, the eldest of his eight children, to go to Yale, Connecticut's only college of higher learning, and scrimped to have him tutored by the local minister, a Yale alumnus. Joseph's sudden death in 1755 ended Ethan's formal education. A local tale remembered Ethan, at seventeen, standing on his father's grave, challenging him to reveal whether there was an afterlife. Ethan started early to dispute religious matters. He did not disbelieve in God, but didn't much like Him. He ridiculed the doctrines of original sin and the divinity of Jesus, taken as holy writ across New England.

Ethan was twenty-four when he married Mary Brownson, who may have been the only woman who would have him. His bride was devout and a half dozen years older, but she came dowered with some land that her father parceled out among his eleven children. She likely couldn't read or write, for she signed their wedding certificate with a cross. Mary would weary of her husband's zest for argument and his contempt for religion. Ethan may have chafed at his wife's piety. Though he would sire four daughters and a son with her, he contrived ways to be absent more often than not. With a family to feed, he quit farming to work a marginal iron mine and forge in Salisbury, Connecticut. He had a violent temper and was charged with assaulting a neighbor who bought his stake in the forge. Profanity got him accused of public blasphemy. He was later ordered out of Northampton, Massachusetts, where he tried to run a lead mine, after quarreling over religion in a tavern. His neighbors could not have been sorry to see him depart for the New Hampshire Grants.

Around 1769, Ethan Allen left his wife and three small children in the care of a brother in Massachusetts, and set out into the Grants beyond the Berkshire hills to join his cousin, Remember Baker, hunting deer and selling their hides. Baker had fought the French and Indians as a teenage ranger before settling in the Grants in 1764. Another cousin, Seth Warner, followed to explore the forest as an amateur botanist, collecting medicinal herbs for his father, the local doctor. Their companion Justus Sherwood arrived later in 1771.

As life grew better for the homesteaders, so did the good life for Governor Wentworth, whose ingenuity in skimming a profit from his land grants made him one of the richest men in New England. Wentworth's success was a source of envy for New York's lieutenant governor Cadwallader Colden, who deemed the unruly Grants less loyal to the Crown than New York, where Hudson River aristocrats followed the English custom of employing tenant sharecroppers to farm their estates. Homesteaders like Ethan Allen, Seth Warner, and Justus Sherwood expected to own what they tilled.

New England's towns skewed toward subversive republican notions, Colden noticed, while New York modeled its government on the English constitution. "Can it then be good policy," he mused, "to diminish the extent of jurisdiction in His Majesty's province of New York, to extend the power and influence of the others?"

So Colden claimed the same property on behalf of New York in April 1765, and ordered settlers in the New Hampshire Grants to pay New York a confirmation fee or face eviction. He sold off titles to 36,000 acres that Wentworth had already granted. The fees alone totaled more than $196,000, from which he pocketed $30,000—a fortune worth more than a million dollars today—until he ran out of the watermark stationery required for legal transactions under Britain's Stamp Act.

Colden knew that New York and New Hampshire's Grants were divided by more than overlapping claims of geography. In colonial America, Yorkers and Yankees were bred in the bone to mistrust each other as ardently as they disliked Virginians or Carolinians. Yorkers disparaged Yankees as vulgar and insolent, and thought their penchant for thrashing out differences in public verged on anarchy. Yankees were contemptuous of Yorkers as subservient and intolerant and feared having their farms swallowed up by New York's feudal system of baronial manors. Ethan Allen would turn their resentments to his advantage.

Governor Wentworth assured his customers that their deeds were legal. New York, he charged, had failed to populate a single township in the Grants. He was shoved out of office in 1767 after granting himself titles to another 65,000 acres—more than a hundred square miles. The Board of Trade and Plantations, which supervised colonial commerce from London, accused him of selling land more for private gain than public good, and replaced him with his nephew. Never mind, for Benning Wentworth, at the age of sixty-four, married his pretty housemaid, who was more than four decades younger. When he died six years later, she claimed his fortune.

In June 1770, lawsuits to eject nine titleholders from their farms around Bennington were bundled together for New York's highest court to decide. Ethan Allen was hired to gather proof of ownership for the lawyer defending their claims. He rode to New Hampshire's capital at Portsmouth, where he seized the chance to buy five hundred acres from Governor Wentworth in a promising new township, named New Haven after Connecticut's, in the foothills east of Lake Champlain. He paid twenty-five Spanish dollars—about five cents an acre.

New York's chancellor Robert Livingston heard the appeal of the New Hampshire titleholders in Albany's city hall on June 28, 1770. He ruled that the documents Ethan Allen provided were not legal and refused to let the jury look at them. His verdict rendered null and void every charter that Governor Wentworth had granted, and relegated titleholders to trespassers on their own farms.

Ethan Allen was advised to settle on the best terms he could, and loaned a horse and expense money to ride back to Bennington, where a surly crowd packed its Catamount Tavern. He exhorted them to fight the evictions. He knew as well as the settlers that they had no chance of surviving, much less prospering, in the Grants if New York took title to land they had cleared and planted. Allen, in effect, was declaring war on New York, organizing his followers into committees of vigilance around the Grants, with himself as their colonel. His captains included cousins Remember Baker and Seth Warner. The vigilantes called themselves "New Hampshire men," but when New York vilified them as "the Bennington mob," Allen embraced that name.

An early warning system evolved to stop New York from seizing land in the Grants. When New York authorities tried to evict a farmer from New Hampshire, Allen's vigilantes rode in to take back the property and mete out reprisals.

Benjamin Spencer, New York's magistrate in one such township, Clarendon, knew who the troublemakers were. "One Ethan Allen has brought from Connecticut twelve or fifteen of the most blackguard fellows he can get, double armed, in order to protect him," he reported. Unless the Bennington mob was stopped, he warned, "there had as good be an end of the government."

Ethan Allen's tactics did not scare New York's royalist governor, William Tryon, who had crushed an earlier frontier rebellion as governor of North Carolina. He threatened to drive Allen's malcontents in the Grants into the Green Mountains. "I conceive it good policy to lodge large tracts of land in the hands of gentlemen of weight and consideration," he declared, and helped himself to 32,000 acres in the New Hampshire Grants. "They will naturally farm out their lands to tenants; a method which will ever create subordination, and counterpoise in some measure the general leveling spirit that so much prevails in some of his Majesty's governments."

Ethan Allen gave his vigilantes the defiant name of Green Mountain Boys. On New Year's Day of 1772, they assembled at Seth Warner's homestead in Bennington, "firing about his house, etc., and drinking good success to Governor Wentworth and all his grants, and damning the Yorkers," according to an informer who heard that "they were enlisting men and putting each recruit under oath to be true in maintaining the New Hampshire Grants."

Governor Tryon boosted a reward for Ethan Allen's capture to £150, and £50 each for his cousins Remember Baker and Seth Warner. The price on Ethan's head did not constrain him. On a bet, he walked into a tavern in Albany, New York, ordered a bowl of potent punch, and handed his "wanted" poster to the landlord, then drained the punch and swaggered out unchallenged.

Tensions were running high when an armed posse from New York arrived on sleighs early one Sunday morning to capture Allen's cousin Remember Baker, and burn down his

cabin. They smashed in the door with axes. Baker's wife, Desire, tried to stop the abductors, who gashed her cheek and
elbow with a sword. Their twelve-year-old son was slashed
when he tried to protect his mother.

Baker, who had been asleep in the loft, jumped up naked
from his bed and fought back with his axe. Outnumbered, he
knocked out a board on his cabin roof and leapt into a snow-
drift too deep to escape. A swinging cutlass hacked off his
thumb. He was beaten senseless and tossed into a sleigh to
be hauled back to Albany. From Arlington and nearby Bennington, a score of Green Mountain Boys saddled up and
gave chase. The attackers, taking them for a larger force,
dumped Baker and fled back to New York.

John Munro, the New York magistrate who led the
failed raid, identified fourteen of the Green Mountain Boys,
among them Seth Warner and his friend Justus Sherwood,
and clapped bounties on their heads. The next day, Sherwood returned with Warner to get Baker's musket back.
Munro grabbed the bridle of Warner's horse, and ordered his
arrest. Warner whipped out his cutlass and, with Sherwood
covering his back, whacked Munro so hard with the flat of
the blade that the Yorker dropped to the ground. The blow,
cushioned by his hat and thick mop of hair, left him stunned
but alive. Warner and Sherwood trotted away.

To enforce his strategy of intimidation, Ethan Allen led
nearly a hundred vigilantes into the town of Clarendon the
next winter to punish the magistrate Benjamin Spencer, who

hid from them overnight in the woods before fleeing to New York. They bashed in his door with a log and hacked his dog to pieces. Convening a mock court, Allen threatened to reduce every house to ashes and leave every inhabitant a corpse if his Green Mountain Boys had to come back. "None but blockheads would purchase your farms and must be treated as such," he warned.

For all his bluster, Allen knew how far to press his threats to advantage, for no one got killed. Instead, the Yorkers and their local collaborators were publicly thrashed with "twigs of the wilderness"—supple birch switches with the bite of a rawhide lash. Whipping was accepted punishment for petty criminals in the colonies.

Ethan Allen's vigilantes in the Grants declared anyone with a magistrate's commission from New York to be their enemy. After one tipped off the authorities in New York City, the Green Mountain Boys tied him to a tree and whipped him two hundred times before jeering spectators. As soon as his bloody back was dressed, he was banished from the Grants with no time to collect his family, and promised five hundred more lashes if he returned.

Even law-abiding Yorkers faced being driven off their land or having houses and crops damaged. One doctor advised his neighbors to buy their land titles from New York. Though armed with a brace of pistols, he was dragged to the Catamount Tavern, tied to a chair, and hoisted by rope above the two-story tavern, next to a stuffed catamount atop the signpost, its teeth bared toward New York. He was left dangling for a couple of hours to the amusement of passersby.

By the following June, 1773, Tryon asked Frederick Haldimand, the Swiss-born general commanding British forces in New York, for regulars to put down the "riots" in the Grants. Haldimand refused, reasoning that New York's militia could suppress the lawbreakers. He would hear more from Ethan Allen and his mob.

Tryon had the New York legislature pass a law in early 1774 prohibiting "tumultuous and riotous assemblies" by more than two people in the New Hampshire Grants. Anyone refusing to disperse could be shot. It amounted to a death warrant for Ethan Allen and his gang. He claimed that "the Bloody Act" was unconstitutional because the Grants had no elected representatives in the legislature. He dared Tryon to take on the Green Mountain Boys, as "good a regiment of marksmen and scalpers as America can afford."

Every Green Mountain Boy was ordered to arm himself with a good musket, a pound of gunpowder, ball or buckshot, and a sharp tomahawk. "They may condemn us to be hung for refusing to place our own necks in the halter," Ethan Allen scoffed, "but how do the fools calculate to hang a Green Mountain Boy before they take him?"

In the autumn of 1772, Remember Baker had led Ethan's youngest brother, Ira, on an exploration of Lake Champlain. Ira knew good land when he saw it and urged his brothers to invest in property along the east coast of the big lake, for as he explained, "that was the country my soul delighted in and where, at all events, I was determined to make settlement." The Allen brothers plunged into the rapacious sort of speculation that they professed to despise. With neither capital nor official contracts, Ethan and his brothers Ira, Heman, and Zimri joined their cousin Remember Baker (though not Seth Warner) to create the Onion River Land Company, which leveraged property that they didn't own to buy land that they couldn't afford and to which New York said they were not entitled.

While Allen lobbied from Bennington, Ira Allen and Remember Baker returned to protect their investment. At the first waterfalls before the Onion River empties into Lake Champlain, they built a log blockhouse and stocked it with muskets and gunpowder to repel Yorkers with rival claims to the land. "We never walked out without at least a case of pistols," Ira boasted.

The Onion River Land Company did not own the property, so Ethan set out to buy titles from the speculators in New York. In February 1773, Ethan and Ira Allen rode with Remember Baker down to White Plains, north of New York City, to buy as much land as a prominent Quaker real estate investor would sell them on extended credit.

Ethan, Ira, and Remember, who were hunted in New York, assumed the disguise of British officers traveling from Canada to catch a ship for London. Their brother Heman booked them into a local tavern. When they settled their bill several days later, the landlord was startled to learn that his jolly guests in scarlet uniforms were Yankee outlaws.

Over three days, the Allens contracted to buy more than

forty thousand acres in the Grants for less than ten cents per acre. The brothers and Baker rode off to do business with another Quaker who was appalled to see the pistols and swords that his visitors were carrying, but put them up anyway. The Quaker investors knew that their titles in the New Hampshire Grants had become worthless in New York, and were eager to dump a sour investment.

The Allens tottered on the brink of bankruptcy as they scrambled to amass as much property as possible between Lake Champlain and the Green Mountains. Their Onion River Land Company could not even afford the basic fees that New York charged to confirm land purchases. Now they listed 45,000 acres of potential farmland available in the fertile floodplain near what is now Burlington, Vermont: "Land for sale on Winooski intervale," they advertised in the *Courant* newspaper in Connecticut, "little or no timber growing thereon, except a few scattering buttonwood, elm and butternut trees. The land rises from the intervale in graceful oval hills, and spreads into swails [*sic*] of choice mowing ground." They recommended the local river's "diversity of excellent fish, particularly salmon."

Between 1773 and 1775, the Onion River Land Company accumulated a little more than 77,000 acres along Lake Champlain, but may have sold only 17,000 acres. The Allens and Remember could not agree on who owned what, and dissolved their real estate speculation in March 1775. They resolved to sort out their differences a year later. But by then, Ethan Allen would be missing at sea aboard a British warship. Remember Baker would have his head cut off. Seth

Warner and his Green Mountain Boys would be fighting for their lives in the frozen wastes of Quebec.

The Green Mountain Boys relied upon a loose network of friends and neighbors, not all of whom shared Allen's hatred of New York. When Justus Sherwood arrived from Connecticut, he made friends with Seth Warner, who was working as a road surveyor in Bennington. Sherwood staked out his pitch in the foothills of Lake Champlain, a fifty-acre plot in the new township of New Haven, where Ethan Allen had bought five hundred acres from Governor Wentworth, and set to work clearing his patch of forest, girdling and burning the trees, pulling out roots, wrestling rocks into boundary walls. The other settlers elected him their equivalent of town clerk, entrusted with keeping New Haven's records.

He was also invited to join a select group of thirty-five speculators promised an additional 150 acres each "for the more speedy settlement of this town" if they cleared and cultivated at least five of the acres by the following June 1775. His partners included Ethan and Ira Allen, Seth Warner, and other Green Mountain Boys whose loyalty Ethan wanted to reward.

Sherwood accumulated up to sixteen hundred acres in the Grants. He built a snug log cabin for his new wife, Sarah, and planted an apple orchard to make hard cider, the most popular beverage. The fields he cleared grew hay to feed his livestock, and wheat and oats to support his family. Corn, potatoes, and green vegetables filled his garden.

Unlike his neighbors in the Grants, where adult slavery would be declared illegal in 1777, Sherwood employed several African slaves. On the eve of the American Revolution, as many as one in four Connecticut households had slaves.

Homesteaders like Sherwood had more in common with their Canadian neighbors than with the Yorkers. The best markets for their lumber, potash and grain, cattle and sheep lay through Montreal, not New York. By 1771, the bulk of oaken barrel staves shipped from Quebec to Britain came from the Champlain Valley. Only the southwestern Grants lay closer to the Hudson River Valley and Albany than to Montreal. This geography would shape loyalties in the revolution to come.

TWO

Seizing Fort Ticonderoga

A merica's war for independence may have begun on the village greens of Lexington and Concord, Massachusetts, on April 19, 1775, but the first blood was spilled five weeks earlier on the eastern rim of the New Hampshire Grants when ten protesters were gunned down in the name of King George in the Connecticut River town of Westminster.

Ethan Allen was not there, but determined not to be left out, he dispatched fifty Green Mountain Boys at a gallop across the Grants to join hundreds of local militiamen seeking revenge for what became infamous as the Westminster Massacre. His defiance of New York's authority had been slow to attract homesteaders who had settled along the Connecticut River, a hard day's ride from the base of Green Mountain Boys. Here was an opportunity to plunge his grudge-fight with New York into the frothing cauldron of a larger revolution against Britain.

Hard economic times and worthless money had left farmers across New England prey to creditors. The popular response in the New Hampshire Grants was to shut down the courts that New York maintained to dispense justice. On Sunday afternoon of March 12, 1775, a hundred protesters gathered in Westminster to block the district court from opening on Monday. They were not bent on violence, though some picked up cudgels from a woodpile as they occupied the two-story clapboard courthouse. The sheriff appointed by New York arrived with a posse of sixty loyalists armed with muskets, pistols, swords, and rocks. He ordered the "rioters" inside to disperse or "be in hell before morning."

The judge allowed them to stay until morning when he would hear their complaints. His Monday docket showed nothing more urgent than a murder. Many demonstrators left.

The sheriff retired with his men to the local tavern. They lurched back to the courthouse an hour before midnight. The sheriff demanded entrance in the name of King George, and was rebuffed. Drawing his sword, he climbed the stairs to the door. "Goddamn you, fire!" he ordered his posse, who shot into the dark courthouse, killing two protesters and wounding eight. In the chaos, most escaped through a side passage. The others trapped inside, including the "wounded and suffering," were stuffed into two basement cells, a witness said, "to bear the insane taunts of the victors, and listen to their vile abuse." The jailer opened a small bar reserved for judges and lawyers and poured fresh shots for the sheriff's men, who resumed their "brawling frolic."

Daylight revealed the carnage. Musket and pistol balls pocked the oak timbers of the courthouse. Bloodstains smeared walls and stairs. The first corpse found was that of a young farmer from nearby Brattleboro. He had been shot in the head, a coroner's inquest ruled, "of which wound he died, and not otherwise."

Pleas for help were answered from both sides of the Connecticut River, which divided New Hampshire from the Grants. Militiamen mustered not just in Westminster but also neighboring towns. By noon Tuesday, Westminster teemed with more than four hundred trigger-itchy gunmen, some from as far away as Massachusetts.

The witch hunt spread for New Yorkers and their loyalist friends. Westminster's roads were sealed off by supporters who, as one New York journal reported, "indiscriminately laid hold of all passengers against whom any of the party intimated the least suspicion. The mob, stimulated by their leaders to the utmost fury and revenge, breathed nothing but blood and slaughter against the unfortunate persons in their power."

Ethan Allen's deputy Robert Cochran rode in with his Green Mountain Boys and dared the crowd to collect a £50 reward posted by New York for his arrest. They carted the sheriff and seven of his posse off to jail in Massachusetts, where New York's chief justice arranged their release.

The vigor with which militiamen poured into Westminster foretold the resistance that awaited British redcoats in Lexington and Concord five weeks later. The massacre frayed the last strands of tolerance toward New York's claim over the New Hampshire Grants. On April 1, 1775, town elders in the eastern Grants resolved to petition King George to annex them to any government other than New York's or allow them to form their own. The law of self-preservation gave them the right, they claimed, "to wholly renounce and resist the administration of the government and New York, till such time as the lives and property of those inhabitants may be secured by all; or till such time as they can have the opportunity to lay their grievances before his most gracious Majesty."

Ethan Allen had his own plans to rid the Grants of New York. He flirted with seeking annexation by New Hampshire, then settled on a more brazen scheme to transform the Grants into a separate royal colony. He found an influential ally in Philip Skene, a retired British officer who, like Ira Allen, saw the potential of Lake Champlain.

Between 1763 and 1771, Skene accumulated 29,000 acres on the lake's southern end, where he built a grand estate with its own sawmills, forge, and a boatyard. Since his property was purchased directly from London, he felt beholden to neither New York nor New Hampshire. He dreamed of governing a royal colony from his fieldstone manor at Skenesborough (now Whitehall, New York). He proposed to Ethan that the boundaries of the New Hampshire Grants be extended as far west as Lake Ontario.

Skene sailed off to London, where he confirmed his royal appointment as the lieutenant governor of Ticonderoga and the satellite fortress at Crown Point, and surveyor of His Majesty's woods and forests along Lake Champlain. It remained only to persuade the locals to formally petition the king to make him their governor. Skene's grand new title tripped him up when the ship sailing him back from England docked on June 7, 1775, in Philadelphia, as the Sec-

ond Continental Congress was in session. The presumptive
lieutenant governor of Ticonderoga and Crown Point was
detained as a British agent after plans to raise a Loyalist regiment were discovered among his effects.

Popular fury over the British raids on Lexington and Concord demanded retaliation and what more enticing target
than Fort Ticonderoga? In a wilderness without roads, the
star-shaped fortress was situated to dominate an inland waterway from Montreal to New York City, with land portages
linking the St. Lawrence River and Lake Champlain to Lake
George and the Hudson River. And Ticonderoga contained
a trove of heavy artillery.

In March 1775, the Massachusetts Provincial Congress
sent a young lawyer, John Brown, north across ice-clogged
Lake Champlain to learn whether the Canadians and Indians would support their American neighbors if war broke
out. Brown thought that only a preemptive action could
stop British troops from striking south toward Boston. "One
thing I must mention, to be kept a profound secret," Brown
confided in a dispatch from Montreal. "The Fort at Ticonderoga must be seized as soon as possible, should hostilities be committed by the king's troops. The people on the
New-Hampshire Grants have engaged to do the business
and in my opinion are the most proper persons for the job."

On April 28, 1775, a half dozen prominent supporters in
Connecticut siphoned £300 from its treasury to finance an
assault on Fort Ticonderoga and the nearby fortification at

Crown Point. Governor Jonathan Trumbull had the money delivered to Ethan Allen and his Green Mountain Boys.

Two days earlier, Massachusetts had authorized an applicant from Connecticut named Benedict Arnold to mount his own invasion, promising to supply him musket balls, flints, gunpowder, some horses, and £100 in cash. To earn his colonel's commission, Arnold was required to sign up to four hundred recruits, deliver them to Fort Ticonderoga, and, as the Massachusetts committee of safety directed, "use your best endeavors to reduce the same, taking possession of the cannon, mortars, stores, etc., upon the lake."

Arnold was instructed to bring back any serviceable artillery and stores for the new Continental Army deployed at Cambridge, outside Boston. He had to procure provisions himself, and present the bill to Massachusetts. Arnold had no military experience, having worked as a druggist, horse trader, and ship owner. Smart and ambitious, he would distinguish himself as one of Washington's best generals.

A race was under way by Massachusetts and Connecticut to grab a crown jewel within a third colony of New York. For deniability, the sensitive mission was contracted out to free-lancers, Benedict Arnold and Ethan Allen, each unaware of the other's plans. Arnold expected to retrieve eighty heavy cannon and thirty or more brass guns and mortars from Ticonderoga. But the fort itself was in "a ruinous condition," he informed his Massachusetts patrons: "The place could not hold out an hour against a vigorous onset."

Fort Ticonderoga had indeed fallen on hard times since the French defeat at Quebec in 1759. Its garrison had shrunk to several dozen British redcoats, some too old or ill for active duty, plus their families. "The fort and barracks are in a most ruinous situation," confirmed their captain, who was grazing eleven cattle and forty-five sheep along its ramparts.

In May 1774, a British military engineer inspected Fort Ticonderoga and deemed only its stone barracks worth repairing. He proposed abandoning the fort and rebuilding another at Crown Point, which had burned down the year before in a fire caused by soldiers' wives boiling soap. Four months after the inspection, a storage chamber inside Fort Ticonderoga caved in, burying supplies and ammunition.

Ethan Allen had finished briefing his officers and Connecticut financiers at a local tavern when a stout stranger uniformed in blue burst in to announce that Massachusetts had picked him to capture Fort Ticonderoga. He introduced himself as Benedict Arnold, but Ethan refused to read the commission that he flaunted. Arnold, who had brought no troops, was stymied when the Green Mountain Boys threatened to go home if they couldn't serve under their own officers.

They arranged to regroup at a shallow inlet across Lake Champlain just north of Fort Ticonderoga. A hundred and forty Green Mountain Boys in farmers' clothes and seventy-some volunteers from Massachusetts turned out, but no boats were waiting to ferry them across the lake. Ethan Allen, impatient with logistical details, had neglected to arrange transport. Only eight-three troops could be shuttled across, packed into a scow whose oarsman had been plied with whiskey, and a borrowed rowboat. The impetuous

Arnold jumped in and ordered Ethan Allen's men to follow, pitching through fierce squalls to safety on the lake's western shore. With dawn about to break, it was too late to fetch another contingent led by Seth Warner, who had to find their own way across the lake next day.

Allen and Arnold bickered over who should lead the assault. Arnold had his commission from Massachusetts, but Allen had the Green Mountain Boys. "What shall I do with the damned rascal? Shall I put him under guard?" Allen asked one of his men, who suggested that they enter Fort Ticonderoga side by side. Allen ordered Arnold to stay at his left hand, but Arnold rushed ahead anyway.

The Green Mountain Boys followed Ethan Allen through a wicket door left open in the main gate. A startled British sentry aimed, misfired, and fled, taking his pursuers to a small parade ground and stone barracks inside the slumbering fort. A second sentry lunged with a bayonet, but Allen's sword struck him. He begged for his life and pointed out the stairway to the quarters of the post commander. Arnold raced Allen up the wooden steps and banged on the door with his sword. A pale British officer appeared, breeches in hand, to ask by whose authority Allen and Arnold demanded his surrender. One of Allen's men heard Allen holler, "Come out of that hole, you damned old rat." He was later credited with a more pungent salutation: "Come out of there, you sons of British whores, or I'll smoke you out!"

Allen had banged on the wrong door. The British officer staring down his drawn blade was not the fort's captain, William Delaplace, but a recently arrived lieutenant, who had been awakened about half past three by whoops and cries of "No quarter, no quarter!" He opened the door to see "armed rabble" pushing their way upstairs. The defenders in the barracks had been caught in their beds. It was over in ten minutes.

Benedict Arnold again presented his orders from Massachusetts. Ethan Allen insisted that Connecticut had authorized him to take the fort. If the British fired a single shot, Allen warned, no man, woman, or child would be left alive.

Captain Delaplace emerged from his quarters to surrender the small garrison, which included two dozen bewildered women and children. They didn't know that war had broken out in Massachusetts. Benedict Arnold offered to treat Delaplace like a gentleman if he handed over his sword and pistols, but never returned them.

Ten miles to the north, Seth Warner ferried a hundred Green Mountain Boys across to take Crown Point and its meager garrison of nine redcoats and ten women and children.

At the southern end of Lake Champlain, thirty more Green Mountain Boys overran Skenesborough and seized Philip Skene's small schooner moored in the bay. They invaded the crypt containing his deceased wife, whose will bequeathed an income to Skene so long as she lay above ground. The Green Mountain Boys yanked her corpse from the lead-lined casket, which they carted off to melt into musket balls. Philip Skene had yet to return but his son and two daughters were captured. The Skene girls were escorted to freedom in Montreal by a Green Mountain Boy who billed the Connecticut legislature £150 for travel expenses. He reported that Quebec's French-speaking peasants were praying for the Americans to liberate them from British rule.

At Fort Ticonderoga, more rough men landed from the lake and joined the search, which uncovered Captain Delaplace's stash of rum. Ethan Allen preempted the liquor, he said, "for the refreshment of the fatigued soldiery." He and his Green Mountain Boys drank dry all ninety gallons. "The sun seemed to rise that morning with a superior luster," Allen recalled of their binge, "and Ticonderoga and its dependencies smiled on its conquerors, who tossed about the flowing bowl"—brimming with Delaplace's rum—"and wished success to Congress, and the liberty and freedom of America." Connecticut had to reimburse Delaplace for the rum.

Benedict Arnold wanted Ethan Allen sacked. "Colonel Allen, finding he had the ascendancy over his people, positively insisted that I should have no command, as I had forbid the soldiers plundering and destroying private property," Arnold complained. "The power is now taken out of my hands, and I am not consulted, nor have I a voice in such matters."

The quarrel over command led Allen and Arnold to draw swords, until a private ordered them to behave. Arnold kicked Allen's deputy for disrespecting him. "Colonel Allen is a proper man to head his own wild people, but entirely unacquainted with military service," Arnold told his Massachusetts backers, "and as I am the only person who has been legally authorized to take possession of this place, I am determined to insist on my right, and I think it my duty to remain here against all opposition, until I have further orders."

Connecticut reminded Massachusetts that Ethan Allen was in charge. A commission written on the spot directed him to "keep the command of said garrison, for the use of the American Colonies, till you have further orders from the colony of Connecticut or from the Continental Congress."

While Ethan Allen caroused with his men, Benedict Arnold took inventory of the captured artillery, counting as many as 130 salvageable guns. Digging among the ruins at Crown Point later, the Americans unearthed nearly a ton of iron and lead shot buried when ninety-six barrels of gunpowder blew up in the 1773 fire. The conquest of Fort Ticonderoga grew grander in the retelling. "The soldiery behaved with such restless fury, that they so terrified the king's troops that they durst not fire on their assailants, and our soldiery were agreeably disappointed," Allen told the Massachusetts Provincial Congress. He gave Arnold no credit.

Both Arnold and Allen were aware how vulnerable the fort was to recapture. When fifty of his recruits at last appeared, Arnold, a seasoned sailor, pressed them into a crew on Skene's schooner, now armed with small cannon and swivel guns. He sailed the schooner past the northern tip of Lake Champlain into the Richelieu River, where Arnold's men boarded a British seventy-ton sloop, anchored off the Canadian frontier town of St. Johns (now called Saint-Jean), and overpowered the sloop's crew. They disarmed a dozen more British troops and their sergeant at the small fort onshore.

The northerly wind whipped around to fill the sails of Arnold's schooner as it escorted the prize sloop and several barges laden with British prisoners, weapons, and supplies.

Fifteen miles below St. Johns, Arnold met Ethan Allen and his men rowing their flat-bottom barges hard against the wind. Arnold shared his supplies and, over a meal, warned that the British were reinforcing St. Johns. Allen wanted to capture it and landed his Green Mountain Boys across the river at St. Johns where they passed a miserable night swatting off mosquitoes. By dawn, they came under cannon fire from British reinforcements. Allen beat a retreat to his barges, abandoning several men, two of whom got captured. He made light of his narrow escape, likening the incoming grapeshot to music "both terrible and delightful."

Allen's escapades prompted more irritation than gratitude in high places. When he asked New York for weapons, ammunition, and provisions—"we are in want of almost every necessary (courage excepted)"—his urgent appeal was forwarded to the dithering Second Continental Congress, which was reluctant to break with Britain. Allen dispatched the British colors seized at Fort Ticonderoga to Congress, which denounced its seizure as "unwanted and unauthorized." Some delegates complained that Ethan Allen had spoiled prospects for a reconciliation with the Crown.

But elsewhere throughout the colonies, the fall of Britain's northern Gibraltar ignited a patriotic pride. On May 10, 1775, Ethan Allen's irregulars, without artillery, bayonets, or uniforms, had forced British regulars to surrender their Union Jack. Britain had squandered blood and treasure—eight million pounds sterling by one estimate—to expel France from North America, only to see Fort Ticonderoga and Crown Point fall into the hands of rustic rebels. A makeshift American navy with two hijacked sailboats was the new master of Lake Champlain, the vital waterway linking Canada and the American colonies. Within weeks, Congress reconsidered its neutrality and selected Ticonderoga as a springboard for a preemptive invasion of Canada.

Cadwallander Colden, now the king's acting governor in New York, blamed it all on the Green Mountain Boys. He informed Britain's secretary of state for the American colonies that "the only people of this province who had any hand in this expedition, were that lawless people whom your lordship has heard much of under the name of the Bennington mob."

Congress, at New York's behest, recommended that Fort Ticonderoga's cannon be moved to the southern end of Lake George, beyond Ethan Allen's reach. To placate London, it ordered an inventory of the captured cannon and supplies, so that "they may be returned when the restoration of the former harmony between Great Britain and the Colonies, so ardently wished for by the latter, shall render it prudent and consistent with the overruling of self-preservation."

Allen had no intention of giving back the spoils of war. Removing the artillery, he argued, would expose settlers on the northern frontier to danger. But he yielded command to a Connecticut regiment that marched to Fort Ticonderoga in early June. When Benedict Arnold refused to step aside, Massachusetts revoked his commission. Ethan Allen sent his British prisoners, including Captain Delaplace with his wife and two children, to Connecticut as a gift to be exchanged for "some of our own friends in Boston" held by the Crown.

Henry Knox, a Boston bookseller on George Washington's staff, supervised the transfer of guns from Ticonderoga. Sixty tons of cannon, mortars, and other field pieces were hauled overland for three hundred miles the following winter to present Washington with "a noble train of artillery" that would force the British to evacuate Boston in 1776.

Once relieved at Fort Ticonderoga, the Green Mountain Boys dispersed to their farms to plow and plant for the short summer season. Ethan Allen wanted to capitalize on his victory by pushing into Canada. "Had I but five hundred men with me," he boasted on May 18, 1775, "I would have marched to Montreal." Two weeks later, Allen proposed that New York support an immediate invasion of Canada. If England shifted more troops to Quebec, he argued, fewer would be left to garrison Boston. He revised his estimate for the Massachusetts Provincial Congress, saying that Canada could be conquered with three thousand men. To spearhead the invasion, he offered to raise a regiment of rangers from the New Hampshire Grants if Congress would commission and pay them.

If Ethan Allen was a reckless military strategist, he had begun to sparkle as a propagandist. Imagine what America could achieve against Britain by besieging Canada, he wrote New York's Provincial Congress on June 2, 1775: "She might rise on eagle's wings, and mount up to glory, freedom and immortal honor, if she did but know and exert her strength. Fame is now hovering over her head. A vast continent must now sink to slavery, poverty, horror and bondage, or rise to unconquerable freedom, immense wealth, inexpressible felicity, and immortal fame." He pledged: "I will lay my life on it, that with fifteen hundred men and a proper train of artillery, I will take Montreal."

Ethan Allen and his cousin Seth Warner rode down to Philadelphia to pitch the plan to Congress and get paid for capturing Fort Ticonderoga and Crown Point. Congress's president, John Hancock, agreed that mustering the Green Mountain Boys into the American army would benefit the patriotic cause. New York's legislators were persuaded to finance and equip the regiment. On July 4, 1775, Congress resolved that "a body of troops not exceeding five hundred men, officers included, be forthwith raised, of those called Green Mountain Boys," and that they could choose their officers.

Town elders from the western Grants decided for themselves who would lead the new Green Mountain Boys. By a vote of forty-five to one, Seth Warner was elected to command the regiment, with the rank of lieutenant colonel. The elders went on to choose seven captains and fourteen lieutenants, among them Ethan's brothers Ira and Heman.

Ethan Allen was passed over for every rank, though Congress had budgeted funds for him to lead the regiment. It was a humiliating rebuff. "I find myself in the favor of the officers of the Army and the young Green Mountain Boys," he groused. "How the old men came to reject me, I cannot conceive, inasmuch as I saved them from the encroachments of New-York." Ethan may have seemed too unreliable to the elders of the Grants, who would have heard about the drunken indiscipline at Fort Ticonderoga and reckless miscalculation against the British at St. Johns.

Seth Warner had no more military experience than Ethan Allen, but he comported well with a new maturity in the New Hampshire Grants. The name of the Green Mountain Boys had come to refer to its tenacious settlers, not just Ethan Allen's vigilantes. Seth Warner stood nearly six foot four inches and was lean and powerfully built. His tousled brown hair, sparkling blue eyes, and thoughtful opinions invited confidence. Ethan might be fun for a night's carousal, but Seth could be trusted to make the right decisions when stakes turned deadly.

So Ethan Allen's Green Mountain Boys, whom he had created to fight New York, went to war in Canada without him, alongside New York troops, in what Congress officially designated as "Colonel Warner's Regiment in the Servis [*sic*] of the United Colonies."

THREE

Congress Invades Canada

Warner's regiment of Green Mountain Boys joined the makeshift army cobbled together to conquer Canada on the cheap and was baptized by fire in September 1775. King George had proclaimed his colonies in open rebellion, and Ethan Allen, Seth Warner, and Justus Sherwood would get swept into the maelstrom of the American Revolution.

Congress, in Philadelphia, did not declare independence for another ten months. But it was inspired by the battle of Bunker Hill, outside Boston on June 19, 1775. Fighting from defenses thrown up overnight on nearby Breed's Hill, Yankee militiamen lost more than 450 killed and wounded, a quarter of their strength. British casualties ran as high as 40 percent. More than a thousand were killed or wounded before the rebels ran out of ammunition and were routed. A British report warned, "the Americans will put the whole army into the grave or hospitals in three or four nights' work, and an hour's fire in each morning."

On June 15, 1775, Congress directed George Washington to raise fifteen thousand men to protect the colonies, pending a possible reconciliation with Britain. To command his northern army, he chose Philip Schuyler, a New York aristocrat of Dutch descent. He had served as a quartermaster in the French and Indian War. His logistical experience was essential to sustain an army in the wilderness.

Schuyler went north with a muddled agenda. He was told to assess the condition of Fort Ticonderoga and Crown Point. Secure their waters and shorelines. Destroy British boats and artillery. Gather intelligence. Parse local Canadian and Indian sympathies. Occupy Montreal and other towns— so long as Canada's French and Indian inhabitants did not object. If he needed more money and ammunition than he could squeeze from New York, he must beg it from Connecticut's governor, whom Congress would pay back later.

Schuyler disembarked at a portage linking Lake George to Lake Champlain, where he was met by a solitary sentry who could not wake up the rest of the night watch. As he stepped through a hundred sleeping militiamen, a second sentry failed to challenge him. With nothing more than a penknife, Schuyler could have dispatched both guards, set fire to their blockhouse, destroyed provisions, and starved out the main garrison to the North at Fort Ticonderoga, as he later told George Washington.

Washington, who regarded colonial militias as unreliable, sympathized. "From my own experience," he wrote from his headquarters outside Boston, "I can easily judge of your difficulties to induce order and discipline into troops who have, from their infancy, imbibed ideas of the most contrary kind."

Certainly the Connecticut regiment sent to occupy Ticonderoga had done little to improve defenses. "I find myself very unable to steer in this stormy situation," confessed its colonel, who did not know how many men or muskets he had at his disposal. His troops pestered him for rum, and molasses to brew their homemade spruce beer. Some days there was not enough flour to bake bread. The overcrowded barracks were filthy. "I think there has not been one pound of soap bought for the army," one Connecticut volunteer despaired.

Tents that Schuyler had requisitioned did not arrive, nor did blankets. Some units lacked pots to cook their rations or kettles to boil water. New York declined to help. "Our troops can be of no service to you," he was informed, "they have no arms, clothes, blankets or ammunition; the officers no commissions; ourselves in debt."

The northern army verged on mutiny as idle troops waited for boats to ferry them down over Lake Champlain to Canada. Connecticut men felt cheated of their rations and assigned menial chores that New Yorkers dodged. When Connecticut provided fifty dairy cows to supply its troops with fresh milk, New York's militias complained until Schuyler withdrew the cows.

Washington's headquarters posted recruiting limits stipulating that British deserters should not be enlisted, "nor any Stroller, Negro, Vagabond, or Person suspected of being an Enemy to the Liberty of America." The ban against African Americans, to placate the Southern colonies, went often ignored in New England, where former slaves and Indians filled out rosters of some regiments.

Anyone younger than eighteen or not born in America was ineligible to serve unless he was settled with a wife and family. Even so, immigrants from England and Ireland signed up with little fuss. The First New York regiment, disparaged as "the sweepings of the York street," included urchins as young as eleven years old. In any case, there were not enough serviceable muskets to equip more recruits. New York paid a bonus of ten shillings to any recruit who brought his own. No molds were at hand to pour enough bullets to fit the variety of muskets. Massachusetts considered hammering scythes into spears to arm some of its troops.

To reconnoiter what the British were up to in Canada, Schuyler dispatched Remember Baker on several hazardous missions. Like his cousin Ethan, Baker had been passed over for rank in the new regiment of Green Mountain Boys. But he obediently paddled north though he was past his prime as a ranger. He sidled at night to the boatyard at St. Johns, and counted 450 redcoats at the fort. On his next mission, he made contact with potential allies in the local tribes of Abenakis and Mohawks. He returned again in August 1775 to spy on British troops at Isle aux Noix north of Lake Champlain, a swampy island of tangled brush named Nut Island for its hazelnut bushes, Baker floated down the river at night and set up surveillance in a thicket four miles from the base. He passed the time by sharpening his flint used to strike the spark igniting the gunpowder in his musket.

A passing band of Mohawk warriors spotted Baker's canoe hidden in the weeds and tried to paddle it away. Baker broke cover to order them to return it. One brave took aim, but Baker pulled his trigger first. The musket misfired. His flint was too sharp, and snagged against steel. Before Baker could shoot again, buckshot from an Indian musket spattered his brain. Baker's killers cut off his head and a hand, which they carried on a pole into St. Johns in hopes of a £50 reward. A British officer, disgusted by Baker's severed head exhibited atop the fort's wall, paid to have it buried with the rest of his body.

General Schuyler disclaimed responsibility for the death of his veteran scout. Baker had gone to Canada to gather intelligence, Schuyler told Washington, "with express orders not to molest the Canadians or Indians." Baker undertook his fatal mission, he insisted, "without my leave."

Seth Warner and his Green Mountain Boys learned of Remember Baker's death as they passed through Crown Point on their way to Canada. "Captain Baker was the first man killed in the northern department," recalled Ira Allen, now a lieutenant in Warner's regiment, "and being a gentleman universally respected, his death made more noise in the countryside than the loss of a thousand men towards the end of the American war."

The Green Mountain Boys joined more than fifteen hundred troops—four regiments from New York and a fifth from Connecticut—who were laying siege to the British fort at St. Johns, where Baker's severed head had been on display. Confusion over whether Ethan Allen or Seth Warner should command the regiment led the invasion's Brigadier General, Richard Montgomery, to doubt that many would show up.

But 170 Green Mountain Boys wearing large green coats reported for duty at the American forward base on

Isle aux Noix. They brought their muskets but no blankets nor money. New York legislators still considered Warner an outlaw and refused to approve his rank. Montgomery had to commission Warner as the regiment's lieutenant colonel with orders that he be obeyed accordingly. "Should Colonel Warner want a little cash for his people, I can now give it to him," Montgomery decided, and advanced £500 to buy blankets and clothing before they joined the siege of St. Johns.

Warner's regiment deployed along a road junction leading toward Montreal, to block British troops from relieving their beleaguered garrison at St. Johns. The Green Mountain Boys were exposed to so much incoming fire that two companies of New Yorkers were sent to reinforce them.

Summer drought gave way to autumn rains that flooded fields for miles, overflowing the siege trenches and dikes around the American cannons shelling St. Johns. The gun crews slogged through muck and mire like "half drowned rats crawling through the swamp," Montgomery wrote his wife. Drenched, they shivered from the chills and fevers of malarial fever. Lice infested their soggy, unwashed clothes. A contagious diarrhea, called the "bloody flux," sapped their morale as well as their strength.

By the second week of October 1775, 937 militiamen asked for medical discharges. Some, homesick or desperate to avoid winter in Canada, feigned illness by swallowing tobacco juice or burning their tongues with hot chocolate. Schuyler accused them of malingering and cut their daily rations to four ounces of meat and a half cup of rice, forcing some soldiers to sell their shirts and blankets, or beg to fill their bellies.

Schuyler himself contracted rheumatic gout and was conveyed in a fever back to Albany, New York. Command of the northern campaign passed to his deputy, Brigadier Richard Montgomery, who had little confidence in the Green Mountain Boys and New Englanders who failed to respect class or rank. "Pray send me Yorkers," he told Schuyler. "They don't melt away as fast as their eastern neighbors." A former British captain who had wed a New York heiress, Montgomery mistrusted Yankees. "The New England troops are the worse stuff imaginable," he said. "There is such an equality among them that the officers have no authority, and there are very few among them in whose spirit I have confidence. The privates are all generals but not soldiers."

And worse, Montgomery's war chest was empty. Congress's advance to Schuyler of $100,000 was spent by October 1775. Congress promised to follow up with twice as much in paper currency, when what Montgomery needed to feed and support his troops in Canada was gold or silver coinage. "Let the hard cash come up as soon as possible, that our reputation may hold good," he pleaded.

Schuyler replied, "None is to be had in Albany. I fear the want of specie will be fatal to us."

Ethan Allen had wheedled Schuyler to take him along, though his only experience with army life was a fortnight of militia duty eighteen years before. So Schuyler sent Allen forth as a civilian to recruit Canadians, forage for provisions, and explain the American invasion of Quebec to its

French-speaking inhabitants. He wore a deerskin leather jacket and red wool cap like a backwoods hunter. He was not entitled to the colors of the Green Mountain Boys.

Though "preaching politics," as he described his duties, carried no military rank, Allen begged to be treated as an officer and permitted to command a detachment of troops when the occasion required. He approached sympathetic Montreal businessmen for ammunition and liquor to sustain the American troops in Canada, and promised to pay £500, which he didn't have, for supplies to be delivered to him as soon as possible.

Canadians were signing up as fast as he could recruit them with 250 already under arms, Allen lied. "You may rely upon it, that I shall join you in about three days, with five hundred or more Canadian volunteers," he wrote Montgomery on September 20, 1775. "I could raise one or two thousand in a week's time." Allen dispatched six hogshead casks of liquor to announce his pending return to American headquarters. Were the Green Mountain Boys still under his command, Allen would have them seize Montreal, he suggested, though "under present circumstances, I would not for my right arm act without or contrary to orders."

Montgomery never again saw Ethan Allen, who met his old friend John Brown, now a major leading a company of American and Canadian volunteers. Allen proposed that they take Montreal together. He hired fifty Canadians to fight for a "half joe"—a little more than four dollars in Portuguese coins—and license to plunder the town. With some rangers borrowed from Brown, he paddled across the St. Lawrence

River. But with blustery weather roiling, Brown failed to show up, and it is doubtful that he had agreed. Rather than retreat, Allen chose to defend his bridgehead. He exhorted his hirelings to hold their ground, that they would soon have reinforcements, which never came. Allen could not retreat, he maintained later, because the St. Lawrence cut him off from Montgomery's main force.

Even so, Allen's arrival threw Montreal into a panic. Canada's Governor General, Guy Carleton, prepared to evacuate his staff to the safety of ships in the river, until a spy discovered how few invaders there were. A counterattack was cobbled from British regulars, Canadian militiamen, English civilians, and some Mohawk warriors. Outflanked, Allen retreated for a mile, but the Mohawks outran his rented Canadians. Some were killed, more deserted. After two hours of skirmishing more characteristic of the wild frontier than of settled Montreal with its churches and stone and wood dwellings, Allen surrendered his remnant of thirty-eight fighters, including seven wounded, and landed in British captivity. Montgomery and Schuyler were furious that Allen had jeopardized their prospects for capturing Montreal, which the British would surely reinforce. Canadian and Indian potential allies would have second thoughts about joining the American cause.

George Washington blamed Allen's disobedience on insubordination typical of New Englanders. "Colonel Allen's misfortune will, I hope, teach a lesson of prudence and subordinating to others who may be too ambitious to outshine their general officers," he told Schuyler.

The other prisoners, manacled in pairs, were shuffled off to jail. Allen was dragged down to the harbor and shackled, hands and feet, to a heavy iron bar inside the hold of a small British schooner. There he languished under guard, too cramped to stand, until transport could be arranged to a trial and execution in England. General Richard Prescott, the British commander at Montreal, was delighted to find the scoundrel who stole Fort Ticonderoga in his custody. "I will not execute you now," Prescott promised, "but you shall grace a halter at Tyburn, God damn ye." Prescott referred to Tyburn's three-legged gallows, set on the highway near what is now London's Marble Arch, which could hang several condemned at one time. The public executions drew spectators into the thousands.

As Ethan Allen lay in the bilges of a British warship, the invasion of Canada proceeded. Resistance was stubborn enough that Montgomery bypassed St. Johns and took a more vulnerable stone fort a dozen miles to the north, capturing its garrison of eighty-three Royal Fusiliers on October 9, 1775. It was the first American victory of the campaign and yielded desperately needed stores, included 120 barrels of gunpowder and more than 6,000 musket cartridges. Seth Warner's regiment was sent north to occupy two villages on the St. Lawrence near Montreal.

General Carleton may have regretted sending the bulk of his regulars to reinforce the embattled British army in Boston. From his remaining fusiliers, Quebec militias, some Scottish settlers, and Iroquois scouts, he assembled eight hundred troops south of Montreal to relieve the trapped

garrison at St. Johns. On October 30, 1775, they crossed
the St. Lawrence in several dozen boats into an ambush
that Seth Warner set up from the south bank. The Green
Mountain Boys, reinforced by a regiment of New Yorkers,
raked Carleton's forces on the river with musket fire and
grapeshot—deadly clusters of small iron balls—from a four-
pound cannon. Carleton's flotilla retreated with scores dead
or wounded. Warner's ambushers, outnumbered two to one,
suffered no serious casualties.

Canadian allies helped the Americans float a pair of nine-
pound cannon on flat-bottomed bateaux at night down the
rapids to Chambly, within range of Montreal. Carleton saw
no recourse but to evacuate his staff officers, and a load of
gunpowder, in ten or so small boats. Disguised as a Quebec
peasant, he was smuggled past the Americans in a boat with
muffled oars, a humiliating escape for His Majesty's governor general of Canada.

The seven-week siege of St. Johns ended with the surrender of five hundred British regulars—more than half of the
redcoats in Canada—and forty-one cannon on November 3,
1775. Such a heavy snow fell that night that tents collapsed.

On November 13, Montgomery's troops entered Montreal to a hearty welcome from its French inhabitants. Allen's
captor, General Prescott, now had to surrender with his garrison and stores, including 760 barrels of salt pork and 200
pair of useful shoes.

With Montreal taken, many Americans assumed their
war was over. Montgomery cautioned against undoing in a
day what they had achieved over months and "restoring to an

enraged, and hitherto disappointed enemy, the means of carrying on a cruel war to the very bowels of their country." He hoped that no one would abandon him at this critical juncture. He promised to replace their summer rags with warmer winter clothing, including blanket-overcoats, shoes, mittens, and caps, plus a dollar's bounty for any soldier who signed on through the winter until mid-April 1776.

To Americans unaccustomed to venturing farther than a day's walk from their hearths, Quebec seemed as remote as the North Pole. "I have had great difficulty about the troops," Montgomery told Schuyler, "I am afraid many of them will go home." Indeed, three hundred men returned to their farms, strewing gear in their wake. The New England troops carried off fifteen hundred muskets taken at St. Johns. But some, stirred by Montgomery's patriotic appeal, agreed to push on, buffeted by snow squalls and icy winds, to Quebec City.

The Green Mountain Boys, after their victory on the St. Lawrence, elected to pull out, too thinly clothed in their green coats to endure the Canadian winter. Montgomery discharged them with thanks for their service, but he was not happy. "The rascally Green Mountain Boys have left me in the lurch after promising to go," he complained. Lieutenants Ira Allen and Robert Cochran stayed on. The rest of Warner's regiment slogged back to the New Hampshire Grants to batten down their farms for the harshest winter in a decade.

Snow blanketed the hills and forests of Quebec and the downpour turned to stinging sleet in the darkness. The roads churned into knee-deep morasses of freezing mud. But an American victory looked inevitable, even without the Green Mountain Boys. Carleton's army was retreating and had yet to win a battle. Montgomery was confident enough to write his wife that he hoped to see her in six weeks.

Ethan Allen's rival, Benedict Arnold, would not be out-flanked. He went to Massachusetts to get paid for his service at Ticonderoga and to lobby Washington, who entrusted him with a command "of the utmost consequence to the interest and liberties of America." Arnold planned to strike with a second army deep into the Canadian woods to surprise the British at Quebec City as Montgomery advanced northeast from Montreal. Washington stressed to Arnold that "upon your conduct and courage, and that of the officers and sol-diers detached on this expedition, not only the success of the present enterprise, and own honor, but the safety and welfare of the whole continent, may depend."

Arnold marched eleven hundred men to the shuttle voy-age up the Kennebec River, where 220 flat-bottomed row-boats had been slapped together from green wood. He was already running late for the season, without enough food, ammunition, foul-weather gear, or helpful maps. He drove his untested troops up the Kennebec into wilderness in what is now Maine, through a trackless maze of forests, swamps, and raging rivers deep into Quebec. By his estimate, more than a hundred tons of supplies, including provisions for six weeks, had to be hauled around waterfalls and up rapids in wooden rowboats. The trek was so grueling that some who lost their way starved to death. When their rations of salted beef and salt fish spoiled, they slurped flour mixed with water into a thin paste that constipated rather than nourished the hungry. A pet Newfoundland dog was devoured, paws and all. Leather cartridge boxes were boiled into a phantom broth. Soldiers too weakened to stand dropped in their tracks. "When we attempted to march, they reeled about like drunken men, having now been without provisions five days," recalled one soldier. Rain, wind, and floodwater battered the column with hurricane ferocity, but Arnold ordered his commanders to press on, leaving the ill and weak to find their own way back. One Continental colonel, short of rations himself, turned his regiment around and marched them home, refusing to continue the death march.

By November 2, 1775, they were met by the first French Canadian peasants who greeted them with an abundance of food. Cattle were slaughtered and eaten. Their hides were stitched into moccasins for the barefoot. Arnold arranged to have beef and potatoes waiting as his column, stretching twenty miles, straggled in. Men too famished to digest meat wolfed down hot bread and butter, milk and eggs. "The politeness and civility with which the poor Canadians received us added to our joy," Arnold's surgeon said.

Arnold emerged at the south bank of the St. Lawrence with 675 gaunt survivors. His audacious trek, he claimed, was "not to be paralleled in history." In eight weeks, they had covered nearly 600 miles, he reckoned, wading nearly 120 miles through water up to their waists. Quebec City's governor ordered all boats removed from the south bank of the St. Lawrence. But Arnold scrounged about thirty canoes and dugouts from local Indians to ferry five hundred men overnight across to the city's outskirts, where he demanded its surrender, threatening that "if I am obliged to carry the town by storm, you may expect every severity practiced on such occasions."

The governor answered with his cannon. A hundred of Arnold's muskets toted through the wilderness no longer worked. Gunpowder had dissolved in the rainwater and slush. "My brave men were in want of everything but stout hearts," he reported, "and would gladly have met the enemy, whom we endeavored in vain to draw out of the city, though we had not ten rounds of ammunition a man, and they double our numbers." In frustration, he pulled back to await Montgomery's arrival in a foot of snow on December 1, 1775, with supporting artillery and three hundred New Yorkers and Canadian allies.

But General Carleton arrived first in a sailing brig on November 19, 1775, to take charge of Quebec's citadel and its small garrison of fusiliers, marines, and gunners. One hundred fifty Scottish recruits shipped in from Newfoundland to join other settlers from Montreal in a new regiment named the Royal Highland Emigrants. Each recruit was promised two hundred acres of land in any British province of America. Carleton pressed sailors from ships in the harbor. Civilians unwilling to fight were given four days to quit the city or be presumed traitors and spies. By December, Quebec's garrison swelled to as many as eighteen hundred untested defenders. Carleton knew his adversary Richard Montgomery. Both had served sixteen years earlier in the British expeditionary force that defeated the French on the same battleground. Carleton was determined not to repeat the mistakes that cost France its empire in North America.

The battleground in Quebec City had frozen too deep for conventional siege trenches, so the Americans built fortifications of ice. They dragged a half dozen cannon and a mortar to within seven hundred yards of the citadel wall, but the defending artillery blew the flimsy ice ramparts apart. Montgomery's attack plans were betrayed by a deserter. Carleton refused to parley with the Americans, who were reduced to shooting arrows over the walls with scribbled promises of safe passage to England if he capitulated.

Montgomery implored Schuyler to "strain every nerve to send a large corps of troops" to his aid as soon as Lake Champlain was navigable. "We are not to expect a union with Canada till we have a force in the country sufficient to insure it against any attempt" to reassert Britain's control, he wrote on December 26, 1775. By the time his appeal reached Congress eleven days later, it was too late. The enlistments of his New Englanders would expire on New Year's Day 1776, leaving Montgomery no option but to attack.

The Americans, outnumbered two to one by the defenders, had to strike before their army melted away. Montgomery unleashed a desperate assault at two a.m. on Sunday, December 31, 1775, in a howling blizzard. Ghostlike in hooded white blanket-overcoats, the Americans approached the city walls behind curtains of swirling snow. They stuck sprigs of hemlock and pieces of white paper in their caps to distinguish one another from the enemy.

The glow of their lanterns alerted British sentinels. Sword in hand, Montgomery led one charge through snow drifting waist-deep down the lower street of the old town, and called for his troops to follow. Grapeshot blasted from a hidden cannon fatally struck his head, thigh, and groin and killed a dozen more. Disoriented, the Americans pressed on in darkness. Ira Allen and his comrade Robert Cochran had been sent to feign an attack on the highest bastion but their guide, lost in the storm, took them in a circle.

Benedict Arnold led an assault from the north with scaling ladders and a pair of cannon dragged on sleds. A musket ball ricocheted through Arnold's left leg, and lodged inside his ankle and heel. "Rush on, brave boys!" he shouted. Snow blinded the Americans to incoming enemy fire. Wet gunpowder rendered as many as nine in ten muskets useless. The attackers dropped from their scaling ladders and fell back.

Had Montgomery not been killed nor Arnold wounded, they might have won the battle. Instead, it was daylight when two soldiers carried Arnold to a hospital inside a Catholic convent where a surgeon dug shards of metal and bone from his leg. He refused to be moved to a safer hideaway or let other casualties surrender or be evacuated. He had his pistols loaded and placed next to his sword. He ordered that loaded muskets be laid on the blood-soaked straw pallets of the men wounded and dying around him. They were his soldiers in a fight to the death if the enemy burst into the ward. Snow was still falling when the American attack collapsed by mid-morning. Carleton prudently kept his troops inside the citadel.

The British-born prisoners of war were told to swear allegiance to the Crown and enlist in the Royal Highland Emigrants or risk hanging in England as traitors. Casualty lists showed that seventy-seven Americans did join the "King's Service." But so many considered the forced oath as not binding that they tried to desert at the first opportunity, and all were tossed back into prison.

Arnold, weak from loss of blood and unable to stand, regrouped the remnants of the northern army, reduced now to eight hundred men, for a blockade of Quebec City. Snow lay six feet deep, despite a heavy rain and January thaw. He lacked the seasoned artillerymen and engineers needed for a fresh assault. He reckoned that five thousand more men were needed to ensure victory in Quebec. "I hope we shall be properly supported with troops by the Congress," he scrawled in a letter to his sister from his bed on January 6, 1776. "I have no thoughts of leaving this proud town, until I first enter it in triumph." By the end of February, Arnold was restless to return to the war. His wound had healed, he assured Washington, "and I am able to hobble about the room, though my leg is a little contracted and weak."

Montgomery's death left Major General David Wooster the senior American officer in Canada, with a command beyond his competence. He was well into his sixties and sipping his courage daily from "flip," a potent alcoholic punch tamed with sugar, egg, and nutmeg to which he had grown addicted. He pleaded for more troops. Washington had none to spare.

From the security of Montreal, Wooster implored Seth Warner to bring his Green Mountain Boys back to the war. "I have not time to give you all the particulars, but this much will show you that in consequence of this defeat our present prospect in this country is rendered very dubious, and unless we can be very quickly reinforced, perhaps they may be fatal, not only to us who are stationed here but also to the colonies in general," he wrote a week after the lost battle for Quebec. "You, sir, and your valiant Green Mountain Boys, are in our neighborhood, you all have arms, and I am confident ever stand ready to lend a helping hand to your brethren in distress, therefore, let me beg of you to raise as many men as you can, and have them in Canada, with the least possible delay. No matter whether they march together, but let them come on by tens, twenties, thirties, forties, or fifties, as fast as they can be prepared to march."

Seth Warner had cause to disregard Wooster, who had tangled with the Green Mountain Boys before the war. Wooster held New York title to three thousand disputed acres in the northern New Hampshire Grants, and had brought a sheriff to eject the settlers holding competing titles. Both were tied to a tree and threatened with a flogging until Wooster agreed not to disturb the homesteaders.

Warner could not order his demobilized Green Mountain Boys to leave their cabins and families in midwinter. So he mustered a fresh regiment and within ten days raised more than 170 men to follow him back to Canada through drifting snow and headwinds to salvage the foundering invasion. They traveled in small bands up the treacherous ice of Lake Champlain, on snowshoes or clinging to sleighs carrying supplies to what remained of the shattered army. During those short, bleak days and frostbitten nights, a southbound traveler reported meeting "many parties upon the lakes hanging upon the sleighs like bees about a hive." By mid-March 1776, 407 men joined the new regiment of Green Mountain Boys in Montreal.

Seth Warner was so persuasive at recruiting men to fight that a Massachusetts regiment from the Berkshires agreed to join them. Congress dispatched more regiments from Pennsylvania and New Jersey on a six-hundred-mile slog to Quebec. A committee canvassed door-to-door around Philadelphia collecting blankets to keep the troops warm. When the Pennsylvanians appeared in late March, the fence posts of Quebec were barely visible under five feet of snow.

About nine hundred American soldiers hung on in Quebec through the winter, awaiting reinforcements, too disheveled to re-form into two new regiments as Congress requested. Of Arnold's eleven hundred veterans, 284 were left by late March, and their enlistments would expire in mid-April. Local Canadians no longer trusted the American army to protect them, and refused to supply food or transport without payment in hard cash.

Snow turned to slush in the spring rain. Smallpox spread among the Americans, who, without adequate clothing or shelter, began to fall sick and die in a widening epidemic.

On April 2, 1776, Arnold was out riding among his troops when his horse fell, injuring his unhealed leg so badly that he had to return to Montreal. The alcoholic Wooster was left to maintain Arnold's blockade of Quebec before the river ice broke up and admitted a flood of fresh British troops from across the Atlantic.

FOUR

This Thievish, Pockey Army

Ethan Allen had disappeared since his capture at Montreal in September 1775. Levi Allen, the third of his five younger brothers, concocted a scheme to find him in England and spring him from prison. Levi imagined that he "could do a great deal, by raising a mob in London, bribing a jailer, or by getting into some service employment with the jailer, and overfaithfulness, make myself master of the key, or at least be able to lay my hand on it some night," as he pitched it to George Washington. An aide replied that Washington did not foresee "even a probability of success in your scheme; it would be running yourself in danger, without a prospect of rendering service to your brother."

Ethan lay shackled in the dank hold of the British schooner in Montreal through the autumn of 1775. Even when he contracted jaundice, his manacles were not loosened. Swinging from the hangman's noose, then hacked apart limb from limb, was the traitor's fate under English law. The doctor examining him concluded that Allen was "at last fully ripened for the halter, and in a fair way to obtain it."

Before Montgomery's army entered Montreal, Allen was moved to a warship whose captain, he said, "treated me in a very generous and obliging manner, and according to my

rank," though he had had none. The next ship, whose "po-
lite, generous, and friendly captain and officers shared their
cramped quarters," took him downriver to a cargo vessel
bound for England. He was jammed with thirty-three fellow
prisoners into a pine cage hammered together between
decks for the rough Atlantic crossing. It measured twenty by
twenty-two feet and was bare but for two excrement tubs. "It
was so dark that we could not see each other, and were over-
spread with body lice," he recalled.

The rations included a daily gill, or half-cup, of rum,
which Allen credited with saving lives. Only when the
green coast of Cornwall was sighted after nearly six weeks
at sea were the captives allowed sunlight and fresh air. The
ship docked at Falmouth in southwestern England. Guards
with swords cleared a passage through crowds that jostled
the filthy prisoners herded a mile uphill to sixteenth-century
Pendennis Castle. Allen still wore the grimy deerskin jacket
and red worsted cap in which he was captured nearly three
months before. An American traveler slipped him a guinea
coin and whispered that bets were laid in London on his
execution.

The stone castle with its large round tower seemed a lux-
ury to the prisoners, who shared bunks with straw to sleep
on. Its commandant sent Allen breakfast and dinner from his
table, with a bottle of wine. Allen wrote home to Congress
describing his ordeal. Let British captives be treated likewise
in America, he proposed, "not according to the smallness of
my character in America, but in proportion to the importance of the cause for which I suffered." Allen wanted his

letter "to intimidate the haughty English government, and screen my neck from the halter."

"Do you think that we are fools in England, and would send your letter to Congress, with instructions to retaliate on our own people?" demanded the officer who opened it. The letter was sent to the acting prime minister, Lord North, a politician loath to sully his career by signing the death warrant for a colonial whose celebrity grew by the day.

The authorities were stumped over what to do with Allen. He could have been hanged briskly enough in Canada, but making him "dance the Tyburn jig" in England was different. Gentry rolled up to Pendennis Castle in carriages to view Allen before he was carted to the gallows. He basked in the attention and harangued his visitors on the futility of defeating the American colonies.

News of his ordeal at sea reached George Washington, who protested that Ethan Allen "has been treated without regard to decency, humanity or the rules of war; he has been thrown into irons, and suffers all the hardships inflicted upon common felons." Since the Americans held British General William Prescott captured in Montreal, Washington warned, "whatever treatment Colonel Allen receives, whatever fate he undergoes, such exactly shall be in treatment of Brigadier Prescott, now in our hands. The law of retaliation is not only justifiable, but an absolute duty."

In London, the curmudgeonly Samuel Johnson declared that Americans were "a race of convicts, and ought to be thankful for anything which we allow them short of hanging." But Ethan Allen was still a British subject, others argued, which entitled him to the rights of any Englishman. The radical mayor of London, John Wilkes, sought a writ of habeas corpus to secure the release of Allen and his fellow captives. "No part of the subjects of this empire will ever submit to be slaves," he told Parliament. "I'm sure the Americans are too high-spirited to brook the idea."

Edmund Burke declared his misgivings about waging war on the American cousins. "We cannot falsify the pedigree of this fierce people, and persuade them that they are not sprung from a nation in whose veins the blood of freedom circulates," Burke told the House of Commons. "An Englishman," he said, "is the unfittest person on earth to argue another Englishman into slavery."

The day after Christmas 1775, Lord North's cabinet considered how to get rid of Ethan Allen. The solicitor general urged that he be not hanged but bribed, as the king did to placate his domestic critics. He suggested that a "person of confidence" in the government offer to pardon Allen's "misdemeanors" in attacking Montreal. If Allen switched sides, he could not only command a regiment of American Loyalists but also preserve his landholdings in the New Hampshire Grants when the rebellion collapsed.

The next day the solicitor general mused, "I am persuaded some unlucky incident must arrive if Allen & his people are kept here." Within two weeks, Allen was removed from England to Ireland before he incited more English sympathy for the American cause. Fear of retaliation saved Allen from the gallows because the rebels held "a considerable number of prisoners," the Earl of Suffolk explained later in Parliament.

Allen was put aboard the *Sole Bay,* a frigate bound for the port of Cork in Ireland, where a British convoy was gathering to cross the Atlantic for an assault on Charleston, South Carolina. He was taken below to a storage closet and forbidden to show himself on deck, which was restricted for gentlemen only. After a few nights, he was invited by an Irish petty officer to share his berth.

Allen's reputation had preceded him. Sympathetic merchants brought wardrobes tailored for thirty-four American prisoners aboard the frigate. "My suit I received in superfine broadcloth," Allen marveled, "sufficient for two jackets, and two breeches." He also got eight shirts from Holland, silk and worsted stockings, two pair of shoes, and two beaver hats, one of which was trimmed with expensive gold lace.

Cork's businessmen also tried to deliver pickled beef, plump turkeys, tea, sugar, and chocolate for the hungry prisoners, plus some Dutch gin and wine and a little cash. The *Sole Bay*'s captain confiscated everything but the clothing, swearing that the damned American rebels should not be feasted by the damned rebels of Ireland.

Weather delayed the convoy in Cork for more than a month. The ships were blown off-course by a winter storm so fierce, as Allen recalled, that "no man could remain on deck, except that he was lashed fast, for the waves rolled over the deck by turns, with a forcible rapidity, and every soul on board was anxious for . . . their lives." The *Sole Bay* limped into the island of Madeira for repairs before crossing the Atlantic. It made land at Cape Fear, near Wilmington, North Carolina, where the first troops to disembark were shot at by snipers and had to decamp to a more distant island in the harbor. "This did me some good to find my countrymen giving them battle," Allen wrote. One of his men jumped overboard and swam to freedom with news of Allen.

Allen was transferred with other prisoners to a ship bound for Nova Scotia. Some sailors and captives contracted scurvy for lack of vitamins. Several crew died. "I was weak and feeble in consequence of so long and cruel a captivity," Allen recalled, "yet had but little of the scurvy."

Seven months had passed in captivity when Allen reached Halifax in August 1776. The prisoners were transferred to the local jail and allowed some medical care. From jail, he wrote to Connecticut's legislature that "the English rascally treatment to me has wholly erased my former feelings" toward England. "I have never asked better treatment than what the laws of arms give to prisoners," he claimed, but objected to not being treated like an officer. "The prisoners have the liberty of the yard; but there is no distinction between gentlemen and others. If I must suffer the vengeance and ignominy of tyrants, it would be more graceful from Turks, Moors, and barbarians."

In October 1776, Allen and the other prisoners were packed aboard a frigate bound for New York City under a more tolerant skipper. "When I came on deck, the captain met me with his hand, welcomed me to his ship, invited me to dine with him that day, and assured me that I should be treated as a gentleman," Allen wrote. The captain told him that "one gentleman never knows but that it may be in his power to help another." Allen hoped that it meant he would be exchanged for a British officer.

He arrived in New York City in late November 1776, and was released on a parole that confined his movements beyond Brooklyn. He was flat broke, in ill health, and starved for news of his family.

If Ethan Allen was ignorant about the outcome of the American invasion of Canada, so was Congress, which dispatched Benjamin Franklin to find out what had befallen its northern army. The grand old patriot was seventy years old and ailing. He landed in Montreal with two delegates from Maryland after a month of hard travel in April 1776. They were greeted by Benedict Arnold, who was now general-in-charge. The news was not good. The Americans sent to liberate Canada had stumbled into a quagmire. Pork, a staple of soldiers' rations, had run out. Wheat and flour were hard to come by without cash. The troops lived hand-to-mouth, grabbing what they could from the locals, often at the point of a bayonet. Franklin's delegation bought thirty loaves of bread to feed themselves. They had failed to bring what was needed most, hard currency. The northern army racked up so many debts that Canadian creditors refused to accept promissory notes. Debilitated by smallpox and unable to pay its troops, the army teetered on collapse.

Franklin left for Philadelphia, where he helped draft the Declaration of Independence. His fellow delegates stayed long enough to report to Congress: "The army is in a distressed condition, and is in want of the most necessary articles—meat, bread, tents, shoes, stockings, shirts." Some nine hundred troops remained by late February 1776, and many were eligible to be discharged. Reinforcements rushed from Pennsylvania and other states raised it to as many as 2,500. But fifteen hundred enlistments expired on April 15, 1776. Disease rendered 500 more unfit.

"You will have a faint idea of it if you figure to yourself an army broken and disheartened, half of it under inoculation or other diseases; soldiers without pay, without discipline, and altogether reduced to live from hand to mouth, depending on the scouts and precarious supplies of a few half-starved cattle and trifling quantities of flour," the delegates reported to Congress.

General Wooster was replaced by John Thomas, who arrived to find his army at fewer than two thousand men, half of them in hospital and verging on starvation. Most Americans had never been exposed to smallpox, but General Washington had forbidden his troops to inoculate themselves for fear that they would be too weak to fight. Thomas, who was a doctor, declined to inoculate himself in deference to Washington's orders. Smallpox had reduced Seth Warner's regiment from 417 to as few as 102 able fighters by March 1776. He showed his Green Mountain Boys how to smear the toxic pus of stricken comrades, or corpses, into knife cuts on their thighs, a court-martial offense.

The melting ice on the St. Lawrence brought a convoy from England carrying advance units of an expeditionary force that would grow to eight thousand British and hired German troops. On May 6, 1776, a British frigate rammed through the ice into the harbor, Union Jack fluttering, followed by two more warships. Two companies of redcoats and a company of blue-jacketed marines disembarked, and by noon had linked up with the citadel's defenders in a battle formation of eight hundred troops with four cannon. The Americans could field barely 250 men and a smaller cannon.

General Thomas planned to consolidate his units on more defensible terrain southwest of Quebec City, but when he sounded retreat, the confused troops broke and ran, leaving behind cannon, muskets, hospital supplies, clothes, and ammunition. Nearly two tons of gunpowder fell into British hands. Thomas's dinner lay uneaten at his headquarters, along with critical papers. A young captain ran back to scoop them up. A hundred smallpox patients tried to flee the hospital. Many were abandoned for the British to treat. General Carleton promised that once their health was restored they could go home.

Montreal had to be abandoned as the last Canadian support for the Americans evaporated. "I tremble for the fate of our scattered, sick, starved Army," Arnold wrote, "as well as for our friends in this country, many of whom will lose their all if we are obliged to evacuate it." Canadians who had risked lives and fortunes to help the Americans were left to fend for themselves. General Thomas died of smallpox on June 2, 1776, on his way to defend Chambly, the key town fifteen miles southeast of Montreal. He left behind what he had described as an army "disheartened by unavoidable misfortunes, destitute of almost every necessary to render their lives comfortable or even tolerable."

Washington had sent one of his best military engineers,

Lieutenant Colonel Jeduthan Baldwin, to shore up the defenses in Quebec. He witnessed what he called the northern army's "cowardly and shameful retreat." Within days, he caught smallpox too. A doctor told Baldwin that he had a good deal more to bear before he felt better. On a rainy June 1, 1776, as General Thomas lay dying, about forty pustules erupted around Baldwin's face with a radiating itch. Despite his high fever, Baldwin knew that he was lucky to survive.

He could barely walk, but he left to lay out defenses at Chambly for the retreating army. He heard that 2,900 men were ill at Chambly and St. Johns, chiefly from smallpox, as they braced for the British assault. Some officers ran off and left their men stranded on the riverbank, Baldwin observed, "to be taken care of by me or others."

He had nearly lost a leg fighting Britain's last war against the French, but the retreat left him disgusted with army life. While he set to work on Ticonderoga's defenses, the campaign chest containing all his clothes, cash, and other valuables was stolen from his tent. Baldwin wanted Congress to discharge him, "as I am heartily tired of this retreating, ragged, starved, lousy, thievish, pockey army in this unhealthy country." General Gates scraped up $98 to buy Baldwin some new clothes, but refused to let him go.

Seth Warner's troops were stationed along Ile d'Orléans, a twenty-one-mile island of farmland in the St. Lawrence, on the easternmost flank of the collapsed American blockade. Now he had to infiltrate his Green Mountain Boys back through British lines. Their enlistments had expired several weeks ago, but Warner wielded them into a mobile rear guard, fighting one skirmish after another to force the British regulars to stop and fight as the American army retreated.

The self-effacing Warner left no account of this grim combat. But one of his captains described years later how Warner exposed himself to constant danger by retrieving casualties during the retreat. "He was always in the rear, picking up the wounded and diseased, assisting and encouraging those who were least able to take care of themselves, and generally kept but a few miles in advance of the British, who closely pursued the Americans from post to post," Daniel Chipman related to his son John in a biography of Seth Warner published in 1858. "By calmly and steadily pursuing this course, by his habitual vigilance and care, Warner brought off most of the invalids, and with this corps of the diseased and infirm, arrived at Ticonderoga a few days after the main army had taken possession of that post."

The Americans, short of ammunition, stopped in St. Johns long enough to tear off two and a half tons of lead sheathing from the roof of the best building to melt down into bullets before torching the town. Baldwin pushed off in the last boat on June 19, 1776, with Benedict Arnold, who had his horse shot so the British could not use it.

The retreating American army had stopped to regroup at Ile aux Noix on the river ten miles north of Lake Champlain. As many as eight thousand troops—"as fine an army as ever marched into Canada," one officer called them—crowded onto the narrow island of 210 acres without shelter from constant rain. Half suffered from smallpox, malaria, dysentery, and other diseases. As many as nine hundred who died on the island were dumped into two mass graves. Their general begged Washington to let him resume the retreat. "One fortnight more in this place will not leave us well men enough to carry off the sick," he warned. The evacuation of Ile aux Noix took eight days.

Scant help awaited soldiers who made it south across the border into New York. Several thousand survivors lay in tents or huts, or on bare ground around the ruined fortifications at Crown Point, without medicine or fresh food. "Everything about this army is infected with the pestilence," remarked its commander, General Gates, "the clothes, the blankets, the air, and the ground we walk on."

John Adams described the returnees as "an object of wretchedness to fill a human mind with horror, disgraced, defeated, discontented, diseased, naked, undisciplined, eaten up with vermin; no clothes, beds, blankets, no medicines; no victuals, but salt pork and flour."

Congress's army, by British estimates, lost to death and desertion as many as five thousand men in their disastrous invasion of Canada. "Our misfortunes in Canada are enough to melt a heart of stone," Adams wrote his wife, Abigail. "The smallpox is ten times more terrible than British, the Canadians and the Indians together."

The Declaration of Independence, approved in Philadelphia on July 2, 1776, boosted morale when a copy reached Fort Ticonderoga. On Sunday, July 28, 1776, General Gates read it out to his troops, who responded with three cheers.

But Washington could no longer depend upon militias. He needed Continental volunteers, regulars, ready to march and fight. On July 5, 1776, Congress created a regiment filled primarily by Green Mountain rangers and led by Seth Warner and other officers who had served in Canada. Warner was promoted to colonel and his deputy, Samuel Herrick, to lieutenant colonel. New York again objected to promoting them. With no colony willing to adopt them, the Green Mountain Boys formed an additional regiment in Congress's own foreign legion alongside two regiments of French Canadians and a battalion of German immigrants.

As the northern army trickled in through the summer of 1776, a new generation of American partisans infiltrated back into Canada to shadow the British army. Ethan Allen's cousin, Remember Baker, had been beheaded on such a mission a year earlier, but he was replaced by new scouts like Benjamin Whitcomb, a New Hampshire ranger who became the eyes and ears of the Continentals, including Warner's regiment.

Whitcomb excelled at long-range reconnaissance patrols a hundred miles north of Fort Ticonderoga. By canoe and on foot, he and his spies snaked along the forested eastern shore of Lake Champlain, floating north to the St. Lawrence River below Montreal. They slept outdoors and avoided cooking lest a wisp of smoke betray them.

Whitcomb was in his late thirties, nearly six feet and "rather thin than otherwise"—so said British posters that offered fifty guineas' reward for his capture. His lank brown hair was tied back with a ribbon. He wore a sleeveless jacket with slash pockets and a floppy hat with a gold cord, and carried a musket, powder horn, and blanket, like other hunters. But he called unwelcome attention to himself when he gunned down a British general on horseback in July 1776.

Benedict Arnold had dispatched Whitcomb to Canada to track British movements and abduct an officer for interrogation. Whitcomb staked out his ambush near a wooded ravine between St. Johns and Chambly, near the road defended by Seth Warner and his Green Mountain Boys the previous September. On July 24, Brigadier Patrick Gordon, resplendent in the scarlet tunic of His Majesty's 29th Regiment of Foot, galloped past. Whitcomb broke cover too late to stop him, and fired, shattering his target's right shoulder. Gordon barely made it back to his unit before falling off his horse. Whitcomb lay in the knee-high brush till dark. He counted upward of forty carts and a regiment of redcoats before escaping into the woods, pursued by Indian trackers.

General Gordon lingered for a week before dying, and was given a hero's funeral in Montreal. Whitcomb knew his bullet had struck an officer whose ornate epaulets confirmed his high rank. He was more upset that a leaf had fluttered across his sight as he pulled the trigger on Gordon. He prided himself on never missing when he hunted deer.

Shooting from behind rocks and trees struck British officers as cowardly. Despite their reliance on colonial rangers for their scouting, generals were the nobility of the caste-conscious British army. A general might lose his life in valiant combat or a foolish duel, but not taking the air on horseback away from the battlefield. A British flag of truce was dispatched to Fort Ticonderoga, demanding that Whitcomb be handed over for "due punishment, which can only be effected by the hangman."

Instead, Whitcomb snuck back to the same spot and snatched Gordon's quartermaster with his corporal on September 13, 1776. Jeduthan Baldwin watched them delivered unharmed by canoe to Fort Ticonderoga for interrogation.

Whitcomb was disparaged as "an unlettered child of the woods from the frontier of the Hampshire Grants," but his scrupulous notes impressed General Gates, who forwarded them to Congress. "I never knew any man more capable of doing good service in the ranging or scouting way, than Lieutenant Whitcomb," vouched Gates. Congress promoted Whitcomb to captain, authorized to raise two more companies of fifty rangers each. Their spy operations were so perilous that Whitcomb's Independent Corps of Rangers seldom exceeded eighty men. And they were paid so erratically that Whitcomb sometimes had to advance their wages from his own pocket.

FIVE

A Green Mountain Boy
Serves His King

Ben Whitcomb could not have missed the fleet that General Carleton was building to reclaim Lake Champlain. Where roads did not exist, armies had to travel by water. Boats sent in sections from England and Quebec were hauled overland for reassembly at the boatyard in St. Johns and pulled by wagon around the rapids. The flotilla included several dozen armed row-galleys and longboats crewed by seven hundred British seamen drafted from ships in the harbor at Quebec City.

To halt the British, Gates chose Benedict Arnold, who hammered together a fleet from unseasoned lumber in the small dockyard at Skenesborough, at the southern end of the 120-mile lake. When promised sailors failed to appear, he pressed militiamen at Ticonderoga, many of whom couldn't swim, into duty as novice seamen, and forbade them to go ashore lest they desert. He complained to Gates that "we have a wretched motley crew in the fleet, the marines, the refuse of every regiment, and the seamen, few of them ever wet with salt water."

Arnold's pocket navy was propelled by sweeps—long

oars—as much as by sails. His four biggest gunboats were hardly more than seventy feet long; other gunboats were fifty feet or less. The gondolas were squat barges up to fifty-four feet long and fourteen feet wide. Some were so cramped that crews had to sleep in shifts on deck. Arnold considered his boats and their crews as expendable as cannon.

In late September 1776 he sailed his pocket flotilla down Lake Champlain and hid out in a shallow channel between a wooded humpback of Valcour Island and the New York lakeshore. The British fleet overshot the Americans and had to tack back against a stubborn northerly wind. Carleton's warships drew too much water to enter the island's shallows.

What ensued from October 11 to 13, 1776, was the most curious naval battle of the American Revolution. For five hours or more, two fleets of glorified rowboats traded broadsides, often at point-blank range, blinded by battle smoke. Arnold had to aim cannon himself when his crews didn't know how. Grapeshot and cannonballs shattered the mast of the schooner *Royal Savage*, which Arnold had captured in May 1775. He abandoned it in such haste that he forgot to take receipts for his expenses in Montreal, without which Congress would not reimburse him.

The British salvaged ten cannon and some swivel guns from the *Royal Savage* before setting it afire. As they watched it burn, Arnold, under cover of a thick fog and moonless night, rowed what remained of his fleet single-file through the blockade. Two damaged gunboats had to be scuttled; a third foundered on a rock. "On the whole, I think we have had a very favorable escape," Arnold reported to General Schuyler.

General Carleton was mortified to have missed the chance to destroy the American fleet. He hoisted canvas to overtake the fleeing boats. Reeling from salvo after salvo, the gunboat *New York* lost every officer but its captain. Three British warships hulled the *Washington*, a row galley seventy-two feet long, with so many cannonballs that it sank in sixty feet of water. Its captain struck his colors and surrendered to spare the *Washington*'s crew. Carleton paroled more than a hundred captured crewmen the next day on their pledge to fight no more.

Arnold traded broadsides with the British for a couple of hours until he ran out of ammunition. With his boat shot to pieces, he raced for the New Hampshire Grants on the eastern shore of Lake Champlain, where he slammed his row-galley and four smaller gunboats aground and set them ablaze, flags flying. He ordered his marines to jump overboard with their muskets, scramble up the bluff, and form a line to defend the burning boats. Arnold jumped last and blew up his boat, heedless that his lieutenant lay dying on the deck.

Arnold led the crews ten miles through the forest, dodging an Indian ambush. He reached the American base at Crown Point before dawn with two hundred survivors. He felt, he said, "exceedingly fatigued and unwell, having been without sleep or refreshment for near three days." The Americans walked a dozen more miles south to Fort Ticonderoga before the British landed at Crown Point on October 15, 1776.

Arnold's fleet was destroyed. Of fifteen larger boats, only

four could float. Eighty crewmen were killed; 120 were cap-tured. But he had stopped a British invasion for another sea-son. "Few men ever met with so many hairbreadth 'scapes in so short a period of time,'" General Gates marveled. The laurels that Ethan Allen had craved were bestowed on his rival, Benedict Arnold.

Crown Point was still smoldering when Carleton's navy arrived. "The rebel fleet upon Lake Champlain has been en-tirely defeated in two actions," he declared in a dispatch to London with a caveat. "The season is so far advanced that I cannot yet pretend to inform your lordship whether any-thing further can be done this year."

Rather than risk becoming snowbound in a hostile wil-derness, Carleton sailed back to winter quarters. He took aboard forty or so Loyalist refugees from New York and the New Hampshire Grants. They had been guided to Crown Point by the Green Mountain Boy Justus Sherwood.

Justus Sherwood left few clues why he remained loyal to Britain. As clerk of the frontier settlement of New Haven, he respected law and order. As an Anglican, he may have revered the king, head of the Church of England. It was enough that in the revolutionary fervor of the New Hamp-shire Grants, neutrality was no longer an option. When he had joined the Green Mountain Boys four years earlier, their declared enemy was New York, which threatened to eject set-tlers from their homesteads in the New Hampshire Grants. He had no quarrel with Britain, which could vindicate his land claims over New York's.

Sherwood was a third-generation American. His grandfather had arrived from England back in 1634. But in the summer of the Declaration of Independence in 1776, revolutionary committees across the colonies required that everyone swear allegiance to the new United States. In the New Hampshire Grants, settlers who refused to prepare for war were threatened with fines. Without written proof of patriotism, it was unsafe to travel without being arrested. Yet Sherwood made no secret of his loyalty to the king and admitted to "exerting his influence to prevent the people in his vicinity from taking arms against His Majesty." He might have hung on had he kept his unpopular opinions to himself. But friends and neighbors could no longer shield him.

In August 1776, his farm in New Haven was invaded by armed intruders who ransacked his cabin. They broke open his chests and scattered all his papers and writing, destroyed the furniture, and carried off clothing and provisions. His farming tools and livestock, ten cattle and seventeen hogs, were stolen. Sherwood, not his assailants, was placed under arrest. By declining to swear allegiance, he had forfeited his right to redress or protection from theft or assault. He was allowed to post bail, probably because of his standing as town clerk in New Haven, and went home to await the judgment of the local committee of safety. Before the night was over, Sherwood was pulled out of his bed by more armed freeloaders. Sherwood no longer had legal grounds to evict this "guard of insulters," as he called them. He was brought before the committee of safety to explain why he had not taken the compulsory loyalty oath.

As the proprietor's clerk of New Haven, Sherwood had

been entrusted with its charter and other documents, kept in his tidy handwriting. The township records vanished, and were never found. Sherwood may have buried them, possibly marking the spot with an overturned pot to retrieve later.

After a month in jail, Sherwood was sentenced to prison for life within a copper mine in Connecticut northwest of Hartford. The Simsbury mines had been converted into a dungeon eighty feet underground, into which enemies of independence could be dumped, to die neglected and forgotten. But before he could be transported to the mines, a shocking sentence that Sherwood considered worse than death, he broke away from his keepers to "fly to the mountains."

Sherwood had already taken the precaution of transferring title to his farm to his father-in-law to shield it from confiscation. He sent his wife, Sarah, now seven months pregnant, to live with her family of sheep farmers. But when he vented his anger in Bennington, he was publicly flogged with twenty lashes. He escaped into the woods, collecting twenty Tories on the run, piloting them and a score more fugitives to Crown Point in time to run across General Carleton, who carried them to Canada. Delivering forty recruits entitled Sherwood to a captaincy in the Queen's Loyal Rangers, a new regiment of American Loyalists raised to fight for the king.

His loyalty to the Crown, Sherwood reckoned later, cost him two thousand acres of land and the season's bumper harvests. The lost bounty of his "honest labor and thrift" included, by his tally, a dozen acres with good haystacks, twelve more acres of harvested wheat, three acres of oats, ten acres of corn, potatoes, and other garden vegetables. But the most painful loss was leaving his pregnant Sarah behind, not knowing whether he would see her again, or their unborn child.

Through the summer of 1776, survivors of the calamitous campaign in Canada converged on Fort Ticonderoga and a log fortress being built on Mount Independence, a rocky bluff across the narrows of Lake Champlain. Without tents to keep them dry, soldiers no longer able to fight lay on boards exposed to sun and rain. Now dysentery swept through the New Hampshire Grants, overwhelming basic sanitation at Ticonderoga. Illnesses thrived in such close quarters: the chills and fever of an ague spread by mosquitoes, typhoid from polluted water, the debilitating "bloody flux" of diarrhea, "bilious putrid fevers," and malignant strep throat.

General Gates ordered more "vaults" and "necessaries"—outhouses and privies—to be built "in such places as are least obnoxious." Soldiers who failed to use the latrines and committed their "nastiness in any other part of the camp," he announced, would be punished on sight with forty lashes of the whip.

Even safe on New York soil, soldiers fell prey to malnutrition and disease. "The wretched condition they are now in, for want of almost every necessary convenience of life, except flour and bad beef, is shocking to humanity and beggars all description," said a Pennsylvania colonel, "Mad" Anthony Wayne, who assumed command of the garrison at Fort Ticonderoga. "We have neither beds nor bedding for our sick to lay on or under; other than their own clothing; no medicine or regimen suitable for them; the dead and dying laying mingled together in our hospital, or rather house of carnage, is no uncommon sight."

The garrison thinned out as the damp lake fog gave way to falling snow, and more men hurried home. In the winter of 1776–1777, ill-clad defenders froze to death in the unheated stone buildings and log huts around the forts. With four weakened regiments totaling twelve hundred men and boys, of whom three hundred were due to depart, their commander could do little more than mount guards, send out some scouts, and scavenge for firewood, which became scarcer as trees were cut down to stoke the fires. Cooped up together, the troops were again at each other's throats. In one brawl, some Pennsylvanians opened fire on their Massachusetts allies, wounding several men. "It had already risen to such a height that the Pennsylvania and New England troops would as soon fight each other as the enemy," said a Yankee brigadier.

Nearly half of new recruits showed up unarmed. Reinforcements promised from New York were delayed for lack of muskets. Departing militiamen balked at turning in their weapons until they got paid. Of nineteen hundred troops in Fort Ticonderoga's garrison by May 1777, one in four had to be armed with spears. Thirteen hundred pairs of shoes were requisitioned for the troops, but only nine hundred were delivered. One third of the "poor wretches" serving in one Pennsylvania regiment turned out for duty barefoot.

Congress was preoccupied with the star-shaped fortress under construction across the lake on Mount Independence, formerly called Rattlesnake Hill for its abundance of vipers. To link Mount Independence with Fort Ticonderoga, Baldwin crafted a floating log bridge a quarter mile long, supported by sunken timber piers, with a boom of logs linked by iron chains to choke off the southern narrows of Lake Champlain to British shipping. South of the fortifications, a wooded headland known as Sugar Loaf rose above the shoreline. John Trumbull, the son of Connecticut's governor, was jeered in the officers' mess when he argued that Sugar Loaf was worth defending. To prove his point, Trumbull fired cannon from Fort Ticonderoga and Mount Independence, hitting Sugar Loaf both times. He also took Benedict Arnold and other officers on a hike up the promontory. The ascent, they agreed, was "laborious, but not impracticable." But Trumbull could not persuade his superiors to include Sugar Loaf in the defense perimeter. Its summit looked too steep to accommodate cannon.

On January 15, 1777, Seth Warner and other delegates from fifteen townships in the New Hampshire Grants slogged through ice and snow to the courthouse at Westminster to arrange the formal break from New York. Warner estimated that three in four residents of the eastern Grants wanted a separate state, as did almost all settlers to the west. The rest were neutral, Warner said, ignoring the minority who, like Justus Sherwood, preferred British rule. With Ira Allen presiding over the small convention, the outcome was foregone. The delegates named their state New Connecticut, because so many settlers came from Connecticut. They resolved to draft a new constitution when they next met in June 1777.

Ethan Allen's brother Heman and three others traveled to

Philadelphia to ask that New Connecticut be seated in Congress as one of the "free and independent American States." The New Hampshire Grants, they reminded Congress, not only fed and supplied the Continental Army at Ticonderoga, but could also muster more than five thousand men capable of bearing arms in defense of American liberty. Their bid to become, in effect, the fourteenth state was vetoed by New York, which warned the other states not to tolerate this "dangerous insurrection." It accused the Green Mountain Boys of "sundry and iniquitous pretensions" and rescinded Seth Warner's rank of colonel.

Congress hastened to assure New York that it never meant "to give any encouragement to the claim of the people aforesaid, to be considered as an independent state." Seth Warner, it claimed, was just one of many officers who had raised a regiment in the service of the United States. More rebuffs followed. New Connecticut was already taken as a name by a district on the Susquehanna River in Pennsylvania. It would be inconvenient, Congress decided, "for two separate districts on this continent to have the same name." It fell to an old mentor of Ethan Allen, Thomas Young, to devise an alternative from the early French explorer Samuel de Champlain's description of the Green Mountains—"les monts verts." Young proposed that the New Hampshire Grants start calling themselves Vermont.

Snow blanketed the ground in March 1777, when General Carleton dispatched Justus Sherwood on a long-range reconnaissance south of Lake Champlain with five scouts. Whatever intelligence these Loyalists could gather would inform Lieutenant General John Burgoyne, who had returned to Montreal from London with a secret plan to end the American rebellion. Sherwood took advantage of his mission to stop by his in-laws' sheep farm where he surprised Sarah, who was nursing their baby daughter, Diana. Their overnight reunion was forgivably passionate, for after he rode off, her belly began to swell again.

For nearly six weeks, Sherwood's spies roamed the villages, pastures, and woodlands north of Albany, New York, gathering intelligence, from the strength and disposition of rebel forces to local political sentiments. Sherwood must have scaled Sugar Loaf, for he prepared detailed sketches of the defenses at Fort Ticonderoga, down to the number and location of artillery and troops. He was nearly undone when a Patriot patrol caught two of his men. Sherwood escaped by sprinting with his other three scouts to the patrol's beached boats and pushing off into Lake Champlain.

Sherwood returned to Canada with a trove of information for the invasion envisioned by Burgoyne, which he would join as a captain in the Queen's Loyal Rangers. His reports drew the attention in London of the secretary of state for the American colonies, Lord George Germain.

Whatever fortune favored the United States in its struggle for independence would have to include King George's choice of an arrogant titled peer to shape his policies there.

Lord George Germain had some talent but more ambition. Other Members of Parliament scorned or feared him. His best generals loathed him, remembering how he had been cashiered from the army. But they couldn't ignore him, because Germain positioned himself at the nexus of His Majesty's most significant decisions, not least General Burgoyne's invasion of the American colonies in 1777.

Germain was ignorant of the rugged terrain on which he deployed his fighting force, envisioning Europe's tidier fields of battle and network of highways that he had trotted as a cavalry officer. He never showed the least curiosity to visit the colonies, but he micromanaged the war, unconcerned that overstretched British regulars could not occupy so vast an expanse as America. "To attempt to conquer it internally by our land force is as wild an idea as ever controverted common sense," the army's adjutant general had told a fellow general in June 1775. It made perfect sense to Germain, with his disdain for the misguided colonists.

His story must begin with his original identity as George Sackville, born in 1716, who after studying at Trinity College in Dublin embarked on a military career. His gallantry earned him promotion in Britain's interventions around Europe. But hubris at the battle of Minden in Germany in 1759 triggered his downfall. As general commanding the British cavalry, Sackville pretended not to understand orders to attack from his German superior. He delayed unleashing his horsemen, who were poised to slash down the wavering French troops with their sabers. The French escaped.

Sackville was court-martialed for disobeying orders and

cashiered from the British army. King George II wanted him shot for cowardice, but settled for pronouncing him "unfit to serve his Majesty in any military capacity whatsoever." The sentence, which the king considered worse than death, was read out in every British regiment.

Banished from court, barred from military office, and ostracized from London society, Sackville plunged into ignominy. Through a private act of Parliament in 1770, he legally assumed the surname of his godmother, Betty Germain, a condition of inheriting her fortune. Over the next fifteen years, now as Lord Germain, he climbed his way back into politics by resurrecting his career in Parliament. He rejected any notion of compromise with the colonies, rising in Parliament in April 1774 to declare: "I look upon America to be our child, which I think we have already spoiled by too much indulgence." Germain curried favor with the new King George III and carved out a portfolio as a leading hawk in his cabinet.

Lord Germain was nearly sixty years old by the time he became secretary of state for the American colonies in November 1775, giving him control as the king's sole commissioner over as many as fifty thousand soldiers in North America. He was intolerant of incompetence among his subordinates and competence among his rivals. He focused upon trivial decisions, such as who among his troops in Canada deserved winter mittens, but was oblivious to strategic details that left him culpable for the eventual loss of the American colonies. While Germain sneered at American generals for calling themselves officers, British generals resented having to salute a scoundrel who had disgraced their uniform. In London society, Germain was referred to as Lord Sackville or, behind his back, as "Lord Minden."

One of Germain's first decisions was to fire General Guy Carleton, who had saved Canada by expelling the American army from Quebec. King George had awarded Carleton the prestigious Order of the Bath for preventing Canada from becoming the Americans' fourteenth colony. Germain's notice of dismissal, dated August 22, 1776, had failed to reach Carleton, who was building his fleet on Lake Champlain. Germain blamed Carleton for not inciting Canada's native tribes to go on the warpath. "The dread the people of New England, etc. have of a war with the savages proves the expediency of our holding that scourge over them," Germain maintained. "The Indians report that had General Carleton permitted them to act last year, Canada would not have been in the hands of the rebels."

Carleton did not learn he was dismissed until Germain's next dispatch arrived seven months later. Germain was bent upon destroying Carleton, a veteran old enough to remember Germain's disgrace at Minden. Carleton's failure to capture Fort Ticonderoga after his naval victory, by Germain's bizarre logic, had left George Washington free to defeat the Hessians down in Trenton, New Jersey, two months later in December 1776.

Germain replaced Carleton with John Burgoyne, a flamboyant cavalryman admired in his own social circle as a witty playwright for the London stage. Carleton had to relinquish most of his troops to Burgoyne, whom he outranked, but hung on to his civil appointment as governor general of Canada. He had reason to feel bitter, but he pledged "every assistance in my power" for Burgoyne's invasion.

General Burgoyne, at fifty-five years, was growing old for military campaigns, but he had great expectations about this one. He sold Germain on his plan for three simultaneous offensives in 1777 to cut New England off from the other colonies. Burgoyne would lead the main force south through Lake Champlain to the Hudson River, to be met by General William Howe's army marching north from New York City. A smaller brigade would strike eastward from Lake Ontario. If Burgoyne's three-pronged offensive succeeded, Loyalists would rise up to join them and the rebellion would fall apart. Burgoyne stressed, and the king agreed, that the success of his plan depended on the invaders from Canada linking up with Howe's troops from New York. But Germain, who had no notion of distances in colonial America, let Howe go off and capture Philadelphia first.

Because not enough Englishmen were enlisting to fight in America, Burgoyne would have to fill out his expeditionary force with four rented German regiments that he considered inferior. General Henry Clinton, who became commander-in-chief of British forces in America, had wanted to hire Russians because, he explained, "They have no language but their own; they cannot desert." But "Cousin Kitty," as King George called Empress Catherine of Russia, refused to lease him twenty thousand of her infantrymen. Instead, the king asked his brother-in-law, the Duke of Brunswick, for 4,300 infantrymen and horseless dragoons. Hiring armies from German princelings who "snuffed the cadaverous taint of lucrative war," as Edmund Burke described them, was routine in European wars.

With Germain predicting that the rebels would sue for peace by the following winter, King George assured the House of Lords on June 6, 1777, that "the operations of this campaign, by sea and land, will be blessed with such success as may most effectually tend to the suppression of the rebellion in America."

As many as thirty thousand German troops, many on the cusp of middle age, would be shipped off to fight in America. They did not consider themselves mercenaries because they served their own rulers. Seth Warner and his Green Mountain Boys would face some of their toughest battles against the rented Brunswickers.

SIX

Burgoyne Bogs Down in Vermont

Washington expected Burgoyne's main force to sail down the St. Lawrence River and attack New York City. He refused to tie down "a useless body of troops" at so remote a backwater as Ticonderoga. "As the garrison at Ticonderoga is sufficient to hold it against any attack," he instructed General Schuyler, "I do not think it politic, under your representation of the scarcity of provisions, to send up troops to consume what ought to be thrown into the fort."

Three hundred miles to the north, preparations for the invasion were visible. Troops, cannon, and supplies filled up the harbor and streets of Montreal. Burgoyne was aghast to find a leaked document "publishing the whole design of the campaign almost as accurately as if it had been copied" from his superior, Lord Germain.

Burgoyne headed south to Lake Champlain in mid-May 1777 with an invasion force including by his count nearly eight thousand British and German troops and four hundred Indian warriors. His train of artillery had 142 cannon, howitzers, and mortars to batter down the defenses at Ticonderoga. The army was led by some of the finest professional soldiers in Europe, eclipsing what backwoods America could field. His deputy, General William Phillips, was Britain's top artilleryman, adept at deploying horse-drawn cannons across a battlefield. The advance guard was led by Brigadier Simon Fraser, who had refined the army's light infantry tactics. The general commanding the Brunswickers, General Friedrich Adolf von Riedesel, had hired out in small wars around Europe and Canada.

Burgoyne had to import his army's food from England, three tons a day, for lack of a dependable local supply. There were not enough wagons and draft oxen to transport his army's baggage, which included his personal stock of champagne. Mounts for his officers and dragoons had been left in England because horses fared badly on Atlantic crossings. He expected to acquire his horses and carts locally, as he would his mistress, the wife of one of his supply contractors.

Burgoyne also had qualms about his force of four hundred mostly Iroquois warriors, drawn from as far west as the Great Lakes with promises of plunder and scalps. They were baffled by his orders to strike fear into Britain's enemies but scalp only the battle dead.

General Gates knew that his army could not hold Fort Ticonderoga and Mount Independence when as many as ten thousand troops were needed to fill out the extensive trenches and fortifications. He had asked Congress for six artillery companies. Two had been sent. The dirt roads were too rutted to haul in supplies by wagon. He passed the buck to his successor, General Arthur St. Clair, a Scot who had left the British army to marry a Boston socialite. When St. Clair took command, he inherited 2,200 men half armed and ill-equipped. Many were barefoot. One in ten had a bayonet. And no paper was available to fold gunpowder and bullets into individual musket cartridges. Storage facilities at Ticonderoga had so rotted that nearly fifty pounds of gunpowder spoiled every week.

St. Clair acknowledged that the "insufficiency of the garrison at Ticonderoga, the imperfect state of the fortifications, and the want of discipline in the troops give me great cause to apprehend that we shall lose that fortress." By June 17, 1777, his garrison numbered 1,576 Continentals, 52 scouts under Ben Whitcomb, 250 Massachusetts militiamen whose enlistments were about to expire, and three New Hampshire militia regiments who "go off whenever they please." Spaced along the winding perimeter they were assigned to defend, St. Clair reckoned that "they would have been scarcely within reach of each other's voices."

Whitcomb's spies found themselves fighting for their lives in small skirmishes with Burgoyne's Indians whenever they sallied forth. Scalps were harvested on both sides. "My scout on which I depend much for intelligence, is not yet returned, nor, I fear, ever will now," St. Clair wrote Schuyler. "It consists of three men only, the best of Whitcomb's people, and picked out by him for that purpose. The woods are so full of Indians, that it is difficult for parties to get through. I shall send off Whitcomb himself presently, for intelligence I must have, although I am very loath to put him upon it, lest he should fall into the hands of the enemy, who have no small desire to have him in their power."

The Americans began their retreat, giving up Crown Point without a struggle. Two British frigates and fifty smaller gunboats sealed off the narrow width of the lake. By July 2, 1777, the British redcoats were advancing along the lake's western coast to Fort Ticonderoga, while the German troops splashed up the swampy eastern shore toward Mount Independence, expecting a protracted siege. "It was impossible—so we said—that the enemy would abandon the fort, which had cost the English many thousands of men in the last war," wrote a Brunswick officer.

Burgoyne ordered his Iroquois warriors, through an interpreter, not to spill blood "when you are not opposed in arms." He declaimed that "aged men, women and children must be held sacred from the knife or hatchet." The Indians cheered—their rum ration was about to be doled out—but Burgoyne's instructions would come back to haunt him.

Some warriors had been drinking his rum when they probed Fort Ticonderoga's defenses. "The Indians were so much in liquor that I found it impossible to bend them to obedience," reported Simon Fraser, who lost two killed and three wounded in a wild shootout with American pickets, possibly some Green Mountain Boys.

As the noose tightened around Ticonderoga, Seth Warner rode out to find more recruits to strengthen its defenses. St. Clair had feared that they would eat up his food rations, but now Burgoyne was expected to attack any hour. Warner rounded up seven hundred militiamen and rangers from

New Hampshire and Massachusetts, as well as the Grants. His cousin Ira Allen was away in the Connecticut River town of Windsor, drafting a constitution to transform the New Hampshire Grants into an independent state-in-waiting. The seventy-one delegates agreed that "the said district should ever be known by the name of Vermont," but bogged down over the details.

Warner asked the convention to rush volunteers, and forty or fifty head of beef cattle, to the aid of the beleaguered defenders of Ticonderoga. "Their lines are so much in want of men," Warner wrote, "I should be glad that a few hills of corn unhoed should not be a motive sufficient to detain men at home, considering the loss of such an important post can hardly be recovered."

But the delegates were desperate to adjourn to protect their families and farms from Burgoyne's invasion, until a violent thunderstorm unleashed such lightning and torrents of rain as to convince some that Jehovah himself was "proclaiming to the convention a duty higher even than the personal protection of family and home." Sheltering inside the meetinghouse from crackling thunderbolts and sheets of rainwater, the delegates rushed through a constitution largely borrowed from Pennsylvania's. But it broke new ground with several reforms unprecedented for the American colonies: Vermont's constitution prohibited adult slavery; granted men without property the right to vote; and mandated a system of primary schools in every township.

* * *

The Americans' failure to fortify Sugar Loaf convinced Burgoyne that they knew nothing about military science. He could not conceive that the rebels would leave the highest ground outside their defense perimeter. "They seem to have expended great treasure and the unwearied labor of more than a year to fortify, upon the supposition that we should only attack them upon the point where they were best prepared to resist," he sneered.

On July 3, 1777, Fraser dispatched forty light infantrymen to take the hill, which they found unoccupied. A British military engineer climbed Sugar Loaf to confirm that it overlooked Fort Ticonderoga and Mount Independence, well within cannon range. General Phillips set four hundred soldiers to work clearing a track up the hill's wooded western slope, out of sight of the Americans. "Where a goat can go, a man can go," he declared, "and where a man can go, he can drag a gun." Using oxen and human muscle, ropes and harnesses, the British hoisted a pair of twelve-pound cannon, each weighing more than a ton, from tree to tree to the summit of Sugar Loaf, which they proudly renamed Mount Defiance.

The appearance of British cannon commanding the heights overlooking Fort Ticonderoga and Mount Independence on July 5, 1777, caused panic among the garrisons below. St. Clair had planned to fall back from Fort Ticonderoga to Mount Independence for a last-ditch defense, but the cannon atop Sugar Loaf made this impossible. He called together his commanders and they agreed to withdraw as soon as possible before the British sealed off the last escape route south.

The United States needed its northern army to fight another day. Justifying his decision before a subsequent commission of inquiry, St. Clair told Congress later that "by abandoning a post I have eventually saved a state." Two militia regiments insisted upon going home when their enlistments expired in two days, "but their conduct was so licentious and disorderly, and their example beginning to affect the Continental troops," St. Clair explained, "I was constrained to send them off,"

St. Clair chose his three best Continental regiments to cover the army's withdrawal and stiffen the spines of the less disciplined militias. Colonel Ebenezer Francis would command the rear guard with his crack 11th Massachusetts regulars as the troops evacuated Fort Ticonderoga and Mount Independence. Then Warner would take command, brevetted to brigadier general for the operation. Warner knew the terrain ahead from his recruiting journeys, and his Green Mountain Boys were accustomed to fighting as a rear guard. And the colonel of the Second New Hampshire Continentals, Nathan Hale (no relation to the American spy hanged in New York City in 1776), would sweep up stragglers and protect the sick and wounded.

By nine p.m. on July 5, the regimental commanders were ordered to quit the ground they had resolved to defend. It was past midnight on July 6, 1777, when several thousand American soldiers tumbled out of Fort Ticonderoga and Mount Independence in a chaotic retreat. A sliver of moon faded with dusk, leaving them to stumble and curse in the dark, which at first spared them from being spotted by Burgoyne's vanguard. They left behind their cannon, ammunition, rations, and battle flags.

Some soldiers wanted to stand and fight, but more were desperate to escape. St. Clair rode back and forth, struggling to form the crowd into the semblance of a formation. Another general threatened to strike a soldier for disobedience, and was deterred when safety locks ominously clicked off on the muskets around him. To no avail, he pleaded that "orders must be obeyed" as the militiamen surged past. With so much disorder, Francis's Massachusetts riflemen could not clear Mount Independence until four a.m., near dawn.

The hasty evacuation was recounted by one of the forty or so African Americans in the garrison, who was told by his colonel to fall in about eleven o'clock that evening. "We immediately obeyed," he recalled. "He then ordered our tents to be struck and carried to the battery. On doing this, the orders were to take up our packs and march, which we also did; passed the general's house on fire; marched twenty miles without a halt, and then had a brush with the enemy."

To obscure their retreat behind the fog of battle smoke, St. Clair had given strict orders that no buildings be torched. But a disobedient French adventurer who had bluffed his way to a brigadier's rank set his cabin afire. The blaze exposed the Americans slipping away over Mount Independence and, one major observed, "gave the enemy an opportunity of seeing every movement we made."

A British lieutenant on picket duty reported that the Americans "set fire to several parts of the garrison, kept a constant fire of great guns the whole night, and under protection of that fire and clouds of smoke they evacuated the garrison." He recorded in his journal that night, "I never before saw such great fires."

James Thacher, the American surgeon's mate, helped load his sick and wounded aboard a flotilla of barges. He remembered the convoy's voyage up Lake Champlain, with three hundred barrels of gunpowder, as a delightful night cruise into a dawn bursting with sunshine. Drum and fife players had serenaded them with popular tunes. Rummaging through the hospital supplies, he said, "We found many dozen bottles of choice wine, and breaking off their necks, we cheered our hearts with nectareous contents."

The rest of the army hiked south with packs and weapons. Some of the reinforcements recruited by Seth Warner did not hear about the evacuation and suspected that St. Clair intended them to absorb the brunt of the British assault.

By daybreak, patrols of Brunswickers advancing into Mount Independence were stunned to find it abandoned. Around the star-shaped stockade, forty or more cannon of various sizes lay intact. At Ticonderoga, the British came upon fourteen more cannon, a half dozen of which had been spiked, and large stores of ammunition. By their estimates, the Americans had left behind several thousand muskets, tents and other equipment, clothing and provisions like rice, coffee, and sugar, even a new battle flag embroidered with gold and silver thread. The bunkers held abundant stores of meat, flour, sugar, coffee, wine, home-brewed beer, and medicine which the invaders consumed.

"Great fright and consternation must have prevailed in the enemy's camp," supposed their commander, General Riedesel, "otherwise, they would have taken time to destroy the stores."

Scattered on the ground were reams of Continental paper currency, which junior British officers used to light their pipes, unaware that it could be spent on small purchases from the locals. The rebels had "done not the slightest damage" to their fortifications and left even their bakeries and breweries intact. "If they had been formally beaten and by force dislodged from their entrenched positions, they could not have left more," observed a Brunswick brigadier.

When Burgoyne learned that the Americans had cut and run, he ordered that a "refreshment of rum will be given to the whole army on consideration of the heat of the weather and the alacrity with which the men have worked." He told London that the rebels were forced to leave behind 175 tons of flour and nearly 72 tons of salt-preserved meat, among other provisions.

Still, Burgoyne worried that his capture of Ticonderoga would not impress the king and his courtiers without sufficient prisoners to show for it. He dispatched his light infantrymen and grenadiers, and Brunswick dragoons and jaegers, hunter-marksmen, in pursuit of the Americans fleeing along a rough military road hacked a year earlier over the wooded hills.

The log-and-chain boom that stretched across Lake Champlain to block British shipping proved flimsier than its designer, Jeduthan Baldwin, expected. British sailors hacked through it in a half hour, freeing Burgoyne's flagship, *Royal George*, and another frigate to sail through in pursuit of the American boats. Where the lake narrows into a channel coursing between steep cliffs, a few artillery pieces strategically positioned might have stalled the British fleet. But the Americans, oblivious to danger, were unloading their boats at Skenesborough when the British warships riding a favorable wind arrived to rake the small harbor with cannon fire.

Three American gunboats blew up. Two others struck their colors and fell intact into British hands. American officers tried to rally their troops, but "every effort proved unavailing," Thacher said, "and in the utmost panic they were seen to fly in every direction for personal safety." As many as two hundred American boats were reckoned lost with their cargo.

The Americans set fire to the ironworks and storehouses before taking flight. The adjacent woods caught fire. Skenesborough became a scene of "complete destruction," General Schuyler learned, and "not one earthly thing was saved."

Burgoyne bragged to Lord Germain that the fires destroyed a great quantity of provisions and some weapons. All American baggage was "burnt, sunk, or taken." Tents and clothing that washed up along the lakeshore were salvaged by British sailors and Indian warriors who held "a kind of country fair with them the next day."

With war parties at their heels, Thacher and his comrades took to the smoking woods, leaving all behind. Walking through the night, they reached Fort Anne, "a small picket fort of no importance," where as many as 400 New Yorkers joined 150 New Hampshire militiamen in a futile counterattack. Low on ammunition and duped by a war cry into expecting more Indians, the Americans burned Fort Anne's blockhouse and stockade and retreated sixteen miles to the relative safety of a ramshackle American base, Fort Edward, near the Hudson River. Trophies collected by the British included a handsome new "flag of the United States, 13 stripes alternate red and white, in a blue field representing a new constellation." That evening, a lieutenant reported, "our Indians brought in two scalps, one of them an officer's which they danced about in their usual manner."

Burgoyne applauded the army's success from his new headquarters at Philip Skene's fieldstone mansion. "Every man must now perceive how essential it may be to the King's service to continue the pursuit of a flying enemy." Burgoyne urged them not to relax, "whatever may be the fatigue, while there is a prospect of overtaking the fugitives."

When General St. Clair learned that Burgoyne's army had overrun Skenesborough and destroyed the American fleet and supply depots, he turned his retreating army south by southeast into the New Hampshire Grants, toward the settlements of Castleton and Hubbardton. Responsibility for the crucial rear guard now belonged to Seth Warner, who commanded his Green Mountain Boys and the Continentals from Massachusetts and New Hampshire as a temporary brigadier general. Their mission was to force Burgoyne's army to stop and deploy its troops, giving St. Clair's force time to escape. Warner and his Green Mountain Boys had battle-tested such tactics in the retreat from Quebec. Now they would fight on home ground in the New Hampshire Grants.

The dusty column tramped through the sultry summer heat down the military road, hardly more than a rutted track winding over steep hills through forests and swamps. The New Hampshire Continentals were hard put to gather in so many stragglers—hundreds of walking wounded, ill or diseased, and other laggards too exhausted or drunk to keep up. Since leaving Mount Independence before dawn, they had hiked twenty-two miles to Hubbardton, a march that left Hale's regiment six miles behind the rest of the army.

Seth Warner was told to keep no more than a mile and a half distant, but two regiments of Massachusetts militia bivouacked between his rear guard and St. Clair's main force. Rather than leapfrog over them or leave the casualties behind, Warner let his troops stop and sleep in the woods.

In pursuit was Brigadier Simon Fraser, at the head of 850 chosen men from the most prestigious units of the British Army. His grenadiers were conspicuous for their imposing height, accentuated by conical headgear. His light infantrymen were selected for their agility and speed to cover the army's flanks and probe its front. Fraser was furious that they had committed "horrible irregularities" by stopping to plunder from abandoned rebel stories.

To make up lost time, Fraser refused to wait for his men to be resupplied with water, rations, and ammunition. Without provisions, he marched them nine miles to the first running water. For lunch, two bullocks were caught and slaughtered on the hoof. His men also rounded up twenty stray rebels, "all very much in liquor."

Some Brunswickers had also helped themselves to booty from the American supplies before overtaking Fraser, who was displeased to see their commander, General Riedesel. These Germans were a helpless kind of troops in the woods, Fraser thought. They could not deliver what he needed: ammunition, food, and medical supplies to treat casualties once he routed the Americans. Riedesel bivouacked for the night to rest his soldiers, but Fraser pressed on a few more miles to the next campsite with water. They agreed to resume their respective pursuits at three a.m. with Riedesel supporting Fraser.

Fraser had covered a couple of miles by daybreak when his scouts bumped into Warner's pickets, who fired and withdrew to their main force a half mile away. His Green Mountain Boys were down to 173 troops by the time they reached Hubbardton. Francis's Massachusetts regiment had 310 Continentals. Warner briefed his officers over hot chocolate at the cabin of a local settler. He was running late because he had sent a large patrol to round up civilians in danger.

Nathan Hale had left his regiment to his deputy as he moved about cajoling hundreds of invalids to keep moving. They were attacked as they cooked breakfast down by a local creek. "The enemy came at us without warning," recalled a captain. "We gave them battle. The engagement held one hour ten minutes, as hot a fire as ever was kept up." Before he was captured, the captain said, "great numbers fell on both sides, for hail never fell thicker."

Warner's and Francis's more seasoned veterans were caught off guard but they pivoted into formation. Warner had chosen his terrain well, placing his Green Mountain Boys astride a cart track running along a ridge of hill. On their flanks were his Massachusetts and New Hampshire infantrymen, many armed with .69 caliber Charleville muskets donated from France, with an effective range up to one hundred yards. Others carried heavier .75 caliber "Brown Bess" muskets, standard issue for the British army, with a shorter range of sixty to eighty yards.

The British regulars sweltered in their red wool uniforms and awkward headwear. Now they encountered Continentals wearing fringed rifle frocks of unbleached linen, which General Washington had authorized to let the enemy think every rebel wearing the homemade battledress was a skilled marksman.

Conventional tactics of eighteenth-century warfare called for tight formations of opposing infantry to trade volleys at close range before a final bayonet charge. Fraser's grenadiers and light infantry had mastered the bayonet over open ground. Here they had to advance uphill against an enemy hiding behind trees, rocks, and thick brush.

The opening volley fired by Warner's and Francis's men dropped twenty-one British regulars in the lead platoon. A Scottish officer climbed onto a tree stump for a better view and was shot dead. The smoking muskets enveloped the battlefield in a fog of war. Warner's rear guard laid down withering fire from behind fallen timber and a high log fence, then withdrew to positions uphill and reloaded before the British could re-form. "We drove them back twice by cutting them down so fast," recalled a New Hampshire teenager. "They couldn't drive us from the fence until they charged us." He fired his musket at least twenty times, reloading at the brisk rate of one aimed shot every twenty to thirty seconds. Some Continentals stuffed their musket barrels with extra bullets and buckshot for scatter-gun damage.

General St. Clair ordered the two militia regiments camped ahead to rush to Warner's aid. They refused and resumed their retreat. Colonels of three other New Hampshire regiments volunteered to help Warner, but were overruled, twice, by their general. Had they joined the fray, Fraser's regulars, lacking artillery or cavalry support, might have been overrun, turning the American retreat from Ticonderoga into a triumph.

The battle grew hotter. The British major leading his grenadiers was hit in the thigh. A Royal Marine accompanying him was shot in both eyes. The Earl of Balcarres, who commanded Fraser's light infantry, was wounded in the hip but survived, his uniform shredded by thirteen bullet holes.

Fraser expected the Americans to run when they saw his colors. Instead, his flank foundered as the Green Mountain Boys and Massachusetts riflemen maneuvered to turn and destroy it. Fraser was saved by Riedesel, who rushed his Brunswick grenadiers and jaegers into battle bellowing a Lutheran hymn played by their traveling band to make them sound more numerous. "The Germans pushed for a share in the glory and they arrived in time to obtain it," Burgoyne conceded.

Unprepared for the firepower with which the Americans greeted the Brunswickers, the jaegers shot back with high-velocity .67 caliber carbines that emitted a frightening crack and whoosh. The battle at Hubbardton lasted an hour and a half. Colonel Francis, fighting alongside his Massachusetts men, took a German bullet fatally in his chest. The British grenadiers scrambled up the ridge, clinging to trees and rocks, to cut off the rebels, who dropped their muskets and melted into the forest.

Outflanked, Massachusetts men quit the cover of a log fence and scattered across a wheat field, ignoring the entreaties of Seth Warner, who sat on a stump and cursed, shouting to his Green Mountain Boys to meet him back in Manchester. There was no time to reload or resist the onslaught of long British bayonets. Few Americans at Hubbardton carried bayonets or knew how to use one. But they did know how to shoot. After the battle, a British captain paused to pull some papers from Francis's body, and was wounded by a sniper who escaped unseen from his perch in a tree.

"In the open field the rebels do not count for much, but in the woods they are formidable," a Brunswick officer wrote. "There they lie like bacon hunters behind the trees and slip from one tree to the next. . . . Generally speaking, the rebel seeks safety in his gun, and this is very long. . . . But to our comfort such a shot carries only eighty yards, and they would be badly off if only our men knew how to hit the mark as well as they do."

Bent upon salvaging his career before a court of inquiry in 1778, St. Clair accused Seth Warner of not maintaining proper distance from the main force. Warner was not charged with dereliction. By forcing the British to break off their pursuit at Hubbardton, Warner, widely admired for his "cool courage and perfect self-possession," had inflicted substantial casualties before breaking contact when his troops were overrun. He disrupted the enemy's advance long enough for two thirds of his own rear guard to get away, while the rest of the American northern army escaped to fight another day.

Fraser now found himself deep in enemy territory, short of ammunition and food, and encumbered with 150 wounded men, 230 prisoners of war, and a stockpile of rebel weapons. "I was then in the most disaffected part of America," Fraser wrote a friend, "every person a spy." He threatened to have his Indians scalp any prisoners who tried to escape and put them to work building him a log bunker. His troops slept with their muskets in a downpour that night, expecting a counterattack while the rebels continued their retreat southward.

For the American prisoners, prospects looked bleaker. "We lay confined all day," said a captain. "It rained that night as hard as it ever rained." At two a.m., Fraser detached two companies of his grenadiers to take the prisoners of war to Ticonderoga. The wounded were left behind with a skeleton medical staff.

Justus Sherwood had come to Hubbardton as a scout and forager for Burgoyne, who doubted that Loyalists would fight. Sherwood had risked his life gathering intelligence for the invasion. Now he was under orders to find food and fodder for an army outrunning its supply lines. He led fifty Loyalist and Indian raiders into Castleton, interrupting Sunday worship, killing three residents and taking four captive. In Hubbardton, his men invaded the farm of a rebel sympathizer. The Indians tied him to a tree, stacked firewood around him, and threatened to burn him alive unless he revealed where he hid his flour. Sherwood had the farmer taken away with his two sons to do forced labor at Ticonderoga. He had more success rustling sixty oxen a mile from American lines.

Burgoyne hailed the battle at Hubbardton as a glorious victory, but it was Pyrrhic. The British and Germans who held the ground at the end of the day had been mauled. Fraser's advance corps, a British officer observed, "certainly discovered that neither were they invincible nor the rebels all poltroons. Many of them acknowledged that the enemy behaved well and looked upon General Riedesel's fortunate arrival as a matter absolutely necessary."

For the first time since Burgoyne launched his invasion, the Americans had stood and fought with such ferocity that the British and Germans broke off their pursuit of the northern army. At Hubbardton, the Americans lost about 370 men killed, captured, and missing. "The prisoners brought in resembled bandits rather than soldiers," a German grenadier expressed his contempt, "but were so perplexed that they begged for their lives like children."

The British and Germans lost about sixty men killed, and 148 wounded at Hubbardton from Fraser's advance corps who could not be readily replaced. For two days, the victors tended to their dead and wounded as St. Clair's main force escaped to safety.

Shallow graves were dug in a warm rain so drenching that it was hard to light a fire. A wounded British officer reported later, "the wolves came down in numbers from the mountains to devour the dead, and even some that were in a kind of manner buried, they tore out of the earth." The stench, he said, was "enough to have caused a plague."

Dying generals fill the history pages of the American Revolution. Ordinary soldiers caught in the thick of the fighting are easily overlooked. But one of the most harrowing tales of survival was related by a wounded Continental fifer captured at Hubbardton. His story made clear that many more Loyalists inhabited the New Hampshire Grants than Justus Sherwood.

Ebenezer Fletcher, sixteen years old, was a casualty of Hale's New Hampshire regiment. He was recovering from a measles epidemic at Fort Ticonderoga when he and other patients were ordered to "strike our tents and swing our packs." He was swept up in the evacuation and managed to walk as far as Hubbardton with his Uncle Daniel, a Continental soldier. "A large body of the enemy followed us all day, but kept so far behind as not to be wholly discovered," he said. "Their aim was to attack us suddenly the next morning, as they did."

Fletcher's comrades were eating breakfast beside the creek in Hubbardton, "and all in a very unfit posture for battle," when the cry sounded: "the enemy are upon us." He grabbed a musket. "My lads, advance," yelled his company captain, "we shall beat them yet." Fletcher followed his Uncle Daniel and sought cover with other soldiers in the trees. Fletcher pulled the trigger, but his musket failed to fire.

He reloaded and aimed again. As he turned to cock his firelock, a musket ball tore into his back. Fletcher crawled toward his uncle, who propped him behind a large tree next to another wounded soldier. Fletcher, bleeding, scrambled on hands and knees into the brush, and hid under a log. The enemy surged past so near that he could touch them. Faint, he expected no mercy if he were taken. "Here is one of the rebels," said a British soldier who pulled off Fletcher's shoes. The teenage fifer, lying among the wounded, begged to be well treated. "Damn you," the thief replied. "You deserve to be used well, don't you? What's a young rebel like you fighting for?"

An officer, "a pretty sort of man" as Fletcher recalled, ordered the thief to return his shoes and help Fletcher into camp, where he joined American prisoners of war. As he lay helpless, everything of value was stripped by his captors, from his fife to his silver shoe buckles and the kerchief around his neck. "Some of the enemy were very kind," Fletcher remembered, "while others were very spiteful and malicious."

That afternoon, a British doctor stopped by to extract the musket ball embedded in Fletcher's back. "Well, my lad," the doctor asked, "think you'll be willing to 'list in the King's service if you get well?" No, Fletcher replied, and asked if he would recover. There was some prospect, the doctor told him, though his condition looked hazardous.

A couple of British regulars, likely teenagers too, took pity on Fletcher, whose fair hair and small stature made him look younger than his sixteen years. They made up his pallet from hemlock bark, padded with coats and overalls stripped from the dead and wounded, under a bark shelter to keep him dry from the rain. A soldier fetched spring water and brought Fletcher tidbits of pork and liver, apologizing that it was all he could find. The next day, the soldier was ordered to march on, and pumping Fletcher's hand, wished him well.

"The difference in mankind never struck me more sensibly than while a prisoner," Fletcher reflected. "Some would do everything in their power to make me comfortable and cheerful; while others abused me in the vilest of language; telling me that the prisoners would all be hanged." Fletcher wanted to escape but the doctor thought that he was too grievously wounded to travel when horses and litters arrived to carry the other casualties to Ticonderoga in a bone-jolting ordeal. Some wounded redcoats preferred to walk out than be jostled on the crude litters. Fletcher did not expect to survive the trek. He stripped the boots off another man who died, "supposing my right to them equal to any other person." After dark, he slipped into the woods.

Without a moon, he became lost. He bumped into rocks and trees, and slipped knee-deep into mire. Shadowy beasts seemed to stalk him. From their howling, Fletcher took them for wolves. He was heartened to see campfires ahead. When he crept near enough to overhear strange voices, he knew they were hostile. He wandered uphill into the dark. His wound throbbed when he lay down and tried to sleep.

The boom of a British morning gun jolted him awake. He felt he had no choice but to surrender. Following the drumbeats from the camp he had skirted, he heard a rooster crow and stumbled across a field to a farmhouse. He identified himself as a wounded Continental on the run.

"You have been rightly directed," its owner replied, "for had you gone to either of my neighbors, you would have undoubtably been carried to the enemy again; you have now found a friend, who will if possible protect you." That man had been forced to swear allegiance to the king. He gave Fletcher food and drink and brought him inside. Armed Loyalists were looting and hunting down rebels, and if Fletcher were to be found, his host would suffer. He had to leave to transport British supplies in his wagon but his wife cleansed Fletcher's gunshot wound with rum and dressed it "with every mark of kindness." She gave him a blanket to sleep outside in the bushes till dark when she let Fletcher back in. Her brother-in-law, another Loyalist who had taken up arms against his country, was staying overnight. He agreed not to turn Fletcher in, but told him to leave at once and hide during the day.

Fletcher limped out that night, tripping over muddy roots and stones. He dodged more Loyalist patrols before locating a friend of his father who thought that he had died in battle. When Tory neighbors came for Fletcher, his host backed them off with a loaded gun. Fletcher set forth anew. Finding the next town deserted, he limped back and begged to be taken in. He recuperated for six weeks in his protector's home until a horse could be hired to carry him to his mother in New Hampshire.

His return did not go unnoticed by a local Continental officer who had Fletcher arrested for desertion. His gunshot wound had not fully healed when he was sent to Pennsylvania to serve out two years left in his enlistment, in a campaign launched by Washington to destroy villages and crops of Iroquois supporting the British.

SEVEN

The Most Active
and Most Rebellious Race

When news of the capture of Ticonderoga reached London, the king burst into the queen's bedchamber. "I have beat them. I have beat the Americans," he announced. But in his colonies, the loss ignited outrage and rumors that Schuyler and St. Clair had been bribed with silver balls shot into their camps.

Washington wanted to know why Ticonderoga had been abandoned without a fight but he did not jump to conclusions. "People at distance are apt to form wrong conjectures," he told Schuyler, "and if General St. Clair has good reasons for the step he has taken, I think the sooner he justifies himself the better." To plug the defenses left by the collapse of his northern front, Washington turned to his New England militias, whom he had once disparaged as "an exceedingly dirty and nasty people." His aide Alexander Hamilton ordered brigadiers in New Hampshire and western Massachusetts to divert a third of their militiamen to Washington's army, which was regrouping near the Hudson River town of Saratoga. Schuyler's force of seventeen hundred or more Continentals had been reinforced with a thousand New Yorkers, but the coming harvest season made it almost impossible to retain troops when their enlistments expired.

There were not enough tents to shelter those who remained. Even cooking kettles had been left behind in the flight from Ticonderoga. "I have not one [musket], and many of the troops are without, consequently cannot give any," Schuyler reported. He had only five rounds of ball and powder for each American musket in his ranks. Burgoyne had authorized one hundred cartridges per soldier in his advance force.

"Though our affairs have for some days worn a dark and gloomy aspect, I yet look forward to a fortunate and happy change," Washington wrote Schuyler. "I trust General Burgoyne's army will meet sooner or later an important check, and as I have suggested before, that the success he has had will prove his ruin."

Burgoyne had put his invasion force at risk by splitting it into smaller detachments. If the Americans could cut off one enemy column, as few as four to six hundred men, a modest victory would boost morale. "In such an event, they would lose sight of past misfortunes," Washington said, and "at the same time by regard for their own security, they would fly to arms and afford every aid in their power."

Washington's hopes would be tested in the New Hampshire Grants where Burgoyne's forces were "killing and robbing the inhabitants and driving off the cattle for their own use," according to a colonel who described the American army as "in a very broken situation."

Burgoyne commanded that every township in the New

Hampshire Grants send at least ten residents to swear allegiance to the Crown and be issued certificates of protection. Several hundred townspeople did show up in Castleton but few would take the loyalty oath. Most wanted to stay neutral. Near the Connecticut River, seven of eight sons in Strafford's founding family enlisted to fight for Burgoyne.

Upon hearing that inhabitants of the Grants were accepting Burgoyne's protection, General Schuyler issued a counter-proclamation that collaboration with the British would be punished as treason. He turned to the Green Mountain Boys as his enforcers. "Thank the troops in my name, for behaving as well as you say they did at Hubbardton," he told Warner. "Assure them that I will get whatever I can to make them comfortable."

Congress still refused to recognize Vermont's declared independence from New York and Schuyler explained that "as an officer of Congress responsible to the thirteen United States of America, I cannot with propriety take notice of a fourteenth state, unknown in their confederacy." Instead, he appealed to Seth Warner to come to the defense of what were commonly called the New Hampshire Grants. "I think it will be right to leave Colonel Warner with his regiment and the militia belonging to the Grants," Schuyler told St. Clair. He sent the Green Mountain Boys a considerable quantity of powder and ball at the expense of other units for, he explained, "lead or balls, there are none arrived as yet." He provided $4,000—"which is all I can at present spare"—to pay back wages for Warner's men.

Schuyler proposed a scorched-earth strategy to prevent

the British from taking food and other provisions. "Secure all the cattle and carriages you can," he told Warner. "Much depends upon preventing them from getting supplies of that kind." Warner must be vigilant and round up known Tories before they could join Burgoyne's invasion force. "If we act vigorously, we save the country," Schuyler said. "Why should we despond? Greater misfortunes have happened and been retrieved. Cheer up the spirits of people in your quarter."

As Schuyler wrote this on July 15, 1777, disease and desertion were thinning the ranks of his troops at Fort Edward, he told Washington, "for we have neither tents, houses, barns, boards, or any shelter, except a little brush. Every rain that falls, and we have it in great abundance almost every day, wets the men to the skin."

Seth Warner was in no position to carry out Schuyler's flurry of orders. Casualties at Hubbardton had whittled his regiment to as few as seventy-nine able-bodied troops who mustered for duty by August 3, 1777. Another fifty-six Green Mountain Boys were missing since the battle, and ten more were listed as deserters, though soldiers often went off to visit their families and farms before reporting back for duty.

Warner guessed that four thousand British and German troops were occupying the New Hampshire Grants. "The number of troops we have at present collected don't exceed five hundred," he noted, "and unless we have speedy help should the enemy approach, we must be obliged to retreat before them and leave them to possess a great deal of what we have."

Vermont's roads were choked with refugees fleeing south,

leaving livestock and households behind. A church congregation, hearing of the rapid British advance, joined the exodus without going home to pack. Warner's own regimental headquarters was in danger of being overrun in Manchester, where two prominent supporters of the Green Mountain Boys went over to the British. Schuyler promised Warner some militiamen from New Hampshire: "I hope when they come you will be able, if not to attack the enemy, as least to advance so near as to bring off the well affected"—who supported the Patriots—"and secure the malignants"—who might join Burgoyne.

Vermont had yet to create a government, but Ira Allen, acting as secretary of state, petitioned New Hampshire and Massachusetts for help. "This state, in particular, seems to be at present the object of destruction," he wrote. Without friends, he explained, "it will soon be out of the power of this state to maintain its territory." He proposed that New Hampshire "make a frontier for your state with our own, which can not be carried into execution without your assistance." A dispatch rider galloped 150 miles to deliver his appeal to the New Hampshire legislature, which voted to raise an army to defend Vermont. The chief executive of New Hampshire announced that three battalions of militiamen were being called up and sent under the local hero John Stark to "oppose the ravages and coming forward of the enemy."

John Stark was a canny ex-ranger whose hawk eyes, beaked nose, and receding hairline gave him the look of a predatory eagle. When he was twenty-three, he was captured by Indians while out hunting and taken to Canada, where he was later ransomed for a pony worth $103. He commanded the New Hampshire militias at the battle of Bunker Hill in 1775. He helped extract the northern army retreating from Quebec in 1777 and by year's end led Washington's vanguard to victory over Hessian troops at Trenton, New Jersey. But when Congress passed him over for promotion to brigadier general, he went back to his farm. Four months later, he agreed to lead New Hampshire men to Vermont's rescue on condition that he suffer no meddling from Congress.

New Hampshire volunteers flocked to join Stark. He dispatched them across the Connecticut River into the Grants as fast as he could enlist and equip them. Many showed up without muskets and Stark, in any case, lacked enough molds to make the bullets. "There is but one pair in town," he said. Leaving one militia company to guard the stores and two others to protect the heights on his right flank, he crossed the Green Mountains and arrived in Manchester on August 9, 1777. He ignored an order from a Continental general to proceed to Fort Edward, making clear that New Hampshire allowed him to deploy his troops where he thought best. After consulting with Seth Warner, he agreed that his brigade would protect the Continental supply depot at Bennington.

The best place for New Hampshire to stand and fight, Warner convinced Stark, was in Vermont. "You may conclude the frontiers will be where there is a body of troops sufficient to stand [up to] the enemy," he said, and reminded Stark to bring some cooking kettles, for he had none to spare.

*   *   *

A grisly murder near Fort Edward jeopardized Loyalist support for Burgoyne and handed a propaganda boon to Washington. On Sunday morning of July 27, 1777, Jane McCrea, a local beauty admired for her lustrous hair, dressed in a fine gown to meet her fiancé, David Jones, a dashing lieutenant who led a detachment of Loyalist sharpshooters under Burgoyne's command. Jane did not arrive at Burgoyne's camp but her long hair did, attached to a scalp flaunted as a trophy by one of his native warriors. Hardly more than a month had passed since Burgoyne had threatened to unleash his native auxiliaries upon the American rebels: "I have but to give stretch to the Indian forces under my directions, and they amount to thousands." He promised them plunder and trophies and defined the scalps they collected as esteemed "pledges of conquest." The gifts showered on his indigenous warriors included, besides rum, scalping knives made in England and stamped with King George's initials.

The Indians' ritual was described by a junior officer on Burgoyne's march: "Whenever they scalp, they seize the head of the disabled or dead enemy, and placing one of their feet on the neck, twist their left hand in the hair, by which means they extend the skin that covers the top of the head, and with the other hand draw their scalping knife from their breast, which is always kept in good order for this cruel purpose, a few dexterous strokes of which takes off the part that is termed the scalp," he wrote; "they are so exceedingly expeditious in doing this, that it scarcely exceeds a minute." The severed scalp with hair attached was strung on a small hoop often painted red, a souvenir of prowess in combat.

The day Jane was killed, a war party butchered a Loyalist neighbor with his family and their slaves. Blacks tended to be spared for sale into commercial slave markets across the colonies. But Jane McCrea, being "of a good family, and some share of beauty" by one account, got the publicity. She had been dragged from her home, shot twice, scalped, and dumped in the bushes with her clothes torn off, as one atrocity tale told it. Another had her tomahawked, scalped, and tied to a pine tree to die.

Subsequent versions added inconsistent details. Jane McCrea and the old lady who would chaperone the tryst had fallen into the clutches of a couple of "savages" hired to deliver Jane to her fiancé in anticipation of a barrel of rum. The Indians quarreled over how to divide the rum and Jane. One sank his tomahawk into her skull, ripped off her scalp, and danced his trophy on a pole into Burgoyne's camp, with Jane's hair streaming a yard and a half long. The Americans blamed her death on Burgoyne's use of Indian "savages." "It was not long before some innocent persons were made victims of savage barbarity, by means of the scalping knife, in the hands of the barbarians under his command," wrote the surgeon James Thacher. Among their victims, he said, "was Miss Jane McCrea, who was murdered in a manner extremely shocking to the feelings of humanity."

Recriminations resounded through both armies. From the northern headquarters of the Continental Army, General Gates professed shock that "the famous Lieutenant General Burgoyne, in whom the fine Gentleman is united with the Soldier and the Scholar, should hire the savages of America to scalp Europeans and the descendants of Europeans, nay more, that he should pay a price for each scalp so barbarously taken.

"Miss McCrea, a young lady lovely to the sight, of virtuous character and amiable disposition, engaged to be married to an officer in your army, was, with other women and children, taken out of a house near Fort Edward, carried into the woods, and there scalped and mangled in a most shocking manner," Gates wrote to Burgoyne. "The miserable fate of Miss Jane McCrea was peculiarly aggravated by her being dressed to receive her promised husband—but met her murderer employed by you."

Burgoyne responded that Jane's death was "no premeditated barbarity." Two native chieftains had escorted her "for the purpose of security, not of violence to her person," but in their dispute over who would guard her, "the unhappy woman became the victim." The charge that Burgoyne paid for scalps, he said, was "diametrically opposed to truth."

Burgoyne made the Indians hand over Jane's suspected killer, a minor chieftain known as the Wyandot Panther. He was released after his tribesmen threatened to rampage their way home, slaughtering any British soldiers they crossed. Burgoyne decided that it would be more prudent to pardon the murderer than sentence him to an "ignominious death" by the hangman or firing squad.

Lurid accounts of Jane McCrea's martyrdom spread over time through the colonies and became a recruitment tool for the Patriots, who were not reluctant to embellish the grisly details. Washington exhorted militias in western Massachusetts and Connecticut to repel the British enemy, "who, not content with hiring mercenaries to lay waste your country to boost recruitment, have now brought savages, with the avowed and expressed intention of adding murder to desolation."

Farmers old enough to remember the terror of Indian raids took down their guns to protect their families and wreak revenge on Burgoyne and his savages. Loyalists realized that an oath of allegiance to the king could not guarantee protection. If the fiancée of an officer in Burgoyne's army could be scalped on her way to the altar, no wife or daughter was safe.

Burgoyne could not shake off the epithet of "hair-buyer." In his orders, he had threatened that his Indian auxiliaries would be paid for hunting down and scalping British and German deserters. His paymaster justified scalping as useful propaganda. "Nothing will bring the people of this country to a proper sense of their situation sooner than having the Indians let loose amongst them, especially those from the Northward," he wrote. "They are very much afraid of scalping, and this it is said is practiced—if not, the report answers fully the design."

Jane's fiancé, David Jones, had to buy her scalp back from the Indians, or so one ending goes. Jones asked to be discharged from the army. Turned down, he vanished into the Canadian wilderness with Jane's hair. Yet three years later, a Loyalist officer identified as David Jones led a raid on Fort Edward, and burned down the house of Jane's Patriot brother. A more credible account of Jane McCrea's death came from her chaperone, who said that Jane had been accidentally shot by Continental scouts chasing the Indians who were leading her away on horseback. An exhumation decades later found several bullet holes but no tomahawk dents in her skull. Her chaperone recognized Jane's scalp, she said, "because the hair was unusually fine, luxuriant, lustrous and dark as the wing of a raven."

Vermont's Council of Safety, the closest to a working government, wanted to raise another regiment of rangers, to be commanded by Warner's comrade-in-arms, Samuel Herrick. After debating how to pay for the new regiment, Ira Allen, the youngest and nimblest member of the council, proposed an ingenious revenue stream that was soon adopted: Why not make the Loyalists who sought protection under the British army bear the cost of defending the lives and property of those they left behind?

Local commissioners of confiscation were appointed to appraise the assets that the Loyalists left and sell them at public auction. This sequestration would prove so profitable that it underwrote Vermont's war against not only Britain but also New York, whose supporters in the Grants now faced having their property seized. The distinction between the British Crown and the colony of New York was blurred in what Ira Allen called "the first instance of seizing and selling the property of enemies of American independence."

Within a few months, Congress recommended that the thirteen colonies follow Vermont's confiscatory example. By shaking down New Yorkers as well as Tories, Vermont did not need to raise taxes to finance its share of costs of the American Revolution.

Burgoyne's war machine took more than three weeks to maneuver through twenty-three miles of Vermont wilderness, dense with swamps and man-made obstacles. Most British provisions were received from faraway England via Canada and hauled south through the northern forests. General Schuyler deployed as many as a thousand woodsmen to chop down trees in advance of Burgoyne's passage, interlocking their limbs into an impenetrable barrier that had to be hacked apart branch by branch. Rocks and trenches flooded the primitive roads with swamp water. British engineers had to build forty or more bridges, and a log causeway stretching for two miles across one swamp.

It would have been quicker and easier for Burgoyne to retrace his steps back to Fort Ticonderoga via two well-used portages around the lakes. But he marched his army overland for fear of the effect that, he said, "a retrograde motion is apt to make upon the minds of enemies and friends." Burgoyne's men swatted at clouds of gnats, mosquitoes, and flies and griped about the absence of pack horses. Their wool uniforms were stifling in the summer heat and soggy from daily rainstorms. A British infantryman slogging through the woods carried as much as sixty pounds on his back, including his musket, ammunition, haversack crammed with provisions, water canteen, and tenting. Soldiers caught malaria from wading through the swamps and food poisoning when their rations turned rancid, "as the heats then were very severe and violent, particularly in a camp," a lieutenant said. "All sorts of meat were tainted in a very short time, and the stench very prejudicial."

Tensions between the British and their German allies erupted into a brawl after some drunken redcoats insulted a German guard. Informed that liquor was to blame, Burgoyne warned that further misconduct would be seriously "punished as a crime the most fatal to the success and honor of the campaign." British regulars mocked the Brunswick dragoons as absurdly costumed in heavy cavalry boots, plumed hats, dragging ten-pound swords and carrying halters in expectation of horses to mount. Their general promised to exchange the stifling leather britches for linen overalls, though it is unclear how many were issued.

With his lines from Canada overextended, Burgoyne was running low on supplies. His personal baggage filled as many as thirty wagons though he scolded his junior officers for piling personal kits, barrels of Madeira and rum, and bags of coffee on the overladen two-wheeled carts, which had been hammered together in Canada from green wood and kept breaking down. His Iroquois warriors robbed horses from local inhabitants and sold them to Burgoyne's officers. He threatened to prosecute any soldier or local caught with a stolen horse.

The prospect of replenishing his livestock, carts, and food

by snatching rebel stores was too tempting for Burgoyne to pass up. He cobbled together a foraging expedition, selecting not Simon Fraser's light infantry, but a multilingual contingent of troops bound to antagonize the local population, German mercenaries looking for horses to ride, American Loyalists with scores to settle, and Iroquois warriors seeking plunder and scalps.

To lead them, Burgoyne chose a German lieutenant colonel, Friedrich von Baum, who spoke not a word of English. Burgoyne envisioned a lightning strike on the American storage depots at Bennington, but Baum's unmounted dragoons had to walk there, carrying their own flour to bake bread, and herding cattle on the hoof to slaughter for dinner. Any pretense of stealth was compromised by the Brunswickers' traveling band. Baum's superior, General Riedesel, had proposed such a raid earlier with a more robust force. Now he criticized it as too little and too late. Burgoyne had altered his plan so much that Riedesel could hardly recognize it. A retired British lieutenant who raised a company of local Loyalists reckoned that the Bennington area could not be safely entered with fewer than three thousand troops.

Burgoyne had assigned Philip Skene as Baum's liaison officer, "to help you distinguish the good subjects from the bad" among the local populace. Skene assured Burgoyne that Bennington's inhabitants supported the king by five to one, and would swell his ranks of volunteers. For neither the first nor the last time, an army was invading a hostile land without understanding either its language or loyalties.

Burgoyne ordered Baum to seize the livestock and other

supplies at Bennington, fill out his units with Loyalist recruits, find horses for Riedesel's dragoons, and requisition cattle, horses, and carriages from the local communities. Baum should take hostages "of the most respectable people" until their quotas in livestock and wagons were delivered. He assured Baum that Warner's Green Mountain Boys "will retreat before you, but should they, contrary to expectation, be able to collect in great force, and post themselves advantageously, it is left to your discretion to attack them or not, always bearing in mind that your corps is too valuable to let any considerable loss be hazarded on this occasion."

Burgoyne, like other British generals, considered the Loyalist allies incapable of any task more challenging than spying, herding livestock, or directing traffic. He had not brought extra muskets, or even shoes, for the volunteers he expected to rally to his standard. Some unarmed Loyalists were issued ropes to round up strings of ten horses each.

Baum's unruly Indian warriors kept grabbing horses to sell for themselves, and killed cows to take their bells for souvenirs. "If your Excellency would allow me to purchase the horses from the savages, stipulating the price, I think they might be procured cheap," Baum asked in vain, "otherwise they ruin all they meet with, their officers and interpreters not having it in their power to control them." Burgoyne turned him down.

Baum set out, leaving his tents and baggage behind. He meant to travel eastward across the Green Mountains to the Connecticut River. But after a mile, he halted, awaiting fresh orders directing him to Bennington.

The Brunswickers deployed from Castleton had been enticed by its big fat cattle and bounteous fields of grain. "The countryside is delightful around here, and we came across fat pastures that could nowhere be more beautiful," a German wrote home. "From time to time, one even saw small hummingbirds." But by mid-August, the Brunswickers passed abandoned fields of wheat and rye withering for lack of harvesters, in the wake of Warner's scorched-earth tactics. The forty-mile walk to Bennington took them over soggy rutted tracks that passed for roads. Baum's underfed horses dragged two brass cannon, and a clumsy ammunition cart. Days were mercilessly hot and humid, swarming with mosquitoes. Nights turned foggy and damp. Burgoyne now directed Baum to march and wait "until the detachment of Provincials under the command of Captain Sherwood shall join you from the southward."

Justus Sherwood's duties had been restricted to scouting and foraging until Burgoyne assigned him to lead the advance scout of fifty Loyalists and thirty Indians, making him Baum's eyes and ears in an area that Sherwood knew. Four miles from Bennington, his raiders caught five rebels guarding cattle. As they rounded up the livestock and a few horses and carts, they came under fire from a patrol of Green Mountain Boys, who shot one of Sherwood's men in the thigh before melting into the woods. In a few days, Sherwood would be fighting for his life against a larger force led in part by his former friend Seth Warner.

*   *   *

From the prisoners that Sherwood brought in, Baum surmised that fifteen to eighteen hundred rebels were at Bennington, and were bound to retreat at his approach. "I will proceed so far today as to fall on the enemy tomorrow early, and make such disposition as I think necessary from the intelligence I receive," he told Burgoyne in a message scrawled in French. "People are flocking in hourly but want to be armed." Skene assured Baum that the locals were friendly and wanted weapons in order to join him. They were instructed to pin strips of white paper on their hats to distinguish them from the rebels. There would be enough muskets for them when Baum scattered the rebels at Bennington.

Burgoyne's artillery had become a burden. He asked whether the road was practicable to move a "considerable corps of cannon," and instructed Baum to send back as many wagons and cattle as he could seize. Burgoyne also ordered another German regiment to march to reinforce Baum.

Stark had arrived in Bennington on August 9, 1777, and deployed his troops two miles west near the New York border. Warner, who had lived in Bennington, left his Green Mountain Boys in Manchester with his deputy, Samuel Safford, to show Stark the area and recommend how to defend it. Volunteers kept arriving without muskets. Stark dispatched a messenger to Boston to borrow weapons from the Massachusetts Council of Safety.

When Stark learned that Baum was approaching, he sent out two hundred New Hampshire militiamen, who bumped into Baum's force and withdrew. Hearing that more German grenadiers were expected, Stark moved up his planned attack from August 17 to 15. Warner sent word to bring in the Green Mountain Boys from Manchester.

Torrents poured down on August 15, 1777, soaking the gunpowder and forcing Stark to postpone his preemptive attack. Baum dug in atop a wooded hill, where he put his dragoons to work erecting fortifications from logs hewn on the spot or torn from nearby cabins. Stark's skirmishers killed or wounded about thirty of Baum's native warriors and their elderly chief. Stark now pulled back a mile to more advantageous ground, and sent out appeals for "all the lead you can possibly collect in your vicinity" to melt into musket balls. More volunteers, untrained and unarmed, arrived to join his growing army. So did some survivors of Nathan Hale's Continental regiment decimated at Hubbardton.

Every militiaman was supposed to bring his musket, plus a tomahawk, bayonet, or sword for close-quarter combat, three pounds of gunpowder, and a pound of lead bullets. Patriot ranks grew to two thousand volunteers without enough guns or ammunition. Some carried fowling pieces, others old muskets that had seen service in the French and Indian War. Their officers carried heavy swords forged from farm tools.

Through the night, several hundred Massachusetts militiamen arrived from the hilly Berkshires to the south. Among them were war-painted Indian allies from Stockbridge with tomahawks and muskets, eager to go out on patrol. The Reverend Thomas Allen, classics scholar in Harvard's Class of 1762, trotted up in the black sulky in which he made pastoral rounds of his congregation in Pittsfield, Massachusetts. Parson Allen roused Stark. "We have been frequently called out, but have never been led against the enemy," the preacher snapped. "We have now resolved, if you will not let us fight, never to turn out again."

"You would not march now, in the dark and rain, would you?" asked Stark, as his son Caleb recalled their exchange. "No," Parson Allen replied, "not just this minute."

"Then if the Lord once more gives us sunshine, and I do not give you a chance to fight," Stark promised, "I will never ask you to come again."

EIGHT

Victory at Bennington

The morning of August 16, 1777, sparkled with sunshine. Through his spyglass, Colonel Baum watched what appeared to be farmers bound for their cornfields. Were they rebels dodging another fight or Loyalists coming to join his ranks? Sherwood and his company of Queen's Loyal Rangers downhill could not help Baum, who was buttoned up with his Brunswickers in their snug hilltop fort. He lost sight of Sherwood's rangers below, isolated with local Loyalists in a lesser redoubt near a shallow ford in the river.

Baum waited into the afternoon for an attack until the opening volley at three o'clock, like a clap of thunder. He was surrounded. Two columns of men broke from woodland cover and opened fire from opposite sides. Three hundred Green Mountain rangers and local militiamen shifted to the right. Two hundred New Hampshire militiamen deployed to the left. A hundred more reinforced the center.

"There are the redcoats," Stark was said to shout. "They are ours, or Molly Stark sleeps a widow tonight!"

Guided by Warner, Stark pushed up the rest of his little army. The wooded hills and gullies provided cover for the Americans, who grew to outnumber Baum's corps. His log fort, erected in haste, had left dead space hidden from the defenders' fields of fire. Snipers zeroed in on the blue-and-yellow uniforms inside the breastworks.

As Baum's cannon fired clusters of cast-iron grapeshot, a cart exploded with the last of his gunpowder. Out of ammunition, the Brunswick dragoons fought their way downhill, sabers swinging. Their heavy scabbards snagged in the bush. They collided with the musket butts of Stark's reserves in hand-to-hand combat. Indian auxiliaries quit the white man's quarrel. Baum took a fatal bullet in his gut. His drummer signaled for a parley to discuss surrender. Stark's men ignored it because they didn't understand the language of drumbeats. The Americans seized both German cannon. Stark dismounted to show his troops how to load and fire them.

"It lasted two hours—the hottest I ever saw in my life," Stark reported to General Gates, "however, the enemy was obliged to give way, and leave all their field-pieces and all their baggage behind them."

Thomas Mellen, a teenage volunteer from New Hampshire, fired his musket until the barrel was too hot to touch. He grabbed another from a dead Brunswicker in which "bullets went down better than my own." He rushed past Germans who threw down their empty weapons and knelt in the rain puddles, begging for water and their lives. A barefoot militiaman pulled the shoes off one corpse. He was killed later.

The fog of war was as thick at the Loyalist redoubt, where Parson Thomas Allen prayed that God teach the hands of his parishioners to wage war and their fingers to fight. Twenty-two men had arrived with him from the Berkshires, and seventeen more followed. The preacher clambered on a fallen tree and beseeched the Loyalists inside to surrender. They responded with a volley of bullets. He jumped down. "Now, Joe, you give me a musket," he told his brother. "You load and I'll fire." He joined the first wave over the breastworks.

New Hampshire men attacked from the right flank. Another hundred made a frontal assault to draw the enemy's fire, then rushed the redoubt before its defenders could reload. The militiamen, recalled a Loyalist ranger, "all came jumping into the midst of us, with such a noise, that we thought of nothing but getting out of the way of their muskets as fast as possible. I saw all my companions going over the wall on the other side, and I went too." They scattered into the fields, to be picked off or chased on foot.

Justus Sherwood saw his company cut down from sixty to twenty-four Loyalist rangers. He ordered the survivors to run for the woods and escape. The commander of the Queen's Loyal Rangers lost all but seventy of the 270 men he led into battle at Bennington, including Sherwood's company. "When the smoke cleared away," Mellen said, "those who had vanquished the Tories beheld, among the captives, their neighbors and in some cases their kinsmen."

General Stark set out a hogshead keg of Tobago rum to refresh his men, who were looting Baum's ravaged redoubt. Before his troops could drink their rum, Lieutenant Colonel Breymann arrived with 644 more Brunswickers. They had fought Warner's Continentals, saving the British flank from collapse at Hubbardton six weeks before. Now Breymann's grenadiers had arrived too late, slowed down by the steep hills, muddy quagmires of roads, and constant rain. By the next morning, his hungry horses could scarcely pull both cannon. As he approached the battle, gunmen in shirtsleeves scrambled up a ridge to his left. Philip Skene assumed they were Loyalists until they opened fire. Breymann ordered his grenadiers to advance. His cannon ran out of ammunition. Skene's mount was shot out from under him, but he swung onto a nearby artillery horse and galloped away.

The Brunswickers' doctor was captured as he treated his wounded. His captor poked him with a bayonet, pocketed his watch, and offered him some rum. The Americans looked healthy, husky, and drunk. Each had a flask filled with rum hanging from his neck and carried a powder horn and musket. The German prisoners were herded down the road past their dying colonel sprawled naked on a cart. Baum begged his captors to go slower but they did not understand German.

The Green Mountain Boys under Warner's deputy, Samuel Herrick, had marched more than twenty miles to Bennington, where heavy rain forced them to dry out their gear and gunpowder, and reload. Revived by a half-cup of watery rum per man, they hit Breymann's column on both flanks. In the dusk, he retreated down the road under fire, abandoning his cannon. "I did everything in my power to save them," he assured Burgoyne, "but the want of ammunition prevented me not only from returning the enemy's fire, but even from getting out of it."

Some of Stark's men wanted to give chase, but he would not risk spoiling a good day's work. Had daylight lingered an hour longer, he reported to Gates, "we should have taken the whole detachment." Stark praised his "brave officers and soldiers for gallant behavior; they fought through the midst of fire and smoke, mounted two breastworks that were well fortified, and supported with cannon.

"Colonels Warner and Herrick, by their superior intelligence and experience, were of great service to me," Stark told Gates. "I would be glad he and his men could be recommended to Congress." Stark's pickup army of Green Mountain Boys, militiamen, farmers, and a fighting clergyman had cut to pieces the best German mercenaries money could buy. At least 207 lay dead, and more than 700, including 30 officers, were captured. The Americans lost 30 killed and 40 wounded.

The corpses littering the road included Seth Warner's brother Daniel. Seth, said Mellen, "jumped off his horse, stooped and gazed in the dead man's eyes, and then rode away without saying a word." Mellen and his battle buddies "lay down and slept in a cornfield, near where we had fought—each man having a hill of corn for a pillow."

Stark's troops didn't know how many enemy they had killed. "One of our scouts found, the beginning of this week, twenty-six of the enemy lying dead in the woods," a soldier wrote home later. In the August heat, bodies decomposed so fiercely that the stench overwhelmed Bennington's meetinghouse, now turned into a makeshift hospital.

The Loyalist dead were the last to be buried. In one grave, Mellen counted thirteen Tories, mostly shot through the head. In Bennington town, the prisoners of war were put on display: first the British, then the Germans and the Indians and "hindmost the Tories." One hundred fifty-two captured Loyalists were yoked in pairs behind horses to be paraded before jeering spectators. A Tory with his left eye shot out was matched with a horse missing a left eye. "It seems to me cruel now," said Mellen years later, "it did not then."

Some Loyalists expected to be hanged. Instead, Bennington's Council of Safety sentenced the most notorious to confinement underground in the same Simsbury mines that Justus Sherwood had evaded two years earlier. Others were compelled to labor the following winter "for the benefit of the traveling public," tramping down snowdrifts wide enough for a horse-drawn sleigh on the road from Bennington.

Burgoyne had nothing to show for the botched raid, neither horses to mount his dragoons nor carts to carry his supplies, nor provisions from Bennington's barns to feed his army. Nearly a thousand of his expeditionary forces were dead, wounded, or captured. His logistical supply route from Canada was severed. Four cannon, a thousand muskets with bayonets, and more than enough swords to equip cavalry across New England had been abandoned to the rebels.

"As I promised in my order that the soldiers should have all the plunder taken in the enemy camp," Stark asked Gates that "your honor send me word what the value of the cannon and other artillery stores above described may be." Thomas Mellen's eventual share of the spoils of war amounted to a little more than four dollars.

"One more such stroke and we shall have no great cause for anxiety as to the future designs of Britain," General

Washington declared when he learned of Stark's victory. "I hope the whole force of that country"—New England—"will turn out, and by following the great stroke struck by General Stark near Bennington, entirely crush General Burgoyne, who by his letter to Colonel Baume [*sic*] seems to be in want of almost everything."

Congress revoked its censure of Stark for refusing to obey orders and promoted him to brigadier general in the Continental Army, the rank denied him seven months earlier. It bought him a new uniform, though not a new horse. His brown mare had been stolen during the battle.

The hero of Bennington posted a twenty-dollar reward in a futile attempt to catch the thief or buy back his horse and saddle. "How scandalous, how disgraceful and ignominious must it appear to all friendly and generous souls," Stark fumed, "to have such sly, artful, designing villains enter into the field of action, in order to pillage, pilfer, and plunder from brethren when engaged in battle."

To Parliament, Burgoyne blamed Baum's defeat on the "impositions of a treacherous enemy" who had feigned allegiance to infiltrate his defenses. He accused Baum of advancing too far and Breymann of moving too slowly. But he shrugged off Baum's waste of ammunition as a misfortune akin to "bad weather, bad roads, tired horses and other impediments."

Burgoyne also disparaged his Loyalist volunteers who had suffered heavy losses, "not half of them armed, who may be depended upon; the rest are trimmers"—opportunists—

whose suspect motives made them worthless as soldiers. "One man's views went to the profit which he was to enjoy when his corps should be complete," he stated, "another to the protection of the district in which he resided; a third was totally intent upon revenge against his personal enemies; and all were repugnant even to an idea of subordination."

John Peters, wounded commanding the Queen's Loyal Rangers, criticized Burgoyne's "slender praise" of his Loyalists. But Burgoyne did single out "the distinguished bravery" of Captain Justus Sherwood, "who was forward in every service of danger to the end of the campaign." Yet Burgoyne reached the curious conclusion that "there is no circumstance to affect the Army with further regret or melancholy, than that which arises from the loss of gallant men."

In a letter to Lord Germain ten days after the battle, Burgoyne complained that of his 3,500 troops left, "scarcely 2,000 were English." The Germans were not his best, he said, as shown by the tardy arrival of Colonel Breymann. "Had my instructions been followed, or could Mr. Breyman [*sic*] have marched at the rate of two miles an hour any given twelve out of two and thirty" miles, "success would probably have ensured; misfortune would certainly have been avoided." This infuriated General Riedesel. His Brunswickers did not get the credit due for rescuing the British infantry at Hubbardton.

Whipping the Americans was not so easy as it looked from London. "The great bulk of the country is undoubtedly with Congress in principle and in zeal, and their measures are executed with secrecy and dispatch not to be equaled,"

Burgoyne reported to Germain. "Wherever the King's forces point, militia to the amount of three or four thousand assemble in twenty-four hours; they bring their own subsistence, and the alarm over they return to their farms.

"The Hampshire Grants, in particular, a country unpeopled and almost unknown in the last war" against the French, Burgoyne warned, "now abound in the most active and most rebellious race of the continent and hangs like a gathering storm upon my left."

Burgoyne had heard nothing from Sir William Howe, with whom he expected to link at Albany. Of the messengers he dispatched, Burgoyne despaired, "I know of two who being hanged and am ignorant of whether the rest arrived" at Howe's headquarters in New York City. Howe had sailed south to capture Philadelphia, leaving Burgoyne in the lurch.

"When I wrote more confidently, I little foresaw that I was to be left to pursue my way through such a tract of country and host of foes, without any cooperation from New York," Burgoyne wrote Germain, "I yet do not despond. Should I succeed in forcing my way to Albany, and find that country in a state to subsidize my army, I shall think no more of a retreat, but at the worst fortify there and await Sir W. Howe's operations."

Germain's letter urging General Howe to wrap up his excursion to Philadelphia in time to assist Burgoyne had failed to reach Howe, who was by now in the Chesapeake region. The defeat at Bennington made clear that Burgoyne's invasion was foundering, but Germain brushed off its significance: "I am sorry the Canada army will be disappointed in the junction they expect with Sir William Howe," he said, "but the more honor for Burgoyne if he does the business without any assistance from New York."

It would become clear why Howe had failed to help Burgoyne implement a plan that King George endorsed. Germain was so impatient to beat the London carriage traffic and drive to his country estate, Stoneland, for the weekend that he had not waited for his secretary in London to draft a fair copy of his instructions to Howe.

"Lord Sackville"—Germain was still addressed by his original name—"came down to the office on his way to Stoneland when I observed to him that there was no letter to Howe to acquaint him with the plan or what was expected of him in consequence of it," Germain's secretary reported. " 'So,' says Lord Sackville, 'my poor horses must stand in the street all the time, and I shan't be to my time anywhere.'" Germain's secretary offered to write to Howe and include Burgoyne's instructions "which would tell him all that he wanted to know, and with this his Lordship was satisfied, as it enabled him to keep his time, for he would never bear delay or disappointment." The copy of the letter to Howe, for which he would not postpone dinner in the country, turned up months later in a cubbyhole at Germain's office.

Until Bennington, the northern army had been in constant retreat since its flight from Ticonderoga. Now John Stark and Seth Warner had changed the fortunes of war. Burgoyne, having dithered four more weeks after the defeat at

Bennington, was running short of supplies. He had the option of retreating to Ticonderoga or Canada, but he resolved to press on, even though his promised linkup with General Howe's forces from New York City loomed less likely by the day. On September 13, 1777, Burgoyne crossed the Hudson River westward and dismantled the bridge behind him, severing links to his garrisons at Lake George, Skenesborough, and Fort Ticonderoga. His objective was Albany, a thriving town on the Hudson River a hundred sixty miles north of New York City.

What he did not realize was that American rangers and light infantrymen were operating behind his lines to interrupt his supplies from Canada, free prisoners of war, and attack Ticonderoga. Their base was Pawlet, a remote hamlet at the end of a wagon track into the Green Mountains. As many as fifteen hundred troops converged on Pawlet. Five hundred Vermonters or New Hampshire men, included Seth Warner's Continentals and Ben Whitcomb's scouts. Others had been drafted from Massachusetts for three months.

For speed and surprise, the Pawlet army took no cannon, ammunition carts, heavy baggage, or tents. Each soldier carried just his musket, two dozen cartridges, and a change of clothes. Cattle on the hoof, called "beeves," were herded along to be slaughtered and eaten on the spot. Mounted militiamen from the Berkshires delivered sacks of flour on horseback from Bennington, thirty-five miles to the south. At passing farms, the soldiers bought, bartered, or pilfered vegetables, colloquially called "sass."

The Americans split into three raiding forces of five

hundred men each under the command of John Brown, the lawyer who had helped Ethan Allen reconnoiter Fort Ticonderoga two years earlier. One raiding force, including Herrick's rangers and Whitcomb's scouts, would attack Ticonderoga, another Mount Independence, and the third Skenesborough, which the British had evacuated.

Before dawn on September 18, 1777, Ebenezer Allen, Ethan's third cousin, scaled Mount Defiance with forty Green Mountain Boys to seize the British cannon and their gun crews on the summit. They signaled by mimicking three hoots of an owl. "Allen and his men scaled the craggy rocks with much danger," Ira Allen wrote. Before they reached the summit, "they found a cliff they could not climb in the ordinary way." Ebenezer ordered a man to stoop, stepped on his back, "and in that way ascended." He let out a hideous yell and "his men came after him like a stream of hornets to the charge." One of the British gunners tried to aim his cannon at the rangers. Ebenezer Allen, with no time to reload his musket, shouted, "Kill the gunner!" The gunner ran off with the match still in his hand. Ebenezer Allen swung the loaded cannon around and blasted the British barracks on Mount Defiance.

At Lake George, Brown's raiders rescued 118 American prisoners of war confined in a large barn. Most had been held since Hubbardton. The raiders also captured more than 330 enemy soldiers, 200 barges, carriages, cattle, and horses, and weapons, as well as plunder valued at £10,000, including rum and clothing. The raiders burned what they couldn't float away by boat.

They demanded the surrender of Ticonderoga and Mount Independence. Its commandant insisted that he would "defend it to the last." British Lieutenant Colonel, Barry St. Leger, after losing a battle at Oriskany in the Mohawk Valley, happened to arrive at Ticonderoga with six hundred troops. These were kept at Ticonderoga for fear of further American attacks, depriving Burgoyne of more reinforcements that he desperately needed.

General Gates was cheered to see John Stark show up with his New Hampshire brigade at the Continental Army's camp. But Stark's troops, with their two-month enlistments expiring, wanted to return to their farms in time for their harvests. Stark let them go, and raised a fresh army of 2,500 volunteers, which he took to the Hudson River. He was determined to destroy Burgoyne's dwindling army and force his unconditional surrender. Burgoyne retreated to Saratoga, leaving behind his sick and wounded to the mercy of the Americans, who swarmed "like birds of prey" around his trapped force. German accounts confirmed daily American attacks: "Hardly any patrol was sent out without losing some men. Provisions ran short, sickness rapidly increased, discipline diminished under growing hardships, desertions increased, in spite of the dreadful punishment on deserters recaptured."

General Riedesel urged Burgoyne to abandon his cannon and baggage and retreat north toward Ticonderoga, but Burgoyne declared it was too late and opened negotiations for capitulation. He had fewer than 6,000 British and German troops. American ranks had swollen to nearly 22,000.

On October 17, 1777, Burgoyne's army tramped to a meadow near the Hudson River to lay down its arms, which included forty-two British cannon and more than four thousand muskets. The capitulation would reverberate through the Houses of Parliament in London. The prisoners included three Scottish lords, an English viscount, and four Members of Parliament. Riedesel wrote the Duke of Brunswick later that "his reputation had been sacrificed by others."

A German officer at the surrender was impressed by the conduct of the American troops, "so slender, so handsome, so sinewy," none properly uniformed but armed with deadly weapons. Despite their lack of spit and polish, he wrote home, "you recognize at first glance the earnestness which had led them to seize their guns and powder horns, and that—especially in the forest—it is no joke to oppose them, and that they can cold-bloodedly draw a bead on anyone." Yet he marveled that "there was not a man among them who showed the slightest sign of mockery, malicious delight, hate or other insult."

The costs of war were visible in Albany, where American, British, and German surgeons labored side by side over their casualties. James Thacher was now one of thirty American surgeons who worked into the night "amputating limbs, trepanning fractured skulls, and dressing the most formidable wounds." No stranger to war, Thacher was shaken by the carnage strewn about the overcrowded hospital. Twenty casualties assigned to him included a youth shot through both cheeks, cutting away his teeth and part of his tongue; a soldier whose face had been ripped off by a cannon ball; yet another "brave soldier" with a musket ball flattened against his forehead, under his skin. "If I turn from beholding mutilated bodies, mangled limbs and bleeding, incurable wounds," Thacher noted, "a spectacle no less revolting is presented, of miserable objects, languishing under afflicted diseases of every description." With "no parent, wife, or sister to wipe the tear of anguish from their eyes, or to sooth[e] the pillow of death," Thacher wrote in his journal, "they look up to the physician as their only earthly friend and comforter, and trust the hands of a stranger to perform the last mournful duties."

Justus Sherwood was wounded in the fighting at Saratoga. His name does not appear in any roster of prisoners of war. He never signed a parole like other officers. When he applied to the Crown years later to be compensated for property and income lost in his service Sherwood swore that he was "employed in various scouts and services under Gen'l. Burgoyne and was in every action and skirmish thro' that Campaign."

What happened was no less dramatic. The Loyalists feared execution or imprisonment if they laid down arms with the rest of Burgoyne's army. On October 16, 1777, the night before his army capitulated, Burgoyne permitted Sherwood's commander, Colonel John Peters, and his Loyalist officers to escape to Canada. Burgoyne had not signed their commissions, which would have included them in his surrender, so they could technically be considered ordinary privates. That same night, Peters and forty of his Queen's Loyal

Rangers infiltrated through American lines back to Fort Ticonderoga. They must have included Justus Sherwood, who, having refused to sign the Patriots' loyalty oath, would not have forgotten his escape from a life sentence of servitude in the Simsbury underground mines. It seems no coincidence that a week later, Vermont's Council of Safety authorized his wife, Sarah, to cross military lines under a flag of truce to join Justus at Ticonderoga. The order permitted Sarah, once again months pregnant, to take only necessary clothes and one bed. Everything else was forfeited to the state of Vermont. Her escort, afraid of being captured by the British, abandoned Sarah near Lake Champlain to find her own way to Ticonderoga with her small children. They made it to Canada in time for the birth of Sarah's second son.

Seth Warner, as a Continental colonel, was invited to attend Burgoyne's surrender in Saratoga, but his Green Mountain Boys were busy elsewhere. Ebenezer Allen's rangers harassed the British troops retreating back to Canada in November 1777. On one raid across Lake Champlain, they seized forty-nine British prisoners, one hundred or more horses, twelve yoke of oxen, and four cows, among sundry other stores. They also caught a British party with a slave named Dinah Mattis, and her two-month-old baby. Ebenezer Allen, "being conscientious that it is not right in the sight of God to keep slaves," freed Dinah and her baby, Nancy, with the consent of his tough frontiersmen who were not so sentimental about the tomahawks they carried.

"I therefore obtaining leave of the detachment under my command to give her and her child freedom," Captain Allen declared on November 28, 1777, "I do give the said Dinah Mattis and Nancy her child their freedom to pass and re-pass any where through the United States of America with her behaving as becometh, and to trade and traffic for herself and child as though she was born free without being mo-lested by any person or persons."

The flinty and profane Ebenezer Allen may have pro-mulgated America's first emancipation proclamation.

Had his troops all been British, Burgoyne insisted, they could have persevered. He had saved his army by arranging for their repatriation to England, where they could replace other British units released to fight in America. The strate-gem was not lost on Congress, which blocked their embar-kation from Boston, detaining the British and Germans as prisoners of war in Massachusetts and later Virginia.

When Burgoyne returned to London, the king declined him an audience. Guy Carleton, the former governor gen-eral of Canada, traced Burgoyne's humiliating defeat to the meddling of Lord Germain. "This unfortunate event," Car-leton wrote, "it is to be hoped, will in future prevent minis-ters from pretending to direct operations of war in a country of three thousand miles' distance, of which they have so lit-tle knowledge as not to be able to distinguish between good, bad, or interested advices."

NINE

Ethan Allen Sails Free

"Order your broken and vanquished battalions to retire from America, the scene of your cruelties," Ethan Allen cheered when he learned of Burgoyne's defeat. "Go home and repent in sackcloth and ashes for your aggravated crimes." He was still on parole in New York City, despairing that he would ever be exchanged for a British officer, "and I hope your Excellency will promote it, the more so that I have suffered a long and severe imprisonment," he wrote Washington. Alexander Graydon, a Continental major also on parole there, remembered Allen as a "robust, large-framed man, worn down by confinement and hard fare" but "now recovering his flesh and spirits." He wore the same blue broadcloth suit and gold-laced hat donated by Irish sympathizers in Cork. Graydon, a Pennsylvania aristocrat, was intrigued. "I have seldom met with a man possessing, in my opinion, a stronger mind, or whose mode of expression was more vehement and oratorical," he wrote. "His style was a singular compound of local barbarisms, scriptural phrases, and oriental wildness, and though unclassic, and sometimes ungrammatical, it was highly animated and forcible."

Allen took upon himself the cause of documenting the plight of American prisoners of war in New York City. He sought out "the most nauseous and contagious places" and beckoned them to come outside and tell their stories, until Hessian guards drove him away with bayonets. While American officers on parole enjoyed "the benefit of free air and the use of our limbs," he reported, "our poor devoted soldiers were enclosed within walls, scantily supplied with provisions of bad quality, wretchedly clothed, and destitute of sufficient fuel, if indeed they had any."

Allen visited camps teeming with prisoners inside churches and other large buildings. He noted the callousness of British warders and "the hellish delight and triumph" of their Loyalist collaborators, "exulting over the dead bodies of their murdered countrymen." He dismissed the Hessian guards as "a people of a strange language, who were sent to America for no other design but cruelty and desolation."

"I have gone into the churches, and seen sundry of the prisoners in the agonies of death, in consequence of very hunger, and others speechless and near death," he claimed in his memoirs. Where latrines were few, or none, human waste besmeared the floors. "I have seen in one of these churches seven dead at the same time, lying among the excrements of their bodies," Allen wrote. Prisoners subsisting on a trifling ration of stale bread and rotten meat begged him for a copper coin, or a crust, but he was penniless.

Allen did not exaggerate when he estimated that two thousand American prisoners perished from hunger, cold, and illness "occasioned by the filth of their prisons." More than eight thousand Americans were believed to have died in the floating prison hulks and churches around New York City.

Lord Germain dictated that "prisoners from the revolted provinces cannot be treated as prisoners of war," or sent home without renouncing the rebel cause. He considered them traitors, not enemy combatants, an ominous status underscored by the gallows erected within sight of one church turned into a jail.

The only way out for common soldiers was to join the British army. In one churchyard, Allen said, he struck up a conversation with a young Pennsylvanian reduced to a near-skeleton, whose brother had starved to death the night before. He took the youth aside and urged him to save himself by enlisting, then deserting at the first opportunity. Those too ill and weak posed a hazard to public health, portending an epidemic of cholera and other diseases that threatened the city. "The prisoners who were condemned to the most wretched and cruelest of deaths, and who survived to this period," he wrote, "were immediately ordered to be sent within general Washington's lines for an exchange, and in consequence of it, were taken out of their filthy and poisonous places of confinement." Hundreds were too frail and some died in the streets when they tried to walk to boats waiting in the harbor.

Allen blamed Joshua Loring, the greedy commissioner of prisoners under General William Howe, the British commander-in-chief in New York City. Loring, a Tory from Massachusetts, had earned his sinecure by pimping his wife as Howe's mistress. So flagrant was Howe's affair with Elizabeth Loring that the Patriot bard Francis Hopkinson mocked them in a harmonious ditty to a tune like "Yankee Doodle":

Sir William, he, snug as a flea
Lay all this time a-snoring.
Nor dreamed of harm, as he lay warm
In bed with Mrs. Loring.

Loring enriched himself, one New York journal charged, on "the groans and famishing" of his countrymen "by feeding the dead and starving the living"—pocketing funds allotted for prisoners who had died and embezzling from the pittance allowed those who remained alive. Ethan Allen called Loring "a monster—there is not his like in human shape. He is the most mean-spirited, cowardly, deceitful, and destructive animal in God's creation below."

When Ethan's prospects seemed at their lowest, in early 1777 he was summoned before a "British officer of rank and importance" and told that his misplaced loyalty commended him to General Howe, who had in mind appointing Allen colonel in command of a new regiment of Loyalists. The officer, whom Allen never identified, invited him to sail for England to be presented to Lord Germain and perhaps the king. He would be well fitted for such an audience and paid in hard guineas. Then he would return to help General Burgoyne subdue the rebellious colonies and be rewarded with a large tract of land in the New Hampshire Grants or Connecticut when British rule was restored.

Allen compared the offer to Satan's temptation of Jesus in the wilderness. "To give him all the kingdoms of the world if he would fall down and worship him; when at the same time, the damned soul had not one foot of land upon earth,"

Allen said, "and the gentleman turned from me with an air of dislike, saying that I was a bigot; upon which I retired to my lodgings."

Allen and other paroled officers were relocated to outlying slums at Flatbush in Brooklyn and New Lots on Long Island, where they were billeted with poor Dutch families for two dollars a week. The modest homes were clean enough, but the fare consisted of half-baked bread, stale butter, occasional boiled meat or clams, and a mush churned with buttermilk and molasses, "as swill is saved for hogs," so Graydon described it. Their days were spent pacing the streets.

Hearing of Ethan's whereabouts, his brother Ira plotted a rescue. Ira wanted some Green Mountain Boys to row a whaleboat across Long Island Sound to the north shore of Long Island, then strike overland into Brooklyn. Their more practical brother Heman pointed out that even if they succeeded, the British could revoke the paroles of other captured Patriot officers and send them all back to prison.

Ethan wasn't aware of Ira's scheme, but other family news filtered through. He was crushed to learn that his son Joseph had succumbed to smallpox at twelve years old. "The death of my little boy closely affected the tender passions of my soul, and by turn gives me the most sensible grief," Ethan wrote his brother Levi.

His captor in Montreal, General Prescott, whom Washington threatened to execute if Ethan Allen were hanged, was swapped in July 1777 while Allen remained on parole. "You will not be surprised that I express some anxious desire for the possession of liberty which I have been stranger to for near two years," he wrote to the Massachusetts Board of War. He was arrested at a tavern for violating his parole and locked up in the military provost's jail in Manhattan. He spent several days in solitary confinement before he was allowed a piece of boiled pork and some biscuit. Later he was moved to a loft shared with a score of Continental officers and some private gentlemen. They became his cell mates for the next eight months.

On February 6, 1778, four months after Burgoyne's defeat, France threw its support behind the new United States of America, signing treaties for mutual defense and another for commerce with Benjamin Franklin, the American representative in Paris. Hearing that France had allied itself against Britain, Allen declared, "My affections are frenchified" and tried to teach himself French.

On May 3, 1778, Allen was ferried by sloop across New York harbor to the British base on Staten Island, where he was wined and dined before being exchanged two days later for a Scottish officer jailed when the British ship bringing him to America sailed into rebel-held Boston. The British now treated Allen well, speaking of "old friendships and affections." He told his British hosts about the suffering he had seen inflicted on Americans, hoping "that their prisoners should be treated in the same manner as they should in future treat ours."

Allen was set free in Elizabeth, New Jersey, on May 3, 1778. He traveled to Valley Forge, Pennsylvania, to thank George Washington, who was impressed enough to suggest that Congress find Allen something to do. "His fortitude and firmness seem to have placed him out of the reach of misfortune," Washington noted. "There is an original something about him that commands admiration, and his long captivity and sufferings have only served to increase, if possible, his enthusiastic zeal. He appears very desirous of rendering his service to the States and of being employed, and at the same time he does not discover any ambition for high rank."

Washington conferred a brevet commission on Allen as colonel in the Continental Army, but with no command. It was the first and only American commission held by Allen, who told Washington that he valued the approbation of "Congress, Your Excellency and my Country" above gold and silver.

Traveling north with Horatio Gates to Saratoga, Ethan hinted that he too yearned to fight once he regained his health. He returned to a hero's welcome from friends in Bennington on May 31, 1778, "for I was to them as one rose from the dead, and now both their joy and mine was complete." Three cannon saluted his arrival. Toasts turned into binge drinking, or as Allen put it, "we moved the flowing bowl, and rural felicity, sweetened with friendship, glowed in each countenance."

Allen had lost more than time during his captivity. Two of his five brothers were dead. Zimri Allen, who looked after Ethan's wife, Mary, and children on his farm in Massachusetts, had died of tuberculosis in March 1776. On his homeward journey, Allen stopped in Salisbury, Connecticut, to visit Heman, to find that he had died a week earlier, also from tuberculosis.

Allen's arrival in Bennington interrupted the trial of a Loyalist charged with stealing horses for Burgoyne's army. Allen was appointed state attorney to prosecute the case. He invited spectators to come back a week later for his verdict. "You shall see somebody hanged at all events," he promised, "for, if Redding is not, I will be hung myself." Allen's gallows justice did not disappoint them. David Redding, a Queen's Loyal Ranger like Justus Sherwood, was found guilty and spent his final hours in the saddle room of the Catamount Tavern before swinging from a noose across the road.

Having missed out on the battles, Allen fell back on his private war against New Yorkers, whom he considered akin to Loyalists. Upon hearing that John Stark had hanged several Loyalists in Albany, Allen informed him that "the hatred and fear with which you are regarded by the Tories, those infernal enemies of American liberty, must be my apology for proposing to visit you in your quarters in Albany, as soon as I can get things a little regulated in Vermont," he wrote Stark. "The Tories, and the friends of Tories, give us some trouble yet. . . . Their management in a great measure keeps alive the anarchy which has heretofore disturbed the peace of Vermont. I am of the opinion that we will never be at peace, while one of them is suffered to remain in the country."

General Stark replied that he looked forward to meeting Allen, "whose fame has been so extensive, and whom I have never had the pleasure of seeing. As for the political matters you now have in hand, I cordially agree with you in sentiment. You may rely upon my cooperating with you in purging the land of freedom from such most infamous and diabolical villains."

Allen's hatred of Loyalists was capsuled in his drunken quip that hell had to exist, because that was where the Tories belonged. And so, he decided, did his brother Levi. While Ethan had speculated in real estate through the Onion River Land Company, Levi became an itinerant trader of ammunition and other goods for animal pelts, traveling as far as Detroit on Britain's westernmost frontier. Levi, eight years younger, had worked tirelessly to get Ethan released after his capture in September 1775. When Ethan learned his own son, Joseph, had died, he asked Levi to look after his daughters and see to their schooling. Ethan also thanked Levi for sending "a very seasonable relicf" of cash to sustain him on his parole.

A year and a half later, Ethan denounced Levi as a Tory and accused him of counterfeiting, a capital crime because Britain was flooding the colonies with bogus paper money. He was angered that Levi had bought a slave, which was legal in New York until 1827. Ethan petitioned Vermont's Court of Confiscation to seize his brother's property. "The said Levi has been detected in endeavouring to supply the enemy on Long Island, and in attempting to circulate counterfeit continental currency," Ethan charged, "and is guilty of holding treasonable correspondence with the enemy"—to help Ethan while he was a prisoner.

Levi, devastated that his brother turned on him, took out newspaper advertisements denouncing Ethan as an "ingrate" and "serpent" who instigated "a piece of solemn mockery, fraud and deceit . . . to ruin my reputation and deprive me of my estate." The counterfeiting went unproven. Levi's neutrality was enough to condemn him as a Tory in Ethan's mind. "Damn his lukewarm soul," he said.

Ethan Allen came home to find Vermont's borders enlarged at the expense of New Hampshire as well as New York. Sixteen towns along the eastern bank of the Connecticut River, feeling neglected by New Hampshire's capital on the Atlantic seacoast, had joined their friends and neighbors across the river in independent Vermont. Fearing a loss of influence if Vermont's political center shifted eastward from their power base in the southwestern Grants, the Allens objected to admitting the towns in the upper Connecticut River Valley. This put them at odds with Dartmouth College's founding president, Eleazar Wheelock, who favored secession from New Hampshire. Wheelock created his own town, named Dresden, from land owned by Dartmouth and asked Vermont to admit Dresden as a separate town.

The Allens tried to block Wheelock's application, claiming that Vermont's legislature had no time to determine "so copious a matter" in its current session. They were blindsided when the legislature agreed to bring Dartmouth College under the protection and patronage of Vermont. Wheelock was appointed Vermont's justice of the peace, and imported a rare printing press and typesetter from Massachusetts, ensuring a local monopoly on the printed word.

The defection of the sixteen river towns alienated New Hampshire, the closest to an ally that Vermont had in Congress. Its governor, then called president, Meshech Weare, who had mobilized John Stark and his militia in the battle of Bennington, beseeched Vermont to give up its so-called Eastern Union for the sake of peace and tranquility. Unless Congress stepped in, Weare said, the sword would probably decide the question.

Ethan Allen rode to Philadelphia in September 1778 to lobby Congress and apologize for "the imbecility of Vermont" in extending jurisdiction over its neighbors. Other states, he warned, would "join to annihilate the state of Vermont" and restore New Hampshire's territorial claims.

Congress gave Allen a sympathetic hearing and agreed to reimburse him for time spent in captivity. At Washington's behest, he was promised $75 a month as a Continental lieutenant colonel. Vermont dissolved its Eastern Union with the river towns "in the fullest and most explicit manner," in hopes of being invited to join the United States as the fourteenth state.

In the wake of Burgoyne's defeat, Britain was searching for opportunities to reconcile with its wayward colonies. The king had cautioned his prime minister, Lord North, "not to bind yourself to bring forward any plan for restoring tranquility to North America." Lord North sent a commission to consider the colonists' grievances. While Britain could force reasonable terms on the Americans, he argued, "it is better to offer a concession to the colonies now, which may end this contest within the year, than to continue the war for three or four years longer." Lord Germain disdained such compromise, and proposed his own to the House of Commons.

"He owned his aversion to treat with the congress, but his hearty desire to treat with the provinces separately," reported the *Gentleman's Magazine* in London. "He seemed to have no doubt of a successful end of the war. His speech was much applauded."

Many settlers in southeastern Vermont who supported the war against Britain continued to owe allegiance to New York. They neither trusted Ethan Allen nor liked his mobsters and balked at serving in a Vermont militia. Governor Tom Chittenden issued a proclamation ordering all residents in the Grants to comply with Vermont's statutes against treason and rioting. Anyone refusing to serve in its militia could have livestock and other property confiscated. Penalties for resisting Vermont's officers in their duties included forty lashes on the bare back, branding on the forehead with a red-hot iron, and nailing a repeat offender's right ear to a post.

Ethan was deputized to enforce Vermont's draft law. He recruited a hundred men into a posse to arrest several dozen prominent Yorkers for what he called "enemical conduct." They included a colonel commanding five hundred New York militiamen so poorly armed, lacking even ammunition, that Allen had no problem throwing two dozen of them into jail to await trial.

Hearing that charges would be dropped against some defendants, Allen pushed into the crowded courtroom and berated lawyers on both sides. The judge agreed to let him speak, but as a private citizen. He tossed his cocked hat on the table, unbuckled a large sword swinging at his side, and declaimed verses by the poet Alexander Pope:

> *"For forms of government, let fools contest.*
> *"Whatever is best administered is best.*

"Fifty miles have I come through the woods with my brave men, to support the civil with the military arm," Allen said, "to quell any disturbances should they arise; and to aid the sheriff in prosecuting these Yorkers—the enemies of our noble state." The defendants, he declared, "are escaping the punishment they so richly deserve. . . . Let me warn your honor to be on your guard, lest these delinquents should slip through your fingers, and thus escape the rewards so justly due their crimes."

Allen put his hat back on, buckled on his sword and stomped from the courtroom, by one account, "with the air of one who seemed to feel the weight of kingdoms on his shoulders." The colonel and other defendants were found guilty of obeying New York's orders over Vermont's, fined up to £40 plus court costs, and set free.

When Vermont confiscated more livestock from Yorkers, New York's governor, George Clinton, threatened to call up a thousand militiamen destined for the defense of the frontiers, "unless the interposition of Congress should render such a measure unnecessary." Congress dispatched its commissioners to defuse the incipient "cow-war" between New York and Vermont, but they could do little more than wring their hands. "In our opinion, it will be wise to abstain from hostilities for the present, and rather suffer a little than shed blood." It hardly mattered, since Vermont's legislators rejected Congress's advice.

Governor Clinton, who was also a Continental general, demanded that Washington return or replace six brass cannon loaned by New York in 1776. He threatened to use flour stockpiled for the Continental Army in New York to feed his militiamen if they went to war with Vermont.

The prospect of civil war between Vermont and New York did not go unnoticed in London, where Lord Germain learned from Frederick Haldimand, the new governor general of Canada, that "the insurgents of Vermont under Allen still give umbrage to what is called the New York Government."

Germain leapt at the chance to exploit the rift. "The separation of the inhabitants of the country they style Vermont from the provinces in which it was formerly included," he replied, "is a circumstance from which much advantage might be derived." Since the Vermonters had declared independence first from New York, and not Britain, Germain expressed "no objection to giving them reason to expect the king will erect their country into a separate province."

TEN

Conniving with the Enemy

The plot to suborn Ethan Allen can be traced to his captivity in England when the royal cabinet, meeting in London on December 26, 1775, considered that he be bribed and not hanged. Lord Germain had agreed that buying members of Congress or generals like Benedict Arnold would hasten the defeat of Washington's army. The lowest-hanging fruit was Vermont, whose claim to independence was rejected by the original thirteen states. The New Hampshire Grants had seemed but a flyspeck on the British Empire until Burgoyne's disastrous campaign in 1777 exposed its significance as an enemy. Vermont looked ripe for plucking. It had no formal ties to sever with Britain.

In July 1780, a British soldier in farmer's clothes stopped Ethan Allen on the street in his hometown to hand him a letter more than three months old. It came from Beverley Robinson, a Tory of prominence in New York, who inferred "that you, and most of the inhabitants of Vermont, are opposed to the wild and chimerical scheme of the Americans in attempting to separate this continent" from Britain, and would be willing to help restore the ties "so wantonly and inadvisedly destroyed by the rebels."

Robinson, who commanded a Loyalist regiment but dabbled in espionage, said: "If I have been rightly informed, and these are your sentiments and inclination, I beg that you will communicate them to me without reserve." He promised that Vermont could have "a separate government under the king and constitution of England, and the men, formed into regiments under such officers as you shall recommend."

Ethan did not reply. He showed Robinson's invitation to Vermont's governor, Tom Chittenden, who agreed that unless Congress supported its independence from New York, Vermont had no reason to remain at war with Great Britain, and was free to make its separate peace. In late September 1780, Chittenden wrote to Canada's governor general, Frederick Haldimand, proposing a cartel, or written agreement, to exchange prisoners captured along Vermont's northern frontier with Quebec. "If you will send a proper person with full power to Major Carleton, at Crown Point or St. Johns, to confer upon this business," Haldimand replied, "I shall authorize the major to receive him."

Major Christopher Carleton was a natural choice, and not because his uncle was the former governor general of Canada. Orphaned at four years when his parents drowned in a shipwreck, Chris Carleton joined the British army when he was twelve, and later lived among the Iroquois, who decorated his body with fanciful tattoos and bedded him with a native wife, an interlude he recalled with nostalgia.

Carleton learned to fight like the Iroquois, daubing his face with war paint and wearing a ring in his nose. In October 1778, he led more than two hundred British soldiers and native warriors on a rampage through Vermont's Champlain Valley, guided to settlements targeted for destruction by Justus Sherwood and his Queen's Loyal Rangers. Over three weeks, the raiders burned farms, mills, storehouses, and crops, slaughtered livestock, and destroyed enough food crops to sustain twelve thousand men for four months.

Now, two years later, Carleton returned with as many as a thousand British troops, including Tories and Indians, surging this time down the New York side of Lake Champlain. They destroyed 200 dwellings and 150,000 bushels of stored wheat along with other grains and fodder, and sent another wave of refugees fleeing south.

Carleton was also tasked with arranging a temporary truce with Vermont before his troops withdrew to winter quarters in Canada. To open talks on a prisoner exchange and persuade Ethan Allen to bring Vermont under British rule, Haldimand was sending his most effective spy, Justus Sherwood.

On the evening of October 29, 1780, Sherwood walked into a frontier post of several hundred militiamen camped near sawmills along the outflow of a lake near the New York border. The mission was dangerous. Sherwood had been banished from Vermont a year ago and faced being hanged if he returned. He traveled under a flag of truce.

It took Sherwood nearly three days to sail from Canada. Leaving several men to guard the beached sailboat, he hiked into the woods with a couple of men and a drummer. His red-and-green coat identified him as a captain of the Queen's Loyal Rangers, a safer uniform than the buckskins worn by a spy.

Sherwood was to arrange a truce with Ethan Allen, who now commanded Vermont's militias as their general. Ethan was a familiar sight in his pea-green coat on the parade ground of a log blockhouse a few miles to the east, where he drilled his men. The militiamen blindfolded Sherwood and hustled him to their colonel, Samuel Herrick, who would have known him from their days as Green Mountain Boys. Carleton had written Allen that Sherwood would open their negotiations to exchange prisoners. Allen agreed to meet him the next morning. "Every respect will be shown your flag and no hostilities will be permitted on my part," Allen wrote Carleton, expecting that "you will extend your cessation of hostilities against any of the northern posts of the state of New York during this negotiation."

Sherwood was received by Allen after breakfast. More than five years had elapsed since they last met at Sherwood's cabin at New Haven in the winter of 1775. Allen had convened a council of ten field officers to help set up a cartel, or mechanism for the prisoner exchange. He let them cool their heels as he took Sherwood for a walk in the woods, on the pretext of wanting to understand better why he had come.

In the private notes documenting his rendezvous with Allen, Sherwood wrote that "after much conversation, I informed him that I had business of importance with him, but before I communicated I must request his honor as a gentleman, that should it not please him he would take no advantage of me nor ever mention it while I remain'd in the country."

Allen agreed to hear Sherwood out "if it was no damn'd

Arnold plan to sell his country and own honor by betraying the trust repos'd in him." Hardly five weeks had lapsed since Benedict Arnold was exposed on the brink of delivering West Point to the British.

Sherwood explained that Haldimand was well briefed about Vermont's troubles with Congress, and believed the best outcome would be for Vermont to become an autonomous British province under the protection of the Crown. Haldimand considered Ethan Allen "a man of too much good sense and solid reason" not to realize that Congress was duping Vermonters and waiting for an opportunity to crush them. Sherwood said that "this was a proper time for them to cast off the Congress yoke and resume their former allegiance to the King of Great Britain, by doing which they would secure to themselves those privileges they had so long contended for with New York"—notably independence and prosperity for Vermont.

Allen demurred that he was "not to be purchased at any rate," but would consider the British offer very seriously. For now, he worried about what his officers might make of his absence. "He then said we must go in for we had already been too long together," Sherwood noted, "that I might rest assured our present conference should remain a secret."

Allen and Sherwood resumed their dialogue later that night. Allen said he felt surrounded by enemies determined to support New York's territorial claim to Vermont. "He is heartily weary of war and wishes once more to enjoy the sweets of peace and devote himself to his philosophical" studies, Sherwood reported to Haldimand.

Allen told Sherwood that he would consider delivering Vermont to Britain under four conditions: First, Ethan Allen himself—and not a British general—must command Vermont's militia army. Second, Vermont must have a government independent of any other province in America. Third, Vermonters must elect their own civil officials and representatives, even as they enjoyed all privileges that the king's men extended to other states and provinces. And fourth, to confirm the land titles of Vermonters, including thousands of acres claimed by the Allen brothers, Britain must declare the New Hampshire Grants free of competing legal charters or claims from New York and other neighbors. He added an escape clause: Vermont reserved the right to join the United States and send representatives to Congress without ever revealing that it considered returning to British rule.

Allen hoped that Haldimand "will not be too anxious to hurry matters on too fast as that will certainly ruin the whole." Sherwood, a Vermonter, understood the risks. "He desires me to inform His Excellency that a revolution of this nature must be a work of time, that it is impossible to bring so many different minds into one channel on a sudden" stroke, he reported to Haldimand.

Even if Allen wanted to switch sides, Sherwood noted, "it is not in his power to do it at present—for in the first place should he now make a declaration of that nature his own people would Cutt [*sic*] off his head." And Vermont would incur more than the wrath of Congress and its Continental Army. Allen felt sure that Vermont's neighbors—New York, Massachusetts, and New Hampshire—"would on such an occasion pour in upon them thirty thousand men in thirty days' time."

Whether out of swagger or bluff, Allen threatened to march his own brigade to capture Albany and invite all friends of liberty to join him. If forced to retreat, he would make his stand at Fort Ticonderoga and ask Canada for help. It would be in Britain's interest, he said, to send at least twenty thousand troops to support him. "This he thinks will be the readiest method of bringing this whole contest to a speedy decision," Sherwood reported.

Twenty thousand troops were a lot more than Haldimand had at his command, but Allen insisted that he could not depend on promises of protection if the British army would not come to his aid.

Sherwood revealed that he had hidden some proposals in writing from Haldimand, which he offered to retrieve. But Allen, he said, "advised me to let them rest." He also asked that Sherwood not communicate their conversation to anyone else.

Before they adjourned, Ethan Allen's military council approved a swap of captured Vermonters for an equal number of British and Loyalist prisoners held by Vermont. As his officers looked on, Ethan wrote instructions to his commanders to call in their scouts and send out no more patrols while the truce remained in effect.

Allen and Sherwood would continue to explore Vermont's reunion with Britain under the cover of the prisoner exchange. Allen wanted their negotiations kept secret from the world, because New York had spies in Canada who "are at present very suspicious of his and Vermont's conduct," Sherwood reported. To allay suspicions, Allen wanted Haldimand to send flags of truce to New York as well as Vermont.

Allen galloped off to Bennington to tell Vermont's General Assembly about the truce and prisoner cartel, but not his secret agenda on reunion with Britain. The legislators let Allen discharge his militiamen, who went home to their farms to plant winter wheat. Their abrupt demobilization raised suspicions beyond Vermont.

"The conduct of some people at the eastward is alarmingly mysterious," General Schuyler told New York's Governor George Clinton, "a flag under pretence of settling a cartel with Vermont has been on the Grants; Allen has disbanded his militia, and the enemy in number upwards of sixteen hundred are rapidly advancing towards us." Allen had done some kind of deal with the British, he wrote General Washington, "and unless a speedy interposition takes place, the consequences may prove extremely prejudicial to the common cause."

A couple of old soldiers in Vermont's General Assembly accused Ethan Allen of disloyalty to the Patriot cause. Allen retorted that he was resigning as general of the militia but would serve Vermont according to his abilities. When the criticism persisted, Allen walked out, calling it beneath his character to have to listen to "such false and ignominious aspersions." The charges were dropped, but he was never invited to resume command. Nor was he offered a civil post, allegedly because he was a Deist and not a proper Christian.

How serious was Ethan Allen about rejoining Britain? As he cast about for a palatable alternative to the only option offered by Congress, Vermont's subjugation by New York, he would later settle upon a third option: Vermont's neutrality as an independent republic that thrived on free trade with all its neighbors.

Sherwood promised to look into the plight of Ethan Allen's brother-in-law Gideon Brownson, who was confined in a Montreal prison with three other officers from Seth Warner's regiment after being wounded in an ambush near Lake George in 1779. Sherwood knew Gideon, having sold him some riverfront property back in May 1772.

Ethan Allen had asked Washington for four paroled British officers to exchange for Captain Brownson and his jailed comrades. Vermont usually handed over the prisoners it captured to the Continental Army. Washington declined to intercede, explaining that "there are a great number who have been much longer in captivity, and have therefore a just right to a preference."

Instead, Washington offered to ask the British to transfer Brownson and his comrades to a prison in New York "where we can furnish them with supplies of different kinds, which we cannot, from the great distance, forward to Quebec, and where they will be exchanged in due course." But Allen, who had witnessed the appalling prison conditions in New York City, bridled at what seemed callous disregard.

Justus Sherwood now had to extract himself from rebel

territory and retrieve the hidden sailboat that would carry his truce party back to Canada. But no sooner had Ethan Allen departed than his cousin Ebenezer Allen had Sherwood detained, in violation of his immunity under the flag of truce. His guards were menacing: "Some said my life should answer for the consequences, some said one thing and some another, but all conspired to make me very uneasy," Sherwood recalled.

Ebenezer Allen was a Green Mountain Boy to his hard core. He had helped Ethan capture Fort Ticonderoga in May 1775, fought under Seth Warner in Canada in 1776, and had been promoted to chief captain in Sam Herrick's Vermont rangers. So when he had intelligence to report, he was taken seriously, and he suspected the worst from Sherwood's meeting with Ethan. "I am afraid the Enemy have out-General'd him," Ebenezer Allen said of his cousin.

That evening, Ebenezer claimed that one of his scouts had sighted British ships sailing south on Lake Champlain—so many "that the lake looked black for a mile in length"—and a great many bonfires were burning on the western shore. "These are to notify you to give a good look out," he advised, "for I believe they intend to make a forced march on the New York frontiers." The British had broken their promises of no more troop movements, Ebenezer reported. Instead of withdrawing, they were regrouping near Fort Ticonderoga.

Sherwood suspected that Ebenezer invented his sightings to undermine the truce, and offered to resolve the misunderstanding. "To this I got no answer," he noted, "and I soon after found that the whole was a farce of Maj. Allen's own contriving on purpose to alarm the country."

The last day of October 1780 dawned sunny and "glorious in autumnal beauties," as a hunter recalled it. Sherwood and his truce party were marched southward along roads that swarmed with militiamen chasing after Ebenezer Allen's sightings. Sherwood was forbidden to speak to passersby, who seemed "much exasperated," he reported, and "very crabbed and insulting to me."

The mellow autumn vanished overnight with a premature blast of winter that reflected Sherwood's misfortunes. On November 1, he and his companions were overtaken by a snowstorm and could march no further than ten miles into the Green Mountains before being allowed to seek refuge. The next day, they stumbled south for another twenty miles through drifting snow.

Governor Chittenden, upon learning that Ebenezer Allen had violated Justus Sherwood's rights under the flag of truce, intervened. That evening, Sherwood wrote, Chittenden ordered "that I should be treated in a manner that an officer of a [truce] flag had a right to expect and by no means to keep me any longer under the least restraint." But Ebenezer would not let Sherwood slip away so easily. He took a few days to obey Chittenden's order before Sherwood hired some horses and his party rode back north though a new snowstorm to reach Castleton.

Convinced that something was amiss, Ebenezer Allen stalled two more days before he finally let Sherwood leave with Ira Allen and his friend Joseph Fay, who purportedly were going along to set up the prisoner exchange. Night had fallen when they found Sherwood's sailboat, frozen in ice two inches thick. The next morning, they chipped the cutter free and began slowly breaking a path through the ice to open water on Lake Champlain. They covered barely three miles the first day, four miles the second day. On the third day, Ira Allen and Joseph Fay turned back, promising to travel by sleigh later to the British base at St. Johns.

Ira Allen and Fay may not have been deterred by the ice. More likely, they had come along to inspect the trove of documents from Haldimand hidden by Sherwood. "I had the day before shewn them the Gen's proposals," Sherwood wrote in his journal. "After perusing them & discoursing largely on the subject, we burned them." The documents, sensitive enough to be destroyed after reading, seemed to confirm that the British offer of reunion was made to Ethan Allen on the highest authority.

Sherwood was unaware that Haldimand feared for his safety. Having heard nothing for a week, he wanted Sherwood pulled out before he was caught and hanged like John André, the British go-between in Benedict Arnold's thwarted betrayal. "The unhappy tale of Major André and the untimely discovery of his mission shews the necessity of secrecy and the total consequences of being frustrated in designs which can never again be attempted," Haldimand wrote Carleton. "Sherwood being in the enemy's power strengthens this necessity and makes it a matter of great risk for him. You would therefore do well to withdraw him."

But Sherwood was unreachable on the treacherous ice

coating Lake Champlain. The next day, he could ram his boat through the ice for only three miles, and just five miles over the next two days. The ice grew thinner, but the cutter had eleven more miles to reach the safety of open water.

Ira Allen and Joseph Fay had left their rations of beef and bread with Sherwood, who was running short of food. By evening, he ordered his crew to sail to Fort Ticonderoga as fast as possible and await him there. Taking one man, Sherwood hiked overland to the town of Skenesborough where he bought five bushels of corn and as many provisions as he could from the locals, and thirty pounds of pork.

Sherwood and his companion lugged the heavy load overland for three miles, and borrowed a skiff to row to the waiting sailboat. They tacked no further than the ruins of an old French fort on the Vermont shore, and spent a day waiting to collect the family of a captain in Canada. Sherwood took aboard two more men, four women, and four children. His overcrowded sailboat rode perilously low in the icy water, now with twenty-five refugees and crew aboard.

They covered barely two miles against a strong headwind in another snowstorm. But favorable winds the next day allowed them to cover a good sixty miles to a sheltering haven called Tea Kettle Island. From there, it was an uneventful voyage to the British forward lines at the northern outflow of Lake Champlain. Sherwood rowed that same night to the British base on Isle aux Noix and a rendezvous with Major Carleton. Together they set off for Quebec City to tell Haldimand that Ethan Allen was ready to negotiate a separate peace for Vermont.

Haldimand, relieved to see Sherwood safe, was considering a proposal from George Washington for a larger prisoner
exchange, which would be jeopardized if he found that the
British were making a separate truce with Vermont. Haldimand also had to consider that "having a cessation of arms
with so extensive a part of the frontier must either deprive
us, in a great measure, of intelligence, or subject us to mistakes and a loss of Reputation."

The abrupt armistice did not go unnoticed in northeastern New York, which was reeling from the latest attacks
by Carleton's marauders. General Philip Schuyler, who still
commanded the Continental Army's northern front, reported to his superiors that the rascally Ethan Allen had
disbanded Vermont's militiamen and sent them home. He
shared Washington's suspicion that Allen had made a com-
pact with the British in demobilizing Vermont's militia.
"Should this really be the case, it will be a most disagreeable circumstance," Schuyler told Washington "and unless a
speedy interposition takes place, the consequence may prove
extremely prejudicial to our common cause."

Schuyler concluded: "Sending a flag to Vermont for the
purpose of exchanging prisoners appears to me only a cover
to some design of the enemy, and gives me much uneasiness,
especially as rumors prevail that the person"—neither general dared name Ethan Allen—"whom your excellency was
informed to have been in New York in July negotiating with
the enemy.

But Schuyler could not find anyone to "positively ascer-
tain any of these facts." He added on November 1, 1780, "I am

this moment informed that the person I have alluded to in this letter has been to Canada, about six weeks ago, but the information is not such as I can depend upon."

Washington faced a quandary. He could not ask Vermont's Governor Chittenden for help because Congress did not recognize Vermont as anything more than a breakaway district of New York. Yet his cryptic dispatch on November 6, 1780, to Schuyler all but identified Ethan Allen as a prime suspect. "I confess all circumstances and previous information considered," Washington said, "that matters in a certain quarter carry a very suspicious face."

Washington wanted secret plans drawn to abduct Ethan Allen for interrogation, "should it appear, upon a further investigation, that there are good grounds for present suspicions." Washington had already broached this with General James Clinton, the brother of New York's governor, without mentioning names, "to seize and secure, with as much secrecy and as suddenly as possible, the person in question with his papers," he told Schuyler. "You know how very difficult a business this is, and I therefore trust to your prudence in the execution of it."

But none of the agents that General Schuyler had sent into Vermont brought back anything more damning than a casual remark by Ethan Allen when he received Justus Sherwood under his flag of truce. On the day the British flag arrived, he was heard to say—"The time is at length come that we shall be free from the domination of New Yorkers."

Schuyler advised against kidnapping Ethan Allen, for now. "That a certain person is engaged in the enemy's interest I make little doubt of," he told Washington, "but I do not think it either prudent or politic that he should be seized at present; a little time will probably furnish us with sufficient testimony for a conviction."

The British, for their part, were eager over the prospect that Ethan Allen could be induced to switch allegiance. "It appears that Ethan Allen has joined the King's troops," Major General Henry Clinton wrote his patron, the Duke of Gloucester, in London. "I have for two years been tempting that chief, and I have offered him what Congress have refused him."

ELEVEN

Green Mountain Boys
Disbanded

"The Green Mountain Boys have never failed to give the enemy a trimming whenever they have come together," Ethan Allen boasted some months after his release. "War has become a science of these people, and I flatter myself, that the Congress have as loyal subjects in these parts, as in any district, of America." He was basking in the glory of his cousin Seth Warner, who had led his Green Mountain Boys so professionally in the retreat from Quebec and at Hubbardton and Bennington that General Horatio Gates had invited him as "an officer of merit" to attend Burgoyne's surrender at Saratoga.

Warner was soon promoted to full colonel and Gates envisioned "a service of much importance, in which Col. Warner's regiment will be very actively concerned." A rumor lingered that Warner had turned down general's rank in the Continental Army because he felt too poorly educated. More likely, New York blocked his promotion. He was listed as sick on his regiment's muster rolls from November 1777 to February 1779. In his absence, his rangers were deployed to defend northeastern New York, not Vermont. When he returned to duty, Warner was ambushed near Lake George by Loyalists and Indians in September 1779. His horse was shot out from under him and he was wounded twice in the arm, but he mounted the horse of a slain officer and galloped free. It was his last firefight. A mysterious illness began to paralyze his limbs.

After the battle of Bennington in 1777, a friend had said, "Colonel Warner was so continuously on the alert that for seventeen days and nights, he never took off his boots, in consequence of which a disorder was contracted in his feet, which proved incurable, disabling him from any further service in the field."

Hard campaigning had left Warner, at thirty-seven, too spent to command what remained of his regiment. Washington may have concluded that he was no longer up to the task. Or he may have tired of the freewheeling ways of the Green Mountain Boys. His headquarters reprimanded Warner on November 22, 1779, for having too many officers in his regiments, now reduced to seventy rangers. A month later, he was scolded for requisitioning more clothing and blankets per man than other regiments in Continental service. Warner's paymaster was accused of selling twenty or more army coats and spending the money in what Washington's aides called "a scandalous manner." Warner, at his best in the field with his troops, was chided for falling behind on his expense accounts, and was instructed to account for all the funds that he had received to recruit his regiment. On March 31, 1780, Washington put a halt to Warner's enlistments.

When he could summon the strength, Warner tried to

rejoin his regiment in northern New York in pursuit of Loyalists and Indians who invaded the Mohawk Valley. New York's Governor George Clinton told Washington that "on my request, I was joined by a party of two hundred and fifty of the militia of the [New Hampshire] Grants under Colonel Warner and Major [Ebenezer] Allen whose behavior in this respect was in every aspect, very agreeable to me."

By October 30, 1780, Seth Warner had bad news for Washington about the "misfortunes which have befallen our troops on the northern frontier," describing his Green Mountain rangers as "few in number and destitute of clothing." Their log fort near Lake George had run out of provisions for two days when its captain dispatched fifty rangers to chase away what looked like thirty or forty intruders, only to be overwhelmed by Major Chris Carleton's invasion force of hundreds of British regulars, Indians, and Tories. Sixteen Green Mountain rangers fought their way to freedom, eighteen were killed, two wounded, and the rest taken prisoner. With just fourteen rangers left to defend the small fort against impossible odds, their captain capitulated. Warner sent the stunned survivors home to recover.

Washington, hard pressed for troops, seemed less than sympathetic. "I am sorry for the unfortunate stroke upon your Regt at Fort George," he wrote Warner on November 12, 1780, "but I cannot but think it extraordinary that you should furlough the remainder at a time when their services were so essentially necessary."

Washington then informed Warner that his regiment of Green Mountain Boys would be disbanded on January 1, 1781, a casualty of Congress's decision to reorganize the Continental Army along conventional European lines. Warner's officers would be retired on half-pay. His troops would be parceled out among regiments of "the states to which they properly belong"—including New York's. Some of Warner's recruits were marooned in a Rhode Island regiment, and could not get paid because Washington's army coffers were empty.

Seth Warner and his Allen cousins had grown apart. Warner was distressed by rumors that Ethan was fraternizing with the enemy and asked him. No, Ethan lied. Well, he admitted receiving two letters from Tory Colonel Beverley Robinson but said he had burned one, which was untrue, and given the other to Vermont's governing council. He made no mention of his secret talks with Justus Sherwood, whom Warner had written off as a "notorious Tory."

"I am persuaded when Congress considers the circumstances of this state, they will be more surprised that I have transmitted them the enclosed letters, than that I have kept them in custody so long," Ethan Allen said, "for I am as resolutely determined to defend the independence of Vermont as Congress are that of the United States, and rather than fail, will retire with hardy Green Mountain Boys into the desolate caverns of the mountains, and wage war with human nature at large." Under pressure, Allen forwarded the letters to Congress, but the packet was intercepted by the British, who were angry that Ethan had leaked their invitation to change sides.

Vermont's covert talks on reunion with Britain resumed in May 1781 with Ira Allen as the chief negotiator. Ethan could not afford to deal directly with General Haldimand, or even Justus Sherwood, he said, "as that would create too much suspicion." Though Ethan had resigned command of Vermont's militias, he couldn't be seen fraternizing with the enemy. The pretext for his absence, to devote more time to his philosophical studies, wasn't plausible. Ethan couldn't be trusted to keep a secret either.

Ira Allen, thirteen years younger and by most accounts smarter than his eldest brother, was content to play second fiddle. Ethan had nicknamed him "Stub" because Ira was eight inches shorter, but he shrugged that he "as cheerfully answered to that name as to any other."

Ira lacked neither brains nor guts. Measles in his youth had weakened his eyesight, but did not prevent him from venturing into the wilderness alone or with his cousin Remember Baker. He taught himself surveying and would become surveyor general of Vermont and, for a time, its wealthiest landowner. It was Ira who had thought up the Onion River Land Company dodge to amass property. When Ethan organized the Green Mountain Boys, Ira was one of his lieutenants and saw action during Montgomery's failed assault on Quebec.

By now promoted to colonel in the Vermont militia, Ira Allen chose May 1, 1781, his thirtieth birthday, to launch the next stage of negotiations. He traveled overland for a hundred or so miles to Lake Champlain and then by boat across the Canadian border to the British base on Isle aux

Noix with an armed escort of eighteen militiamen and their lieutenant.

Why, his British hosts wondered, did Ira Allen bring a musket-toting platoon under the flag of truce, but no diplomats with pens and paper? The truth was that Ira preferred negotiating alone, convinced that "one person was better than more, as cross questions might arise, and no one could divine what questions and propositions might come from the British."

Major Alexander Dundas, commandant of the British base on Isle aux Noix, welcomed Ira Allen and invited him to the officer's mess. Dundas, whom Haldimand disparaged in his diary as "stupid and silly," was not privy to the reason behind Ira's visit, but he deduced that Vermont's truce was meant to show Congress and the colonies more that "they are tampering with us than to settle with us any material business."

Ira Allen and Justus Sherwood shared sleeping quarters at the fort with the Vermont militia's lieutenant, whom Sherwood sized up as a "downright illiterate zealous-pated" Yankee. His clumsy attempts to eavesdrop on their conversations annoyed Sherwood, who wanted him and his platoon removed to a ship anchored in the river.

Ira had been "cautious not to mention a syllable of any kind of business in his presence," Sherwood said. "When we walk out, he most commonly attends us closely and has just breeding enough to listen and look over a man's shoulder when he is writing." But Major Dundas, unaware of their agenda, left the lieutenant bunked within earshot of Allen and Sherwood.

Six months had lapsed since Sherwood discussed Vermont's return to Britain with Ethan Allen. Sherwood was disappointed to find Ira Allen so ill-prepared. He seemed to have no instructions and could not even provide a list of captured British soldiers required for the prisoner exchange. "After the closest scrutiny we find ourselves perplexed and much at a loss what to think of him," Sherwood told Haldimand.

Sherwood found Ira "cautious and intricate" when they walked and talked in private conversation. "I urged him to make some proposals, telling him that it is now in the power of Vermont to become a glorious government under Great Britain, to be the seat of peace and plenty with every degree of liberty that a free people can wish to enjoy," he reported.

But Ira Allen objected that the British would not let Vermonters choose their own governor, "a privilege they could never relinquish with propriety." Vermont could not venture beyond neutrality during the war, he said, "at the end of which they must, as a separate government, be subject to the then ruling power" of either the United States or Britain. He echoed his brother Ethan's threat that his Green Mountain Boys would retreat into the mountains and, as he put it, "turn savages, and fight the Devil, Hell and human nature at large."

Sherwood scoffed that any "affectionate husband, father, wife and mother could ever be persuaded to leave their happy possessions," and subject their families to "a savage and wandering life, surrounded by enemies of the human and brute creation, exposed to every inconvenience attending those inhospitable mountains." He told Ira that General Haldimand had too much experience and good sense to take notice of such provocations "than by that contempt they merited."

By the fourth day, Ira Allen sounded a little more candid. Vermont preferred neutrality and independence from the United States to being carved up between New York and New Hampshire, he explained. For its defense, Vermont was expanding its boundaries to take in the border towns that wanted to secede from New York and New Hampshire, in good part because their residents objected to paying the burdensome taxes levied by Congress to finance its war with Britain. He asked if Haldimand was authorized to arrange Vermont's reunion with Britain. The governor general would not exceed his powers, Sherwood replied, nor accept a neutral status for Vermont, "which must either be united in constituted loyalty with Britain, or continue at enmity with it."

Ira Allen asked whether Britain's Parliament had drafted the necessary legislation. Sherwood snapped that Vermont was not of sufficient consequence yet to deserve Parliament's attention. Ira insisted that Parliament must pay attention for a reunion to happen. Vermonters favored the American colonies to win the war, but if Congress continued to mistreat them, he said, self-interest and self-preservation would lead them to "fight like devils against their oppressors" and support Britain. Then he begged Sherwood not to convey his objections in a manner that would cause Haldimand to break off negotiations.

When Ira tried to write Haldimand directly, proposing to meet him in Quebec City, Major Dundas threatened to clap him in irons. Instead, Haldimand sent his own adjutant, who conversed privately with Ira for hours in a secluded part of the island. Sherwood was relieved to have another gentleman assist in what he called "this perplexing and shuffling business."

Ira would not venture beyond what his brother Ethan had already told Sherwood six months earlier. Vermonters were justified in calling for a truce, he said, because "the frontiers of Vermont have been left naked and exposed to the wasting sword of British troops." Then he cautioned that "this business requires time and moderation," and refused to write anything down, lest it put him in danger and jeopardize his standing back in Vermont. "He gives reasons which he refuses to sign and then writes himself, but still refuses to sign," Sherwood said.

Though he did not meet General Haldimand, Ira Allen spent two and a half weeks at the base on Isle aux Noix as he hammered out terms in the cartel that would exchange British soldiers taken by Vermont for its citizens held in Canada. He was disappointed that the British refused to include Continental soldiers or women and children because, he said, "notwithstanding we have taken more than three times the number from them, it is at present out of our power to return equal numbers." They had been turned over to Washington's army.

For all their bickering, Ira parted amicably with Sherwood, who arranged coded signals for exchanging messages with the Allens more befitting a conspiracy of spies. Three puffs of smoke and the hoisting of a small white flag after the second puff would signal a request to meet at a designated rendezvous on Lake Champlain's eastern shore. If Haldimand needed to contact the Allens before the next round of talks, a trusted courier would carry the secret message on a piece of paper small enough to swallow "if in danger of being taken by a scout from New York."

Major Dundas supplied the visitors with ample rations for their journey home on May 25, 1781. Once back in Vermont, Ira closeted himself for three days with its innermost circle of leading citizens. Their discussions were so secret, a Loyalist spy said, that "no man of the King's friends nor of the rebels of high or low degree could come to the knowledge of a syllable of it."

Ira had acknowledged that it was in Vermont's "interest and safety" to accept Haldimand's terms when negotiations resumed in another eight weeks. "I told him he talked well, however much I may be convinced of his candor," Sherwood reported, but Ira's changeable attitude "gave some suspicion that he now acts from design."

Publicly, Ira assured Vermont's General Assembly that he had arranged a cartel to swap friends imprisoned in Canada for British agents and Tories. He claimed to have left the documents at home and offered to retrieve them the next day. In fact, he had nothing to show beyond the draft of an unsigned agreement. But he told his critics what they wanted to hear, that he found a fervent wish for peace among British officers as weary of war as the Americans. His glib misrepresentation satisfied most legislators that he had done nothing in Canada to betray Vermont's interests.

Some details trickled out later. Vermont would return to Britain if its settlers could keep their land granted by Benning Wentworth, plus the borderlands extending into New Hampshire and New York. Property confiscated from the Tories would be returned, but no damages would be paid. Failing this, Governor Chittenden deemed it "the business of Vermont to spin out this summer in truces, and in the meantime fill their magazines with arms, ammunition and provision, by which, with the continual increase of the inhabitants, he hoped to be able next summer to defend Vermont against invasion from Canada."

On June 18, 1781, more than three weeks after Ira returned from Isle aux Noix, Governor Chittenden asked again for a sufficient number of prisoners of equal rank to swap for Vermonters in British custody. But General Washington said he would "give no countenance to any cartel" involving Haldimand in Canada.

Washington demanded that no other business be transacted under the cover of Vermont's flag of truce beyond the exchange of prisoners. He charged that the Vermonters, after behaving well in the war, now flirted with becoming an appendage of Britain. If they persisted, he threatened to turn his back on their common enemy, and send in his Continentals to punish Vermont. But if Vermont would stand by him in the common cause until the close of the war, he promised to ensure it would become a fourteenth state.

Even before Ira Allen visited the British base at Isle aux

Noix, New York's Governor George Clinton had been informed of "more serious" misgivings about what he still called the New Hampshire Grants. "I have no positive evidence of a criminal communication between them and the enemy in Canada," Clinton wrote a friend, "but there are circumstances sufficient to justify at least suspicion."

General Haldimand, from his vantage in Quebec, surmised that "Ethan Allen is endeavoring to deceive both the Congress and me." He would not let Ethan and his mobsters near Quebec "in its present weak and disaffected situation" for fear that under the pretense of joining the king's troops, Ethan Allen "may watch his opportunity and with the assistance of the Canadians, or upon the appearance of a French flag, seize . . . the Province."

Still, if the Allens could be coaxed into delivering Vermont to Britain—neutrality was insufficient—Haldimand would have the buffer zone he needed to forestall an attack from the south. "All the intelligence we have received of the designs of the enemy leave Canada out of the plan," Lord Germain assured Haldimand from London. "I trust you will appear in considerable force upon the frontier which will be the surest means to give efficacy to the negotiations with the Vermont people. Nothing indeed should be omitted to attach them to His Majesty and I assure you that no expense that shall be found necessary for that purpose will be grudged."

But Haldimand had little confidence in his British garrison, which he described once as "a small army widely dispersed, composed in general of very inferior troops." Since his arrival in Quebec in July 1778, he had come to realize how vulnerable Canada was to an American invasion. "The reb-els have explored every part of the country, and know it well." His British and German regulars were ill-prepared to cope with their most formidable foe, the Canadian winter.

"Should the rebels undertake a winter expedition, against the province, they have many advantages over us," Haldi-mand had reported earlier to London. "The Germans are heavy troops, unused to the snowshoe, to handling the ax and the hatchet, only fit for garrison duty; the English troops have only been two winters in the country, and there-fore cannot be so expert as the Americans; these are trained to the woods since infancy, know well how to shelter them-selves from the cold, and are excellent marksmen."

Even now, the garrisons required to protect Haldimand's headquarters left few reserves for patrolling a backyard of wilderness stretching from the Atlantic Ocean to the Great Lakes. Haldimand called it "one of the most common and flagrant violations of the principles of war—stretching a thin line, everywhere inadequate, over an immense frontier." To keep the Americans off-balance, Haldimand adopted a pre-emptive strategy of patrols, Indian raids, and border incur-sions that Major Chris Carleton and Justus Sherwood would execute.

Haldimand may not have realized that Vermont was in worse shape. It had declared independence from New York in 1777, only to be invaded and looted by Burgoyne. Its Green Mountain Boys who fought so tenaciously for the Ameri-can Revolution had brought Vermont no closer to being accepted by the United States. Key forts at Ticonderoga,

Mount Independence, and Crown Point remained in British hands. Nearly half of the Vermont republic was a no-man's-land, compelling settlers to pull back to a more defensible line of five log forts to the south.

When Ethan Allen began to conspire with Justus Sherwood, Vermont had few friends in Congress. It had neither money, nor surplus wheat, a popular currency for barter, but it did have land confiscated from Loyalists, which Ira Allen promised to provide to "some of the leading men in New England" in return for their support.

Typical among them was John Sullivan, a general who had campaigned against the Iroquois in 1779 and was now chosen to represent New Hampshire in Congress. But New Hampshire could not afford to send Sullivan to Philadelphia, or pay his room and board there. More than two thirds of its towns east of the Connecticut River had opted to join Vermont, and rather than paying taxes to New Hampshire, were billing it for services rendered in the war. New Hampshire could not meet the quotas set by Congress for men, money and provisions because it faced financial ruin, and "we cannot tell how far the contagion may run," said its president, Meshech Weare.

Ethan and Ira Allen's contacts with Haldimand's agents had become too blatant to ignore. "The conduct of the Vermontese is mysterious, and if the reports which generally prevail are well founded, their measures will certainly be attended with dangerous consequences to this and the other United States," General Schuyler told Washington on May 4, 1781, before Ira Allen arrived at Isle aux Noix. "I cannot, however, believe that the bulk of the people are in on the secret." He conjectured that "the person whom we suspected last year to have been in New York"—who would be Ethan Allen—"and some others, are the only culpable ones."

Washington's suspicions of Vermont's motives increased. "At present they are at least a dead weight upon us," he told Schuyler. "It is greatly to be regretted, that they are not by some means or other added to our scale, as their numbers, strength, and resources, would certainly aid us very considerably, and make the enemy extremely cautious how they advance far in that quarter. The bulk of Vermont people, I am persuaded, must be well affected," Washington added. "Should it be otherwise with any of the individuals, I ardently wish they may be detected in their villainy, and brought to the punishment they deserve."

In Canada, Haldimand was no happier with Ethan and Ira Allen, whose negotiations had failed to bring about any event beneficial to "humanity"—much less to Britain. Still, the door lay open to accept Haldimand's terms for reunification. "Any time therefore, that proposals shall be made by the State of Vermont, such as I can with honor & propriety accept a flag of truce, shall be received," Haldimand wrote Governor Chittenden.

One July day in 1781, a neighbor told Ethan Allen that some friends from Canada were waiting to speak with him in the dusk of the evening. Ethan strolled to the appointed spot to find a British patrol delivering a packet from Canada. He returned the next evening with his reply for the waiting couriers. A British sergeant and his men commuted more than a hundred miles between the garrison town of St. Johns in Quebec and the Allens' farmhouse in southwestern Vermont.

Ethan and Ira used this back channel to keep in touch with Haldimand's headquarters through Sherwood. They greeted their favorite courier, a Loyalist corporal named David Crowfoot, "with every mark of friendship," Sherwood reported. "General A"—a code name for Ethan Allen—"told him for God's sake for his own and their safety to take care of himself, for the [Bennington] mob were watching every motion." Colonel A—a code name for Ira Allen—visited Crowfoot hiding in the woods "and offered him any assistance he could require in money, provisions or anything else in his power, cautioned him to take care of himself while on his way." Crowfoot was caught in February 1782 returning from a rendezvous with Ethan Allen. He managed to destroy his incriminating dispatches and escaped, resurfacing two months later.

Ira also promised to pass along "whatever may take place at Congress," employing the smoke signals worked out with Justus Sherwood. Their negotiations would involve Sherwood for nearly two more years.

The confidential chatter passed on by Ira Allen, who lived with Ethan at their farm, included his observation to Haldimand that many Vermonters came from Connecticut, and would "expect to remain a reasonable time in a state of neutrality. However, I hope there will be no difficulty on those accounts."

Congress spent several days that spring debating what to

do about Vermont, Ira Allen informed Haldimand, and decided to make no determination during the current military campaign.

Frederick Haldimand, as governor general of Canada, was well qualified to preside over Britain's secret negotiations with Vermont, in a military and diplomatic career limited only by his foreign birth in Switzerland. Fluent in French and German though not English, Haldimand refused to involve himself directly in Sherwood's negotiations with Ethan and Ira Allen, insisting "that the strictest secrecy must be punctually observed. Under these circumstances, I could not think of risking my sentiments in writing, among a people who, whether from necessity or inclination, had given up similar letters to Congress."

Justus Sherwood was directed to channel all correspondence on the secret negotiations with Vermont through Haldimand's military secretary Robert Mathews, a British army captain so discreet that a single anecdote survives to lift the veil of anonymity from hundreds of dispatches bearing his name.

While he was shuffling Haldimand's correspondence with Vermont, Mathews courted Mary Simpson, a belle of Quebec society. The rival for her affections was a dashing British captain who spent a month in Quebec City in 1782 while his frigate, the *Albermarle*, was repaired and its crew recuperated from scurvy. Mary Simpson so beguiled the frigate's captain that when time came to sail, he refused to leave her. His shipmates had to drag him to his frigate, by one account, and the heartbroken Horatio Nelson sailed into history, becoming Britain's foremost naval hero, mortally wounded in the battle at Trafalgar against the French and Spanish in 1805.

Mary Simpson married the reliable Robert Mathews, who was promoted to major and ended up governing the Chelsea Hospital for war invalids in London.

TWELVE

Spy Base on the Lake

Justus Sherwood was summoned to General Haldimand's headquarters in Quebec City for promotion on June 18, 1781. After five years of scouting, foraging, and fighting for the Crown, he was placed in charge of Britain's espionage operations along the strategic Canadian frontier, from Lake Champlain to the Connecticut River, entrusted with the "fitting out and dispatching of scouts upon secret service."

For his base, Sherwood chose Dutchman's Point, a secluded peninsula of what is now North Hero Island (named, ironically, to honor Ethan Allen). He arrived with twenty-three Loyalists, old men and boys among them, to build a log fort on a knoll with a panoramic view south on Lake Champlain, and a channel deep enough for boats. He named it the Loyal Block House.

Dutchman's Point was treeless. Timber had to be cut down a mile away and dragged to the site by draft horses, whose fodder must be carted in. Sherwood requested some prisoners sent from St. Johns to build the blockhouse, but was turned down because its isolation made escape too easy.

"I have built a very good and large block house & on the most advantageous spot of any on the lake," Sherwood reported to Haldimand. "It is my humble opinion that there is not so proper a place on the frontiers as this for the residence & departures of secret scouts & I think when the block house is picqueted"—enclosed within a stockade—"50 men may defend it against 300 with small arms and two or three light swivels [cannon] may be placed in it to advantage."

Sherwood set about recruiting a network of secret agents familiar with Vermont and New York next-door. By mid-July 1781, he had enlisted seven spies, "all good and resolute." For Sherwood's deputy, Haldimand assigned George Smyth, an Irish-born doctor who had fled to Canada after being caught spying in Albany, New York. He took the code name of "Hudibras," a character in a seventeenth-century satirical poem by Samuel Butler. Older than Sherwood, Smyth felt he deserved to be in charge. "I am happy to find so willing and hearty an assistant as Captain Sherwood," he quipped.

Sherwood's mission was to eliminate enemies of the Crown, and his first target was Jacob Bayley, a feisty Patriot in his mid-fifties who farmed the rich flatland along the upper valley of the Connecticut River dividing Vermont from New Hampshire. Bayley believed that Vermont belonged in New Hampshire. "For my part, I am determined to fight for New Hampshire and the United States as long as I am alive and have a copper in my hand." And Bayley, who held brigadier general's rank in the militia, was itching to invade Canada again, "that harbor for spoils, thieves, and robbers."

Bayley loathed Ethan Allen and mocked the exploits of the Green Mountain Boys as "the Green Men's Diabolical Acts." From Abenaki neighbors on the northern frontier, he had picked up inklings of treasonable conduct by the Allen brothers. He tipped off Washington about "six or eight rascals in Vermont" who seemed too cozy with the British.

General Washington needed harder evidence. "If instead of vague and random information of insidious designs of the Allens, any positive direct proofs could be adduced, there are means sufficient to check their attempts," he wrote Bayley. "I should recommend your accusations, if they can be proved, to be made to Congress, who I doubt not will take the measures to prevent their effecting any mischievous designs."

Sherwood lacked enough couriers to keep in touch with British headquarters at St. Johns. Its colonel-in-command was not briefed about Sherwood's clandestine role and sent out his own scouts. As Sherwood prepared to resume the next round of reunion negotiations with the Allens, a Loyalist captain stopped by the Loyal Block House with eight men to say that he had been ordered to abduct Jacob Bayley to Canada, or, if Bayley couldn't walk, "to kill him and bring his papers." Sherwood persuaded him to gather intelligence instead on towns along the Connecticut River. A second plot to kidnap Bayley in October 1781 collapsed when he went to Philadelphia to visit Congress.

On the third attempt, Sherwood said, "the whole business miscarried." As Bayley plowed his fields, a note dropped by the furrows warned him: "Samson, the Philistines be upon thee." He bolted for the woods and hid as Loyalists searched his house. After that, he never slept without bodyguards and remained a thorn in the Allens' side.

Sherwood's and Smyth's missions were rarely successful. In early August 1781 one of Smyth's agents led a raiding party of Loyalists and Indians into Albany to abduct General Schuyler, now retired. Forewarned, he barricaded himself upstairs and shot his pistols through the bedroom door and out the window. The raiders carried off the family silverware and a couple of hostages. Schuyler, a New York aristocrat whose daughter, Elizabeth, married Alexander Hamilton, told Washington that the raiders had written orders from Lieutenant Colonel Barry St. Leger, commanding at St. Johns.

Smyth later pitched a grandiose scheme to torch a seventy-four-gun warship being built, with French financing, at Portsmouth, New Hampshire, for the American captain John Paul Jones. Two Loyalist saboteurs were planted in the boatyard but could not set the *America* afire because it was closely guarded, some nights by Jones himself.

Hanging was the fate of spies on both sides who got caught. Sherwood was upset to learn that one of his best agents had been "lately taken and hanged by the rebels whilst on secret service," in Albany, on orders from General Stark. He asked Haldimand that the destitute widow be awarded a small pension.

His other agents were a mixed bag. The most notorious, Joseph Bettys, had fought under Benedict Arnold in the 1776 naval battle off Valcour Island before changing sides. He was cold-blooded and cruel, as an acquaintance described him— "his bosom cold as the marble to the impulses of humanity." Assigned to kidnap a prominent doctor, he carried back instead a girl who struck his fancy. He was finally caught bearing a coded cypher for the commander of British forces in New York. "I am a dead man!" he exclaimed and was hanged in Albany with another spy. Sherwood believed that they "died like soldiers in the just cause."

Some of Sherwood's scouts went deep into Vermont and were seen attending public dances next door to Governor Chittenden's residence. One was deemed "in danger of causing some mischief as he is much given to drink," but Sherwood considered him "a very brave, loyal fellow" and hoped that his carousing would not affect his usefulness.

Sherwood's most effective spies hid in plain sight behind respectable lives. Elnathan Merwin, code-named "Plain Truth," lived quietly just a few miles from Ethan and Ira Allen. Sherwood also handled James Breakenridge, an old gentleman whose farm Ethan Allen's vigilantes had protected eleven years before.

Another Loyalist informant, Luke Knowlton, a Princeton graduate and lawyer from New York, infiltrated Ira Allen's inner circle. When Washington sent an officer to arrest Knowlton for "intriguing with the enemy" by passing letters to New York, he fled and joined Sherwood later at the Loyal Block House. "Saint Luke," as he was nicknamed, returned to Vermont and resumed a political career. When Knowlton was abducted to Massachusetts, Ethan Allen intervened to secure his release.

Justus Sherwood gave his scouts a broad list of questions to ask. They sent back what newspapers they could find for clues to what was going on in the colonies. Sherwood wrote his assessment of Vermont's leaders, where they lived and how far from local forces. His agents trafficked in hearsay and eavesdropping. The Loyalist John Savage guessed that one third of Vermont's leading men inclined toward the British government and another third were motivated by their attachment to Vermont and aversion to New York. The rest, he supposed, "will be guided by the fortunes of war."

Recruiting spies grew harder as peace approached and Loyalists were left to fend for themselves. Sherwood had to explain later why three of his trusted spies had deserted. Two more were Continental Army deserters who, he feared, would change sides again if given the chance.

On July 20, 1781, Joseph Fay reappeared as Vermont's new commissioner of prisoners with instructions to resume the negotiations. Justus Sherwood knew that Fay came from a family of Green Mountain Boys. His father, Stephen Fay, was landlord of the Catamount Tavern. His elder brother, Jonas, was a surgeon in Seth Warner's regiment on the retreat from Quebec. Joseph Fay had fought in the battle of Bennington where Sherwood's company of Queen's Loyal Rangers was routed. Now he resurfaced as Vermont's state adjutant at twenty-eight years old. Sherwood pronounced him "young in everything but rebellion."

So Haldimand expected that Fay would have "sufficient authority finally to negotiate and settle a reunion of Vermont with the Mother Country." But like Ira Allen, Fay had nothing to offer beyond hopes for a prisoner exchange. "I wish it was in my power to remove every suspicion you may have against the good intentions of the people of Vermont," he wrote Haldimand, "but I can only assure you of my own, and that I have not the least doubt you may rest equally assured of the sincerity of such of the others as are made acquainted."

Sherwood suspected that Fay wanted to drag out negotiations into November, past the season for military action. "He professes so much honesty, accompanied with so many gestures of sincerity that he seems to overact his part," Sherwood reported. While Fay seemed "candid, sincere, and open, we are sorry to find him as unprepared as Colonel [Ira] Allen was to close with the proffered terms. He has no written instructions on this subject."

Lacking British soldiers to exchange, Fay was said to have turned over thirty German deserters from Burgoyne's army to an uncertain fate. He acted surprised that the British would not accept prisoners from towns that Vermont had annexed in New Hampshire and New York. And they balked at releasing Gideon Brownson, Ethan Allen's brother-in-law. When Fay returned home, he recommended exchanging the wounded Brownson for the son of Sherwood's deputy, George Smyth, jailed in Albany.

Haldimand realized that Joseph Fay did not have the authority to decide crucial matters. "We do not think Vermont expects by procrastinating to strengthen herself as a state," Sherwood had reported, "but we believe sincerely they design to secure to themselves this campaign from invasion of King and Congress, by spinning out the summer and autumn in truces, cartels and negotiations."

Even so, when Fay left, he took a copy of Alexander Pope's *Essay on Man*, which Ira Allen had lent Sherwood in May. Sherwood's thank-you note testified to the civility with which the reunion talks, for all their duplicity, were conducted, as well as to Sherwood's friendship with the Allen brothers before the war.

"I find Maj. Fay the gentleman you represent him to be, and however different our political sentiments are, you may be assured that my former personal friendship for you and him remains inviolate," Sherwood wrote to Ira Allen on August 21, 1781. "As I have requested the major to present my compliments to governor Chittenden and the gentlemen of Vermont in particular, [I] have only to request that you will remember me to my former good friend General Allen, with compliments and best respects to Mrs. Allen and the young lady"—Ethan's sickly eighteen-year-old daughter, Loraine.

Sherwood and Smyth understood their influence was not enough to bring the rebels to accept reunion with Britain. "In this our fears are strengthened," they told Haldimand, "when we consider that the majority of those leaders were men of low character and no consequence in the country until they made themselves popular in the present rebellion by actions at which a man of honor and integrity would revolt."

Haldimand did not share his superiors' contempt for Vermont's homespun army. "They are in every respect better provided than the Continental Troops and in their principals [*sic*] more determined," he wrote Lord Germain. "They are in their hearts inveterate rebels, and if once united with Congress would be very formidable enemies, having been from their early contests with their neighboring Provinces, continually in arms."

But he was fed up with vacillation from Ethan and Ira Allen, and now Fay. "If it is the intention of Vermont to trifle with me, she will find herself deceived," Haldimand said. And he scrapped further negotiations. "The prisoners, or the greatest part of them, being now exchanged," he concluded,

"I shall not expect a flag of truce from Vermont upon any other business than to signify her acceptance of my offers, and at all times to consist of no more than five persons, who will keep their flag constantly flying."

To conclude their prisoner exchange, the British and Vermont commissioners agreed to meet in mid-September. Fay promised to bring "certain important papers and documents" about what was happening in Vermont. In the meantime, hostilities would remain suspended.

While Joseph Fay resumed negotiations, his brother Jonas traveled to Philadelphia with Ira Allen and Bezaleel Woodward, a future president of Dartmouth College, to formally ask Congress to admit Vermont into the United States. On August 14, 1781, they paused for refreshment at a tavern where they read in the popular *Pennsylvania Packet* a leaked top-secret dispatch from Lord Germain to Gerneral Henry Clinton, commanding British forces in North America. Dated six months earlier, the incendiary document revealed how plans were already under way to absorb Vermont into the British Empire, by force if necessary.

"The return of the people of Vermont to their allegiance is an event of the utmost importance to the king's affairs; and at this time, if the French and Washington really meditate an irruption"—violent invasion—"into Canada, may be considered as opposing an insurmountable bar to the attempt. General Haldimand, who has the same instructions with you to draw over these people, and give them support, will, I doubt not, push up a body of troops, to act in conjunction with them, to secure all the avenues through their country into Canada; and when the season admits, take possession of the upper parts of the Hudson's and Connecticut rivers, and cut off communications between Albany and the Mohawk's country, etc."

Germain's dispatch had been intercepted at sea by the French, who passed it to Benjamin Franklin, the United States representative in Paris. Franklin sent it to Philadelphia, to be read to Congress on July 31, 1781, and published four days later in the *Pennsylvana Packet*. It prompted Congress to reconsider Vermont's application to join the United States.

The exposure of Britain's designs on Vermont did more to influence the "wisdom and virtue" of Congress, Ira Allen contended, than the capture of Fort Ticonderoga, Crown Point, and two divisions of Burgoyne's defeated army.

On August 7, 1781, Congress appointed a commission to consider under what terms Vermont might be properly admitted as the fourteenth state. A preliminary condition was that it give up jurisdiction over the lands and towns it annexed in New York and New Hampshire. Ira Allen and his companions refused to budge and Congress shelved their application for statehood.

In Vermont, the Allens' negotiations with Sherwood concluded with an exchange of prisoners in September 1781. Jails were combed for qualifying British subjects. One hundred thirty men, women, and children were assembled in Skenesborough for repatriation to Canada. Some Americans held in Canada, desperate not to be left out, claimed to be from Vermont.

Sherwood sweetened the offer of reunion: the king must choose "a subject of the colony" for governor, but Vermonters could elect their lieutenant governor and counselors. The British offered to add a Vermont general and a couple of colonels to the king's rolls, to command two regiments of Vermont troops who could accompany British regulars on a joint strike against Albany. Haldimand was determined not to lose another campaign season to inactivity. If nothing was settled before the negotiators parted, Britain would cancel its armistice with Vermont.

A separate peace is a two-edged sword. If the Americans could no longer invade Canada through Vermont, Haldimand reminded General Henry Clinton, "the obstacle will equally affect us in acting against the colonies."

Justus Sherwood, who had wondered if it were worth negotiating with such "equivocating faithless Yankee scoundrels," continued his negotiations as he juggled his spymaster duties. The Queen's Loyal Rangers, in which he had served, was so depleted by casualties and dissension that Haldimand had to disband it. To preserve Sherwood's rank of captain, he was reassigned to a new corps of rangers under a Loyalist major from New York who also suspected that Ethan and Ira Allen were "playing a double role." He proposed that Ethan be abducted. His proposal was rejected because Haldimand needed the Allen brothers to deliver Vermont.

By May 1782, Sherwood reckoned that he had "no less than 47 men in different parts of the rebel frontier on secret service." He resorted to the subterfuge of bringing them to work on his Loyal Block House, where he dispatched them quietly on their covert missions.

But Haldimand was unhappy by "the vast expense you have incurred on that service by paying such high wages to persons regularly subsisted and provisioned by [the] Government." Sherwood explained that volunteers for dangerous missions did not come cheap. They could end up on the gallows. They were in fact paid sporadically, and Sherwood had to ask for them to be issued blankets, mittens, and warmer clothing. His Loyal Block House ran habitually short of other essentials like medicine, for which he sometimes paid the bills. He moved into his Loyal Block House at the end of 1781, leaving his wife, Sarah, and their children in St. Johns. George Smyth continued working there, putting them even more at cross-purposes.

Some senior officers still didn't fathom what Sherwood was doing at the Loyal Block House. He carried sixty-one troops on his roster, but only fifteen were present for duty when he was directed to send a ten-man detail to cut wood, and another fifteen or twenty to perform menial chores for General Riedesel, commander of the Brunswickers, whose contract exempted them from manual labor. At Sherwood's urging, Mathews countermanded the work order.

The British statesman Edmond Burke had warned Members of Parliament, including Lord Germain, about the pitfalls of waging war long-distance. "Three thousand miles lie between you and them," he had declared in the House of Commons on March 22, 1775. "No contrivance can prevent the effect of this distance in weakening government. Seas roll and months pass between the order and the execution, and the want of a speedy explanation of a single point is enough to defeat a whole system."

And that is what happened six years later, in 1781. Germain had not given up on a royalist Vermont, but he now expected the war to be won by a campaign that his best general, Lord Charles Cornwallis, was waging in the Carolinas and Virginia. "If we succeed to the southward, I shall not be afraid of a failure in our negotiations with the people of Vermont," he told Clinton.

"All the intelligence we have received of the designs of the enemy leave Canada out of their plan," Germain wrote Haldimand on July 26, 1781, "and therefore as you have nothing to apprehend for the safety of the province, I trust you will appear in considerable force upon the frontiers, which will be the surest means of giving efficacy to your negotiations with the Vermont people. Nothing indeed should be omitted to attach them to His Majesty."

Neither German, in London, nor Haldimand, in Quebec, seemed aware of the grand plan unfolding to the south. In June 1781, General Washington began to withdraw his Continental regiments from New England to attack the British defenses around New York City. Germain thought Washington had hardly enough troops to protect his own headquarters on the Hudson River. "Our successes in the southern provinces, and the low, wretched and weak state of

Washington's Army, and the vast superiority of the King's forces under Sir Henry Clinton put it out of the power of the rebels to give you any disturbances," he assured Haldimand.

France had been aiding the United States since 1778, sending its surplus muskets and two hundred field cannon. The French fleet in the West Indies was expected to sail for New York. When its admiral diverted to Chesapeake Bay, Washington changed plans and gambled on overtaking Cornwallis. By mid-September 1781, the Continentals linked up with a French expeditionary force to trap Cornwallis's 7,500 troops in the tobacco port of Yorktown, Virginia. It was months before Germain learned what had happened.

To cover his northern front, Washington summoned General John Stark. "I am induced to appoint you to this command," he wrote, "on account of your knowledge of, and influence amongst, the inhabitants of that country"—the Green Mountain Boys and their kin. He asked Stark to "use all your utmost exertions to draw forth the force of the country from the Green Mountains and all the contiguous territory. And I doubt not your requisitions will be attended to, as your personal influence must be unlimited among those people, at whose head you have formerly fought and conquered with so much reputation and glory."

General Stark was now fifty-two years old and hobbled by arthritic rheumatism. New Hampshire had yet to reimburse him for raising its brigade of volunteers and leading them to victory at Bennington. He was so broke that he begged Washington for a loan. Washington, strapped for cash, could offer only sympathy. "But as there is not a single farthing in the military chest, it will be absolutely impossible to furnish any part of the sum solicited," he apologized. "I have not been able to obtain any money, for my own expenses or table, for more than three months."

Only a few months had passed since Congress disbanded Seth Warner's regiment of rangers. Now Washington needed the Green Mountain Boys and their kin to shore up his exposed northern frontier and block incursions from Canada. If the country had been in sad condition in 1778, it was tenfold more so in 1781, contended Stark, who described it as "overrun with spies and traitors."

Stark agreed to stop in Vermont on his way to assume command of the Continental Army's northern headquarters in Saratoga, New York, "and on my passage shall hold a treaty with the Green Mountain Boys," he told Washington on July 15, 1781, "but not having seen or been acquainted with those turbulent sons of freedom for several years I am at a loss to determine my reception, but hope it will be such as shall lead to the general good."

Stark's stopover in Bennington was a success, for Governor Chittenden and his council agreed to help. "I have reason to believe from their conduct that their promises are not fallacious," Stark told Washington on August 9, 1781. Indeed, 150 armed volunteers had turned out on horseback within a few hours of a false alarm of enemy movement near Saratoga.

Vermont had been holding its northern frontier together since the truce expired, but the forlorn state-in-waiting felt "torn by intestine divisions and the intrigues" of its enemies in Congress. The New York government had moved to Lake George "all the cannon, nay, every spade and pickaxe taken by her valiant sons," recalled Ira Allen.

John Stark found his northern front stripped bare. On August 9, 1781, he applied to Washington for rum, "as large as would amount to our proportion." It was accepted wisdom that an army with no rum was in no condition to fight. "Your excellency must know that if I do my duty, I must keep scouts continually in the woods, and men on that service ought to have a little grog in addition to their fresh beef and water," he explained. And he needed armorers to repair the broken muskets because "when a gun is out of repair (though perhaps a trifle would put it in order), a soldier is rendered unfit for duty."

When Stark settled into his northern headquarters, he reported, "My situation in this department is the most disagreeable I was ever in. There is no forage for horses, no horses to transport any kind of provisions . . . no camp kettles for the use of the troops. And unless some of the above-mentioned grievances are redressed, and very speedily, I shall expect the troops on the frontiers will disperse and go to their homes."

On September 14, 1781, Stark calculated that "we have ten rounds of cartridges per man, and no more ammunition in store." For lack of horses, he could not circulate his orders, "unless by detaching a soldier on foot, with his provisions on his back," he told Washington. "This, sir, requires good horses and horsemen. Neither of them are to be had here; and were there any horses, there is no money to pay their fodder, nor forage to keep them on; nor any of either can I get."

Six days later, Stark had run out of ammunition. "We have not even paper to transact our business with, nor can we obtain it," he complained to Washington.

THIRTEEN

A Fake Invasion Canceled

Governor Haldimand had more on his mind than the negotiations over Vermont. He was living aboard a cargo ship in the harbor of Quebec City while his residence was redecorated in the English style, with vegetable gardens and fruit trees. But strong headwinds were blowing from the west, and "five or six stout" American privateers were cruising for booty in the gulf of the Saint Lawrence, giving him cause to fear that the next supply ships expected from England, "should they get so far safe, cannot escape their vigilance."

And Canada was running short of grain. The year's crop had been sold off at extravagant cost, and the new crop was infested by caterpillars. So much hay was damaged that farmers had begun slaughtering or selling off their cattle.

Rumors of fresh war were rife in New York City, where General Henry Clinton expected an imminent attack by a joint French and American force and sought Haldimand's help. "I need not therefore say of how much importance a diversion upon the frontiers of this province and the speedy decision of Vermont in our favor would be."

Haldimand decided to create the diversion by staging an invasion of Vermont, with the collusion of Ethan and Ira Allen. In a secret dispatch carried by a backwoods courier, he assured General Clinton, "I have determined to shew a strong detachment upon the frontier about the first of October," when Vermont's newly elected General Assembly was due to meet.

The lieutenant colonel in command of the mock invasion, Barry St. Leger, would read out a proclamation from Haldimand enumerating the benefits of reunion with Britain. The proclamation, with input from the Allens, promised that "upon their cordially and effectually reuniting themselves as a government under the Crown of Great Britain," Vermonters could form "a separate province, independent of, and unconnected with every government in America," free to "enjoy every prerogative and immunity promised to the other provinces" in the British Empire.

In contrast to Congress's demand that Vermont submit to the authority of New York, Haldimand promised that the king would recognize and protect their land claims that "in consequence of grants from New Hampshire, had been cultivated by the labour and industry of the inhabitants of the Green Mountains." Territory annexed from New York and New Hampshire would be included, "to all intents and purposes, as belonging to the Province of Vermont."

Free trade with Canada, the most profitable market for Vermont farmers and their goods, would be encouraged. And British regulars would reinforce Vermont's militias, who would enjoy "every present and future advantage in common with the provincials now serving with the King's Army." In return, Haldimand expected Vermonters to set "a virtuous example to their countrymen" by renouncing their erroneous rebellion against the Crown "and putting stop to a ruinous and unnatural war" that had destroyed harmony and affection between Britain and its American colonies.

According to the script, Haldimand's proclamation would be delivered by his invasion force sailing south along Lake Champlain. Ethan and Ira Allen's cabal would persuade a newly elected legislature to accept his offer. If Vermont rejected terms this generous, it must bear "the melancholy consequences," he warned.

Ira Allen did not doubt that Vermonters would rather be governed by the Crown than by New York. He proposed that Haldimand's proclamation be opened and read out in the presence of Vermont's General Assembly, which would have no option but to approve the magnanimous terms.

Haldimand's invasion plan also called for St. Leger's army to capture and hold Crown Point on the west coast of Lake Champlain, for as long as the season would permit. He would send more troops south from the British base at Niagara in New York to the Mohawk River, the largest tributary into the Hudson River, to support the main force. If the invasion failed to produce the intended effect of delivering Vermont to British rule, he said, "it cannot fail to alarm and distress the enemy by ravaging the frontiers, and diminishing their supplies."

The Americans were suspicious. Stark had learned from a spy at Crown Point that the British intended "to make a push upon this place, to alarm the New Hampshire Grants . . . and gather all the Tories in this quarter, who are to be met by General Howe's army near this place."

Colonel St. Leger could not have known that Cornwallis's army was surrendering at Yorktown as he launched the mock invasion of Vermont on October 20, 1781, with British troops crammed aboard ninety barges under the protection of four gunboats. No sooner had they sailed south up Lake Champlain than plans went awry. Vermont's militia general Roger Enos had played a supporting role in the charade by sending out his patrols to shadow St. Leger's regulars. Sherwood and Smyth dispatched a British sergeant and a dozen troops from their spy base to catch one of the scouts, then release him with Haldimand's proclamation to hand-deliver to Governor Chittenden. On October 23, 1781, a half dozen Vermont scouts were surrounded near Fort Ticonderoga. Their sergeant was shot dead when he resisted.

It was a fatal example of ordinary Vermonters' ignorance of their leaders' collaboration with the British. St. Leger rushed to make amends, directing that "the last decencies be paid" to the sergeant, who was buried with British military honors. His bloody clothes were sent to his widow under a flag of truce. The five scouts captured were fed and freed with as much food and liquor as they could carry, and a rare letter of apology.

A New Hampshire militia colonel wondered what had prompted St. Leger to apologize for the sergeant's death. Ira Allen's explanation that "good men were sorry when good men were killed, or met with misfortune" sounded lame. The militia colonel persisted. Why should the enemy commander say he was sorry when his foe was killed? Sharper words flew before Ira Allen ordered the colonel to go back to his regiment and not waste time eating up the country's provisions while the frontier was under invasion.

General Stark was no less skeptical. He asked Governor Chittenden for "the most authentic information" about the slain sergeant and demanded to see the letter of apology written by Colonel St. Leger. Stark meant to send it to Congress as proof of Vermont's collaboration with the enemy. While he did not doubt that the principal portion of the people of Vermont were zealously attached to the American cause, Stark acknowledged that Vermont "contains its proportion of lurking traitors."

Ira Allen urged Haldimand to postpone his announcement of Vermont's reunion with Britain since the American victory at Yorktown would make it "hard and some dangerous" to continue. "To publish these matters before they are fully ripe," Ira wrote, "might at last endanger the whole system so well calculated for the happiness of the people and on which I have placed my ambition."

Haldimand's proclamation was not made public. Chittenden and Ira Allen called in the undelivered letters and forged fresh copies that excised incriminating details. Allen put a self-serving spin on the cover-up, contending that the aborted invasion of 1781 had cost but one life at little expense.

As confirmation of Cornwallis's surrender trickled in, Colonel St. Leger took advantage of a fair wind to load his troops on their barges and sail them back to Canada. Governor Chittenden conceded to General Washington that Vermont had indeed been talking to the British, but only to prevent the invasion and get its prisoners back. The revelation seemed not to surprise Washington, who took the British apology calmly.

Haldimand understood that "the conduct of Vermont will be entirely regulated by events in the Chesapeake." On November 18, 1781, he wrote that Cornwallis's defeat left no hope of successful resolution to the talks. Germain had yet to absorb the facts by January 2, 1782, when he prattled on that negotiations with Vermont were "in so fair a train as to afford good grounds to expect that country would speedily be restored to the King's obedience."

"At any rate," General Henry Clinton wrote in his memoirs, "I have little doubt that, had Lord Cornwallis only remained where he was ordered, or even after his coming into Virginia had our operations there been covered by a superior fleet as I was promised, Vermont would have probably joined us."

Governor Chittenden congratulated George Washington on his "glorious victory" at Yorktown over "the haughty Cornwallis and his army," but also reminded him of Vermont's contributions to the cause of American independence. "That the citizens of this state have by nature an equal right to liberty and independency with the citizens of America in general, cannot be disputed. And that they have merited it from the United States by their exertions with them in bringing about the glorious revolution, is as evident a truth as any other, which respects the acquired right of any community."

Washington sent an emissary to find out whether Vermont would be satisfied with independence or seriously contemplated joining the enemy. Chittenden replied that Vermonters were "zealous supporters of independence" who wanted to join the United States. But rather than having to submit to New York, they would take up arms, and join the British in Canada.

If the Allens' fraternization with the British had been a ploy to stave off invasion, then victory at Yorktown offered Vermont the opportunity to declare its true sentiments. Washington held Vermont to its pretext for negotiating with Britain. "I will take it for granted, as you assert it, that they were so far innocent," he told Chittenden, and chose to infer that "there was never any serious intention of joining Great Britain in their attempts to subjugate your country."

Yet, the Allens kept chasing after Haldimand. Ira pleaded that Vermonters were fast "losing sight" of joining the United States. If Haldimand remained patient, he told Sherwood, "these matters may yet crown our most sanguine expectations."

For his part, Haldimand was frustrated by a lack of instructions from London. But he recognized that "the prejudice of a great many of the population, and the prevailing influence of Congress are too powerful to admit of a chance" of a successful conclusion, given the surge of patriotic fervor among Americans, not least Vermonters.

Shaken by news of Cornwallis's defeat in Virginia, Sherwood advised Haldimand that unless "affairs take a more favorable turn to the southward," further negotiations with Vermont would be but "time and labor lost."

Ethan Allen had resigned his command of Vermont's militias more than a year before, but could not pass up the chance to revive his grudge against New York. The final military action escalated their quarrel to the brink of a pocket civil war that Stark, who still commanded the Northern Department of the Continental Army, lacked manpower to prevent.

After the British invaders sailed away, Vermont resumed annexing neighboring towns in New Hampshire and New York. In retaliation, New York drafted Samuel Fairbanks, a lieutenant colonel in Vermont's militia, into its militia as a private, then jailed him for refusing to comply. His supporters tracked down Fairbank's captor to a New York tavern and whisked him and his drinking companions off to Bennington to be mistreated, they complained, "in a most scandalous manner."

Vermont sent its own militiamen to protect New Yorkers who preferred allegiance to Vermont. "If your honor cannot find the militia of Albany some other employment," one Vermont general told Stark, "I shall march my regiment to that quarter, and try powder and ball with them, which I have as well as they." Fairbanks later escaped in a gunfight that wounded three New Yorkers shot by their own side.

New Year's Eve of December 1781 found Vermont militiamen facing down a smaller contingent of New Yorkers deployed across the Walloomsac River, not far from the Bennington battlefield of 1777. Ethan Allen arrived with an old cannon borrowed from Fort Ticonderoga. "I am weak, only about 80 men, and the insurrectors about 146," concluded New York's field commander. The New Yorkers packed up and went home.

Afterward, Allen submitted his expense account for eleven pounds denominated in British currency. This amounted to ten shillings "to my attending on the Militia at the Siege of Vallumcock" on December 31, 1781, and nine pounds, two shillings "to cash paid for my Expenses and for the Militia at the same time." Vermont did not get around to reimbursing Ethan Allen until 1785.

Even after hostilities were suspended, Ethan and Ira Allen urged Haldimand not to lose interest in Vermont, a neutral republic unaffiliated with the United States. "The last refusal of Congress to admit this state into union, has done more to awaken the common people to a sense of their own interest and resentment of their conduct than all which they had done before," he wrote under the pseudonym of "C." "By their own account, they declare that Vermont does not and shall not belong to their confederacy. The consequence is that they may fight their own battles. It is liberty which they say they are after, but will not extend it to Vermont."

He added an intriguing invitation: "If it should be Your Excellency's pleasure, after having conversed with the gentleman who will deliver these lines"—likely Sherwood—"that I should wait on Your Excellency at any part of Lake Champlain, I will do it, except that I should find that it would hazard my life too much. There is a majority in Congress, and a number of the principal officers of the Continental Army, continually planning against me."

Ethan concluded with this promise: "I shall do everything in my power to render this state a British province."

But the British were weary of an unpopular war. On March 25, 1783, four months after the United States and Britain worked out preliminary terms for a peace treaty, Haldimand delivered his final thoughts on the failed negotiations to Ira Allen. He regretted that Vermont had missed its chance to return to Britain. While that "happy moment" of restoring the blessings of reconciliation could not be recalled, he took consolation that he had "not omitted any opportunities." If reports of peace were true, he said, "a very short time will determine the fate of Vermont." Should anything favorable present" itself, he added through his secretary, "You may still depend on his Excellency's endeavours for your salvation."

Ethan Allen claimed to be "half over seas," or half-drunk as an old song put it, when he used his cypher code name— XX XX XX XX—to scribble a rambling note to Sherwood a few weeks later. The die was cast, peace was taking place, and the United States was acknowledged to be independent of Britain. "The scene has changed and Vermont must do as well as she can," Allen wrote from a tavern in Manchester, "and in the menetime [*sic*] feel the highest obligations to their Friends and will not confederate with Congress come on what will but will be Independent of Independency.

"But our enemies are busy. And so are our friends," he observed, "which will produce something by and by." Ethan Allen was already hatching a scheme to encourage American Loyalists to converge on northern Vermont in sufficient numbers "to bring about a revolution" in favor of uniting with Canada. The coup could be pulled off, he assured Sherwood, "without touching or injuring the faith of the British government, as the King, nor parliament, need not be concerned in this matter." It was hardly coincidence that some of the land proposed to accommodate the Loyalists was owned by the Allen brothers.

Haldimand, who wanted the Tories resettled as far from Vermont as possible, was ordered to end negotiations lest they jeopardize the pending peace treaty. "No assistance can be given to that state"—Vermont—"to enable them to act against the Americans," the British prime minister Lord North declared.

"They are really a hardy, enterprising people," Haldimand reflected, "and, though it was in my power with the greatest ease during the war to destroy such of them that should settle on Lake Champlain, it was with great difficulty that I could deter them from attempting it."

The peace treaty, signed in Paris on September 3, 1783, was ratified by Congress in January 1784, but not exchanged until May. Benjamin Franklin, who helped negotiate the treaty, wanted Quebec ceded to the Americans, to prevent border incidents, but the British refused. Loyalists such as Sherwood had hoped to find Vermont demarcated on the British side of the northern border in the peace treaty. Instead, the self-styled republic of Vermont was tucked inside the boundaries of the new United States.

When news of the ratification of the peace treaty reached Vermont, Ira Allen and Joseph Fay vied to feed the British army that they had fought as Green Mountain Boys. The time had come to look to their own interests. The best prospects for Vermont's economic survival lay in free trade with its northern neighbor.

"Since the war has closed, it becomes every one to turn his eye towards the objects of peace in the pursuits of an honorable support," they wrote Sherwood on May 29, 1783. "In this we shall not enter into politicks—but propose for your consideration a contract for supplying the troops in Canada with fresh and other provisions; which will be done upon as reasonable terms as possible, to be delivered at such times & places as shall be agreed upon."

They pitched a business plan for Haldimand to consider: "Since the powers at war have concluded on a general peace, which opens the way for a general commerce, we take the freedom to propose to your excellency, to contract for supplying the troops in Canada under your command with fresh and other provisions, which shall be done at as cheap as possible, and delivered at such times and places as shall be agreed upon."

Ethan Allen weighed in, recommending his brother Ira and Joseph Fay "as proper persons to procure and deliver the beef" to Canada. Before mid-July, he estimated, their "young cattle will be tolerable beef, and the late settlement of the war I suppose will admit of a free trade."

Mathews replied that once a ratified peace allowed a "mutual intercourse, and free trade between Vermont and this Province, General Allen's recommendation in your favor would be attended to." Ira Allen's bid was not accepted, George Smyth claimed, because the king's stores were already well stocked with provisions and no fewer than twenty-one business competitors had already arrived with foodstuffs that lay moored in the river.

Smyth proposed to Ira Allen "that should it be worth your while to send in any quantity of beef or some milch cows to take the chance of the market, that his Excellency would not be averse to it. Nevertheless, I believe he would not wish to have it hurried into execution, as a very short time must ultimately determine the affairs still pending, or at least, at yet, unknown to him."

Joseph Fay also herded his cattle and sheep to sell in Canada. He thanked Haldimand for arranging their transport across Lake Champlain, although, he added, "the market has not proved so advantageous as was expected."

Haldimand could not open Canada to cross-border trade without the king's instructions. But he hinted that he would let Vermont cattle and grain be imported "for the convenience of the people," as well as clothing and other goods necessary for Vermont. "I shall have no objection to you & your brother sending in cattle," he told Ira Allen, "but it must be entirely to take the chance of the market, as I cannot enter into any contract for government on this account."

Ira had hoped for "business of more consequence" between Vermont and Quebec. "P.S.," he added, "I expect to have some Cattle at Onion River this fall that I should be glad to drive to this province provided your Excellency would favor me with a permit therefor."

Ira Allen hustled Sherwood to help him secure a loan in Montreal of 1,000 guineas at 6 percent interest, to invest in prime farmland. "I will make you a present out of the lands I purchase," he promised, "sufficient for each of you on a good farm and its situation will not be bad."

Justus Sherwood, who had built and fortified his Loyal Block House to repel attackers, now found it under commercial assault. In January 1783, a trader appeared with five hundred pairs of shoes to sell in Canada. He was sent away with a message that when his people returned to their rightful sovereign, they would be welcomed with open arms, but no trading could be allowed until then. When a couple of Yankee peddlers showed up with a wagonload of fresh beef, Sherwood dumped it in Lake Champlain.

Ebenezer Allen visited the Loyal Block House in March 1783 and pretended to be "much attached to the King's Government," but Sherwood guessed that he was interested in commerce. Sherwood found it hard to be "commonly civil," recalling how Ebenezer had him arrested after his talks with Ethan Allen. He turned Ebenezer back on the pretext that melting ice had made Lake Champlain impassable.

Four days earlier, Sherwood had learned that the colonies had won. Six years of sacrifice and peril in the king's service had come to nothing. He could not risk going home to Vermont, nor did he wish to. "I think no Loyalist of principle and spirit can ever endure the thought of going back to live under the imperious laws of a Washington and his mignons [*sic*]," he wrote Mathews.

Sherwood didn't know what lay in store now that his war was lost, how long he must stay at the Loyal Block House. "And as every appearance is gloomy on the part of the American Loyalists," he wrote Mathews, "I am anxious to look out some settlement for myself and a few loyal friends, as well as all those faithful fellows whom I have so long employ'd in the Secret Service line and who naturally look for assistance."

His deputy, George Smyth, talked of going home to Ireland. "My day of life, joined to a brittle constitution, forbid new beginnings [in] this country," he said, "and my only wish is to see my Native Country once more, and hope, in a proper time to obtain liberty to go to Europe, where I am wont to spend the rest of my days." In the end, he retired to a suburb of Montreal.

Sherwood asked what Haldimand thought of the Gaspé Peninsula in easternmost Quebec, where a fellow Loyalist officer had invited him to settle, or "whether I had best look for a tract of vacant land on the Southern frontiers of Canada. Your candid friendly advice on these subjects is much oblige[d], dear sir."

Haldimand advised Sherwood that he was "more eligible to seek a retreat as far removed as possible from the scenes of chaos and discord that must unavoidably subsist, Lord knows how long, in the Colonies." He should tour other locations "as soon as possible to decide upon your future situation," and not tell anyone. "You can at no time be so well spared as at present," Haldimand said.

Sherwood visited Canadian settlements along the Atlantic from the Gaspé to Nova Scotia, but he knew nothing about fishing. He toured the St. Lawrence River west of Montreal. On October 14, 1783, he sent back word that the best land he had ever seen lay along the north bank of the St. Lawrence to its inlet on Lake Ontario. "The climate here is very mild and good, and I think the Loyalists may be the happiest people in America by settling this country."

Haldimand wanted Sherwood to assist Loyalist refugees who had fled the United States. Sarah's brother Elijah Bottum brought back to Canada two slaves that Sherwood had left in the custody of his in-laws in Vermont. He used them to help him survey the backcountry of Upper Canada, Quebec's boundary with present-day Ontario, billing the government one shilling and sixpence a day for each slave's labor.

Sherwood never explained why he practiced slavery when so many Green Mountain Boys opposed it. Slavery was tolerated in Canada though on a far smaller scale than in the United States. Loyalist refugees brought about three hundred slaves into Quebec and five hundred more into what is now Ontario. When Britain prohibited slavery in 1833, slaves in Canada won their freedom. But some slave owners packed theirs off to slave markets in the United States.

On December 6, 1783, Sherwood was stricken with smallpox. George Smyth, a doctor, diagnosed him as "dangerously ill" and "delirious" but added, "there are now favorable symptoms." Sherwood's wife and two of their children contracted the disease from him. Sarah became so ill that he could not leave her side, but all survived.

In March 1784, Sherwood sold his farm on Dutchman's Point, while reserving the blockhouse as "King's property." The new owner asked when the garrison next door would be withdrawn. Sherwood told him "not to expect any information from me on that subject without permission or direction from his excellency," General Haldimand.

Governor Chittenden also wanted the commander of the Loyal Block House to certify its evacuation, so that "an officer from this state may take possession thereof." Washington sent his German drill-master Friedrich von Steuben to verify Britain's surrender of its chain of forts along the northern frontier. But as late as September 1792, a British sergeant with eight soldiers occupied Sherwood's Loyal Block House. The British posts on Lake Champlain were not evacuated until 1796.

FOURTEEN

A Bastard Joins the
United States

How could Congress reason with a nuisance as contrary as Vermont? A bastard state-in-waiting unwanted by the United States, it felt under no obligation to pay the costs of a war in which its Green Mountain Boys had bled. It had survived since 1777 by confiscating and selling off the property of its Loyalists. Continental Army deserters found asylum in its backwoods with other fugitives who, if not on the wrong side of the law, were fleeing burdensome taxes and their messy pasts.

Vermonters preferred to live under benign British rule, or so Ethan and Ira Allen claimed, to being dismembered by New York and deprived of their right to keep what they had cleared and settled in the New Hampshire Grants. As from the beginning, their rebellion was about the land.

Congress's failures had tarnished the luster of joining the United States. "Their currency had failed, their revenues were exhausted, their armies were dissatisfied and unpaid, the debts they had contracted were unfunded, the public creditors were everywhere full of complaints against their proceedings, and they had no resources to answer the demands that were perpetually made upon them," wrote Samuel Williams in his earliest history of Vermont, published in 1794. By contrast, "Vermont was happy in being free from the load of debt, which lay upon the United States; and was not perplexed by the constant calls of Congress, to raise the necessary sums of money." Vermont had affordable land to sell homesteaders and speculators from across New England and beyond.

Congress blamed Vermont for squandering its time and resources. The United States could not afford to be torn apart by secessionist movements. The overlapping claims of New York, New Hampshire, and sometimes Massachusetts to the New Hampshire Grants were only part of a tangle of land disputes plaguing Congress, such as Virginia's claims to the Appalachian wilderness that would become Kentucky.

Yet Congress could not "in honor or justice" put off settling its Vermont problem, argued Joseph Jones, an influential delegate from Virginia who compared Vermont to a boil or other hideous growth on America's body politic. He told his colleague James Madison that "such execrencies should be taken off on their first appearance as then the work is easy and less dangerous than when they have grown to a head." Had the claims of New York and New Hampshire to the Grants been settled earlier, he maintained, Vermont "would not at this day have been known—delay has given them a name and made them formidable." Jones worried about "designing ambitious men" manipulating popular discontent. He advised Madison to "fix the boundaries of these states and let the people who live within their respective limits know they are their citizens and must submit to their government."

By August 1781, Vermont's chances had improved enough that Madison reported, "The controversy relating to the district called Vermont, the inhabitants of which have for several years claimed and exercised the jurisdiction of an independent state is at length put into a train of speedy events." Massachusetts had agreed to drop its claims to Vermont. New York and New Hampshire made little headway with their own rival claims.

George Washington believed that Vermont would do less damage inside the United States than outside. "It appears to me," he wrote Governor Chittenden, "that the dispute of boundary is the only one which exists, and that being removed, all further difficulties would be removed also, and the matter terminated to the satisfaction of all parties."

Despite his misgivings about Vermont, Madison ventured that "there is no question but they will soon be established into a separate & federal state." But Congress overruled Washington's recommendation in April 1782. Vermont's admittance could not be considered "until the pulse of nine states beats favorably for it," wrote Madison.

Washington had his own reasons for helping Vermont. He had envisioned following up victory at Yorktown with a lightning strike deep into Canada, wresting away Britain's lucrative export market in beaver fur and other pelts of fashion in Europe. Such an invasion overland would need the complicity of the unpredictable "Vermontese." "I shall say nothing of the benefits which America would derive, and the injury Great Britain must sustain by the fur and other trade of Canada shifting hands," he explained. "Nor of the immense importance it must be to the future peace and quiet of these states, especially the Western part of them, to annihilate the British interest in that country; thereby putting a stop to their intriguing after peace shall be established."

On May 4, 1782, Washington proposed his plan to France's minister to Congress, the Chevalier de La Luzerne, who made clear that France had recognized a United States formed of thirteen colonies and did not want it expanded with a fourteenth state. Having lost Canada to Britain a generation earlier, France objected to being replaced in Canada by the United States.

Unaware that the British cabinet had decided a few weeks earlier to suspend hostilities, Haldimand dusted off his threat to invade Vermont. "The crisis is arrived when coercion alone must decide the part Vermont will take," he wrote General Henry Clinton in New York, by deploying troops to their frontier, and "by laying waste their country if they do not accept the terms offered."

What gave Haldimand pause was "the multitude of militia men in arms ready to turn out at a quarter of an hour's notice." Early melting ice on Lake Champlain made the terrain too soggy to support an invasion. And harvest failures had left Quebec without enough flour to bake bread. Haldimand had been diverting flour allocated for Upper Canada, which must be replaced. He reckoned that another invasion of Vermont would not be feasible before the summer of 1784.

That left Congress, which resolved in December 1782 to

send an army to starve the Vermonters into submission. An earlier memorandum had envisioned confiscating its livestock and grain stores, which could be returned if Vermonters displayed good and faithful behavior toward the United States. Otherwise their property could be forfeited and the country laid desolate, leaving Haldimand with lots of "useless mouths" to feed.

Washington dreaded the bloody consequences of invading Vermont. "Let me ask, by whom is that district of country principally settled? And of whom is your present army . . . comprised?" Washington asked Joseph Jones on February 11, 1783. "The answer is evident—New England men."

"The country is very mountainous, full of defiles, and very strong," Washington continued. "The inhabitants for the most part are a hardy race, composed of that kind of people who are best calculated for soldiers; in truth who are soldiers—for many, many hundreds of them are deserters from this army who having acquired property there, would be desperate in defense of it." He concluded, "I cannot at this time undertake to say, that there would be any difficulty with the army, if it were to be ordered on this service, but I should be exceedingly unhappy to see the experiment made."

Jones reminded Washington that the Vermont legislature had rejected Congress's offer to consider its application to join to the United States once it returned to its boundaries within the New Hampshire Grants. Jones and his fellow Virginians in Congress worried that admitting Vermont would set a dangerous precedent for secessionist movements.

But, he argued, its principled stance need not lead to war. "If Vermont confines herself to the limits assigned to her, and ceases to encroach upon and disturb the quiet of the adjoining states, at the same time avoiding combinations, or acts, hostile to the United States," Jones proposed, "she may be at rest within her limits, and, by patient waiting the convenient time, may ere long be admitted to the Union."

In a resolution drafted by James Madison, Congress denounced "every attempt by force to set up a separate and independent jurisdiction" within any of the thirteen United States as "a direct violation of the rights of such [a] state, and subversive of the Union of the whole under the supervising authority of Congress." It directed "people who assumed an independent jurisdiction" to desist immediately, until their claims could be determined through an election, subject to the approval of New York, New Hampshire, and Massachusetts.

By March 1782, congressmen representing seven of the thirteen United States—Massachusetts, Rhode Island, Connecticut, New Jersey, Pennsylvania, Delaware, and Maryland—were inclined to recognize Vermont's sovereignty if it kept to its original boundaries. Delegates from New York and New Hampshire were opposed, of course, as were those from the four Southern states—Virginia, North and South Carolina, and Georgia—who feared New England would be overrepresented in Congress.

After the Haldimand negotiations collapsed, business difficulties led Ethan and Ira Allen to reconsider the commercial benefits of joining Britain. Vermont's leaders were not "sentimentally attached to a republican form of government," Ethan contended. A majority of Vermonters opposed statehood, he claimed, and would fare better under British rule.

"In the time of General Haldimand's command, could Great Britain have afforded Vermont protection, they would readily have yielded up their independency, and have become a province of Great Britain," he declared, as late as July 16, 1788.

The folly of reversing the rebellion against New York by Ethan Allen and his Green Mountain Boys was not lost on Alexander Hamilton as a New York legislator. Vermont had been severed from New York for years and any attempt to recover it would incur "certain and serious calamities," Hamilton said. "Can any reasonable man suppose that New York, with the load of debt the Revolution has left upon it, and under a popular government, would be able to carry on with an advantage against a people half as numerous as itself, in their own territory; a territory defended as much by its natural situation as by the numbers and hardiness of its inhabitants? Can it be imagined that it would be able, finally, to reduce such a people to its obedience? The supposition would be chimerical, and the attempt madness."

In 1789, New York's legislature moved to resolve its quarrel with Vermont. New York creditors wanted $600,000 to buy out their overlapping land titles. Vermont refused to pay more than a nickel an acre. In the end, they agreed on

$30,000 in Spanish-milled silver or gold coins. When Vermont came up $5,000 short, New York granted an extension. With the final settlement, New York dropped its opposition to Vermont's existence. On January 6, 1791, a convention in Bennington ratified the United States Constitution and applied for Vermont's admission into the United States.

George Washington, president since April 30, 1789, presented Vermont's petition to Congress and signed the act making Vermont the fourteenth state. Southern objections were placated by adding Kentucky, which had split off from Virginia, as the fifteenth state.

On May 8, 1791, a new American flag, with two more stars, representing Vermont and Kentucky, was hoisted over the town of Rutland, Vermont. Artillery volunteers fired fifteen salvos. The drinking began with fifteen formal toasts. A local choir sang an anthem composed for the occasion:

> *Come each Green Mountain Boy,*
> *Swell every breast with joy,*
> *Hail our good land,*
> *As our pines climb the air,*
> *Firm as our mountains are,*
> *Federal beyond compare,*
> *Proudly we stand.*

Barely two decades had lapsed since Ethan Allen, Seth Warner, and Justus Sherwood bonded as Green Mountain Boys. Their friendship forged as homesteaders in the New Hampshire Grants, and outlaws in the sight of New

York, had been consumed in the vortex of the American Revolution.

Seth Warner was the first to die. At thirty-two years old, he had been picked over Ethan Allen to take the Green Mountain Boys to war, where he distinguished himself for courage and competence. As a lieutenant colonel, he was chosen over three brigadier generals to cover the northern army's chaotic evacuation of Ticonderoga. His ingenious tactics limited the British and their German allies to a Pyrrhic victory at Hubbardton and utter defeat at Bennington. Warner triumphed by out-thinking and outwitting his enemies, only to be defeated in the end by paralysis and dementia.

Warner's degenerative illness went undiagnosed, though speculation about its cause has included the deadly effects of mercury poisoning known as "mad hatter's disease." Mercury vapors were used to separate fur from the skin of beavers and other small animals to make the felt hats popular at the time. Mercury was also prescribed in the folk medicine of eighteenth-century America as a panacea for a spectrum of ailments from wounds to syphilis.

Warner did not recover from his illness after the battle at Bennington in 1777. As his biographer Daniel Chipman, son of a Green Mountain Boy, memorialized him in 1858, Seth "struggled long with complicated and distressing maladies, which he bore with uncommon fortitude and resignation, until deprived of his reason, after which he was constantly fighting his battles over again, not in imagination only, but by the exertion of a preternatural physical strength, so that it required two or three to take charge of him."

Warner died violently incoherent in Roxbury, Connecticut, on December 26, 1784. Several men were needed to confine him on his deathbed. Thirty Green Mountain Boys and their friends mounted a tearful vigil of honor around his body, and mourners packed his funeral three days later. He died penniless, leaving his widow, Hester, destitute after twenty years of marriage, with three children to raise. In begging Congress for a pension due as widow of a Continental colonel, she wrote of herself that, "Notwithstanding your petitioner had the chief care of looking after her dear companion, it yielded her some consolation that she had the opportunity of looking after the colonel in his last sickness."

Nearly two years after Seth's death, Hester wrote an indifferent Congress from their home, "Had it been the colonel's fate to have fallen in battle, as many did that were engaged with him, your petitioner is informed that she should be entitled to receive some gratuity from your honors. Your petitioner, therefore can hope inasmuch as the death of her dear companion was in consequence of the wounds and hardships he received in his country's service in the late war."

Her petition was supported by Ethan Allen and ten other Green Mountain Boys and prominent Vermonters. Had Colonel Warner retired earlier from military service, he might have recovered his health, they contended, "but it being the trying time of American affairs in this quarter, there was no room in a mind like his to attend such a proposition and accordingly he persevered until his important and memorable actions at Hubbardton and Bennington." The petition was denied.

Warner had been so intent on saving his country that he neglected to save for his family. What land he owned was sold for unpaid taxes. Three years after his death, Vermont's legislature begrudged his widow and heirs a wedge of two thousand swampy acres abutting a rock-stubbled hill. Hester's inheritance was worthless.

Nine lines chiseled on his gravestone paid homage to a gallant life ended at the age of forty-one:

TRIUMPHANT LEADER AT OUR ARMIES' HEAD,
WHOSE MARTIAL GLORY STRUCK A PANIC DREAD,
THY WARLIKE DEEDS ENGRAVEN ON THIS STONE
TELL FUTURE AGES WHAT A HERO'S DONE.
FULL SIXTEEN BATTLES HE DID FIGHT,
FOR TO PROCURE HIS COUNTRY'S RIGHT.
OH! THIS BRAVE HERO, HE DID FALL
BY DEATH, WHO EVER CONQUERS ALL.
WHEN THIS YOU SEE, REMEMBER ME.

Except for rabble-rousing in the secession-minded Susquehanna and Wyoming Valleys of Pennsylvania in 1786, Ethan Allen enjoyed playing the country squire at his fourteen-hundred-acre riverside farm in northern Vermont, near present-day Burlington. His prison memoir had been widely popular. But when he published "Reason the Only Oracle of Man," a diatribe against organized religion lifted in part from his old mentor Thomas Young, it sold only a couple of hundred copies.

After his long-suffering wife, Mary Brownson, died in 1783, Ethan courted a brisk young widow. Frances Buchanan was more than twenty years younger, and the stepdaughter of Crean Brush, a vindictive Loyalist who had helped get Ethan outlawed in New York as "a dangerous leader of lawless banditti." In late 1777, Brush had suffered a reversal of political and financial fortunes and put a pistol to his head, "besmearing the room with his brains," as one account of his suicide put it.

Ethan Allen cherished his spunky new bride, who was land-rich, as "the partner of my joys, my dearest self, my love, pride of my life." He installed Fanny in his snug farmhouse, where she bore him two sons and a daughter. Hannibal and Ethan would graduate from West Point and join the United States Army. Their daughter, Frances, would be cloistered as a Catholic nun in a convent in Montreal.

"I suppose our friend Ethan will be one of the first members" of Vermont's delegation to Congress, predicted an acquaintance. But Allen never saw it admitted into the United States. As his brother Levi was sailing to London in futile pursuit of a commercial treaty with Britain, Ethan suffered a stroke in February 1789. He had spent the night visiting his cousin Ebenezer Allen at his farm on the southern tip of South Hero Island across Lake Champlain. He was sledding back through the snow with a load of Ebenezer's hay, when the driver heard Ethan gasp.

As he lay dying, an improbable anecdote had a clergyman at his bedside assuring him: "The angels are waiting for you, General Allen."

"They are, are they?" Ethan was said to have murmured. "Well, goddamn them, let them wait."

His death elicited a range of emotions. At Yale, which young Ethan could not attend, its president, Ezra Stiles, jotted in his diary on February 13, 1789: "Died in Vermont the profane and impious Deist Gen. Ethan Allen," and presumed that "in Hell he lifts up his eyes, being in torment."

Ethan Allen was mourned as a hero though the only war he waged had led to his surrender and capture in Quebec. "His remains were decently inter'd with the honours of war and a large circle of military men attended from all parts of the state," Ira Allen wrote to their brother Levi in England. Cannon were discharged over Ethan's grave, whose location was soon forgotten. No headstone or portraits survived.

He was eclipsed by economic depression and westward emigration from Vermont. But hard times would spawn a belated nostalgia for a legendary Ethan Allen that never quite existed in his raucous lifetime. He reentered history as the most celebrated of Vermonters.

Ethan's flaws masked his virtues. He could be loud, impetuous, and self-serving. He was also charismatic, bold, and resourceful. He was a bully with a soft spot for the downtrodden. He was a clumsy military leader but a masterful propagandist who inspired, or coerced, settlers to throw their lot in with him. He withstood for thirty-two months the harshest treatment that his British captors could inflict, to prove himself their equal. Yet half a decade later, Vermont's favorite patriot vowed to do everything in his power to make it a British province.

Historians have been hard put to parse the motives of the Allens, who seemed to shift with the winds of change between fidelity to the Patriot cause, stubborn neutrality, and longing for the British rule that might have been.

"When Ira Allen declared on his honor that he preferred union with Great Britain and implicated Ethan in that statement, he may or may not have been telling the truth. Neither of the brothers paid much attention to that when it served their purpose to ignore it," wrote the historian James Truslow Adams. "When [Ira] Allen said bluntly that what he was after at all costs was to save his property, he was probably nearer the truth than at any other time in the negotiations."

Justus Sherwood could not go home to Vermont. His wife, Sarah, recovered from smallpox, was permitted to visit her family there. Justus filed a claim with the British government for £1,209 for the loss of his farms and possessions in Vermont, documenting how "his little property which he had accumulated by honest industry was forfeited and sold or otherwise taken for the use of the Rebels." In the end, his royal compensation amounted to $229 for his original farm. Yet he continued to own land in New Haven, where his brother-in-law offered to buy two hundred acres. His service as a Loyalist captain also entitled him to a pension on half-pay plus three thousand acres in Canada from the Crown, but he never received his proper share.

So Sherwood homesteaded twice, this time on the north bank of the St. Lawrence River, east of Lake Ontario, as he had done back in New Haven, Vermont. He built his new cabin in Augusta township, one of many that he had surveyed. He competed with other refugees for scarce axes, hoes, and other farm tools. He encouraged other Loyalists who hoped to settle in Montreal and resented being exiled to the Canadian woods. Even as he helped others, he lamented that "no man can need money more than I do at present."

In a summer drought in 1787, he slaughtered most of his livestock to sustain his family through the next winter. He fell back on logging, to sell lumber that could be exported to Britain. In what is now Prescott, Ontario, he re-created what Vermont might have looked like had he reunited it with Britain. He became a local legislator, justice of the peace, and a respected surveyor. He established a small Anglican church and struggled to find an ordained priest. And he quietly held on to 150 acres back in New Haven, Vermont.

Justus Sherwood was still logging in 1798. Ferrying a load of lumber down the St. Lawrence, he tumbled off his raft and drowned, at the age of fifty-one. His body was never found.

General Frederick Haldimand retired to London and was knighted for his services to the Crown. "You are always a soldier and always right," King George told him. His foreign birth barred Haldimand from further promotion. He hung around the royal court, yearning for the king's approval while admiring the ladies-in-waiting. "The court was crowded, and it seemed to me that I had never seen so many beautiful women there," he noted in a private diary. He was furious to find that other generals in America had lined their pockets by skimming allowances for their troops. His superiors Sir William Howe and Sir Henry Clinton always drew "upwards of one hundred rations a day and as much wood as they could burn," another general told him.

Haldimand harbored belated regrets about a lifetime of duty to Britain. "The more I know of this country, the more I see that it is the height of folly to trust to the generosity of the nation," he confided to his diary. "Services are forgotten the moment there is no longer need of us."

The canny Tom Chittenden served a dozen years as Vermont's first governor while he farmed his extensive wheat fields watered by the Winooski River. Visitors who called on him were fed around a common table with his hired hands. In the evening, Chittenden interrupted affairs of state to pour stiff drinks for customers who frequented a small bar that he had installed at one end of the room.

Levi Allen drifted between St. Johns in Canada, and England. "I am quite weary of living in the manner for ten years past," his wife, Nancy, scolded, "you have made me completely wretched by being so much absent." On a trade mission for Vermont in December 1789, Levi visited Philip Skene in London and offered to raise a regiment of Green Mountain Boys to serve the king in America. The black sheep among the Allen brothers was not taken seriously.

Ebenezer Allen padded alone on snowshoes across frozen Lake Champlain in 1783 to homestead on South Hero

Island, south of Sherwood's Loyal Block House. He became a neighbor of his cousin Ethan, whose farm lay just across the lake, and later opened a tavern. But Ebenezer never lost his crust as a Green Mountain Boy. Once he visited the British officer's mess in Montreal, where a regular challenged the scruffy stranger to a duel, daring him to choose the time, place, and weapon.

"The time is now," snapped Major Ebenezer Allen. He pulled out his horse pistol and spat out his rules: You put your pistol in my mouth. I put my pistol in your mouth. At the command to fire, we both pull the trigger! His challenger did not pursue the duel.

Ira Allen was the wealthiest man in Vermont until his creditors turned on him. The Vermont legislature refused in 1784 to let him enact a commercial treaty with Quebec that might have saved his lumber business. A year later, the legislature annulled his land surveys, claiming they were too sloppy. Without a duty-free commercial outlet for Vermont's products in Canada and Britain, the Allen brothers' financial empire shriveled.

Ira sailed to England and lobbied for a canal that would open direct passage from Lake Champlain to the St. Lawrence River and Atlantic Ocean. Rebuffed, he hatched an audacious plot for a French-American invasion of Canada, to be renamed the Republic of United Columbia. He traveled to Paris in 1796 to seek financial and political support from France's revolutionary government to finance the insurrection.

The French government agreed to sell Ira twenty thousand muskets and two dozen cannon, ostensibly to equip Vermont's militia. But the ship he chartered in the Belgian port of Ostend, the *Olive Branch*, could load only fifteen thousand muskets and twenty-one cannon. The Royal Navy intercepted the *Olive Branch* off southwest England and assumed that the muskets and cannon packed aboard were destined for rebels in Ireland. To get his guns back and recoup his investment, Ira had to prove otherwise.

He traveled to France, but as details of his plot to seize Canada tumbled out, he was arrested on suspicion of spying as well as gunrunning. After a year in Paris's jails, shivering in the filthy Pélagie prison, Ira returned to Vermont bankrupt. Rather than get locked up again for indebtedness, he fled to Philadelphia where he died alone, destitute and crippled by gout, on January 15, 1814, "without a groan and without pain," as a neighbor told it. Ira was buried in an unmarked pauper's grave in a potter's field bequeathed by the Quakers, four hundred miles from the Vermont that he had labored to create. He was sixty-two years old.

An obituary notice in Burlington, Vermont, for this most turbulent of sons was brief: "Mr. Allen, citizen of this town, died in Philadelphia."

-AFTERWORD-

Rev. Samuel Williams, a friend of Ira Allen, thus ends his 416-page *History of Vermont*, hand-printed and published in 1794. It remains no less relevant today.

"Ye people of the United States of America, behold here the precarious foundation upon which ye hold your liberties. They rest not upon things written upon paper, nor upon the virtues, the vices, or the designs of other men, but they depend upon yourselves; upon your maintaining your property, your knowledge, and your virtue. Nature and society have joined to produce, and to establish freedom in America. You are now in the full possession of all your natural and civil rights; under no restraints in and acquiring knowledge, property, or the highest honours of your country; in the most rapid state of improvement, and population; with perfect freedom to make further improvements in your own condition. In this state of society, everything is adapted to promote the prosperity, the importance, and the improvement of the body of the people. —But nothing is so established among men, but that it may change and vary. If you should lose that spirit of industry, of economy, of knowledge, and of virtue, which led you to independence and to empire, then, but not until then, will you lose your freedom: Preserve your virtues, and your freedom will be perpetual!"

-ACKNOWLEDGMENTS-

As a journalist I learned there is no such thing as a dumb question, but I tried the patience of many people who opened their lives to me in writing this book. It was a reporter's curiosity that emboldened me to poke into this unfamiliar corner of the American Revolution, an inquiry that began around 2006. I was also alerted by a whopping property tax when I retired to Thetford, Vermont, and bought an old farmhouse with sixty acres dating back to 1784, when Vermont was still an independent state-in-waiting. In real estate as in furniture, antiques cost more.

I took advantage of wide-ranging access to the stacks and collections of Dartmouth College's Baker-Berry Library and its satellite Rauner Library as a visiting professor and alumnus. I am indebted to the courtesies extended by Peter Carini, the college archivist, and Jay Satterfield, head of special collections at Rauner, and their supportive staffs.

I value the Vermont Historical Society as one of this nation's finest—and friendliest—and served as a trustee for several years alongside eminent local historians such as Frank Bryan and Nicholas Muller, under its directors from Kevin Graffagnino (more recently at the Clements Library at the University of Michigan) to Steve Perkins today. The Society's librarian, Paul Carnahan, and assistant librarian, Marjorie Strong, displayed remarkable patience with my repetitive questions. Its editor, Alan Barolzheimer, let me serve on the publications committee.

Gregory Sanford, Vermont's retired State Archivist, embraced my project with ebullience and introduced me to a trove of original research, including the Mary Greene Nye Index and Henry Stevens Papers stored at the state archives in Middlesex, Vermont. Professor Peter Teachout at Vermont Law School shared his legal writings on the origins of Vermont's ground-breaking constitution.

At the Newberry Library in Chicago, its President and Librarian, David Spadafora, whom I had previously known as the president of Lake Forest College, extracted documents from Newberry's archives on American colonial history that I did not locate in Vermont, including the memoirs of the teen-aged Continental fifer Ebenezer Fletcher. I also thank the British Library at National Archives of Britain for admitting me to their reading rooms.

Fort Ticonderoga sets the scene for this book and, faithfully restored, deserves a visit by anyone seeking to understand the northern front of the American Revolution. Rich Strum, the director of education at Fort Ticonderoga, and Beth Hill, the museum's resourceful CEO, invited me to their dynamic seminars on the American Revolution.

I turned to my friends and neighbors to share their insights into Vermont's unique history, including Tony Mastaler's pitch-perfect quips and Betty Smith's cool edits as my favorite producer at Vermont Public Radio. Locally, I learned from Laurie and Wes Burnham, Pat, Don, and Jack Henderson, and

Acknowledgments

Clark and Jill Graff. Jack Shepherd, my best friend and collaborator on two earlier satires for Simon & Schuster, encouraged me to rethink some of my assumptions in framing this book.

At Dartmouth's MALS (Master of Arts in Liberal Studies) program, Don Pease, Wole Ojurongbe, Amy Gallagher, and Maisey Bailey helped juggle my teaching schedule to facilitate the writing of this book. I feel likewise indebted to the creative writing chair at MALS, Barbara Kreiger, and my neighbor Cynthia Huntington, former poet laureate of New Hampshire.

At Simon & Schuster, the brilliant Alice Mayhew undertook our fifth book together. Her focused and persistent associate editor Stuart Roberts kept my manuscript on track.

I was fortunate to have my longtime literary agent, Sterling Lord, foresee the potential for my book and broker my contract back in 2008. Sterling continues to offer a wealth of timely suggestions.

My Oxford-educated wife, Jaqueline, who never met a book that she didn't want to read, learned forbearance during five foreign postings together for the *New York Times*, and was relieved that I found myself something else to do when I gave up daily journalism. She has been living since with piles of unsorted research spilling underfoot from every corner of our farmhouse and barn.

My son Chris, a Vermont Law School graduate, bequeathed his 1860 first editions of Frank Moore's two-volume *Diary of the American Revolution*, and scavenged second-hand bookshops and libraries for me before his life was cut short by a brain aneurysm in 2014.

Acknowledgments

And foremost, my dutiful daughter Celia Wren, who started out in book publishing, found time in her career as a theater and arts critic to compile and organize the notes and bibliography for this book and made its publication a reality. Without her persistent encouragement and tender tough love, I could not have brought this to fruition.

-BIBLIOGRAPHY-

"An Account of General Montgomery's Burial." Collections of the Massachusetts Historical Society; reprinted on capecodhistory. us.

Adams, James Truslow. *New England in the Republic: 1776–1850.* Vol. 3 of *The History of New England.* Boston: Little, Brown, 1926.

———. *Revolutionary New England: 1691–1776.* Vol. 2 of *The History of New England.* Boston: Little, Brown, 1927.

Aichele, Gary J. "Making the Vermont Constitution: 1777–1824." *Vermont History* 56, no. 3 (1988): 2–37.

Allen, Ethan. *A Narrative of the Captivity of Ethan Allen.* Walpole, N.H.: Thomas & Thomas, 1807.

Allen, Ira. *The Natural and Political History of the State of Vermont.*

The Allen Letters. Vermont Historical Society, Montpelier, Vt., 1920.

Anburey, Thomas. *With Burgoyne from Quebec.* Edited by Sydney Jackman. Toronto: Macmillan of Canada, 1963.

Arch, Stephen Carl, ed. *A Narrative of Colonel Ethan Allen's Captivity.* Acton, Mass.: Michigan State University, Copley Publishing Group, 2000.

Baldwin, Jeduthan. *The Revolutionary Journal of Col. Jeduthan Baldwin, 1775–1778.* Edited with a memoir and notes by Thomas Williams Baldwin. Bangor, Me.: The De Burians, 1906, reprinted by Ayer Company Publishers, North Stratford, N.H., 1995.

Barbieri, Michael R. " '. . . they will not trouble us here this summer': An Account of Some Incidents That Took Place 17 June 1777 near Fort Ticonderoga." *The Bulletin of the Fort Ticonderoga Museum* 16, no. 3 (2000): 252–71.

Bellesiles, Michael A. *Revolutionary Outlaws, Ethan Allen and the Struggle for Independence on the Early American Frontier.* Charlottesville: University Press of Virginia, 1993.

Bellico, Russell P. *Chronicles of Lake Champlain: Journeys in War and Peace.* Fleischmanns, N.Y.: Purple Mountain Press, 1999.

Belcher, Henry. *The First American Civil War.* 2 vols. London: Macmillan and Co., 1911.

Bill, Alfred Hoyt. *The Campaign of Princeton, 1776–1777.* Princeton: Princeton University Press, 1948.

Burns, Brian. "Carleton in the Valley, or The Year of the Burning: Major Christopher Carleton and the Northern Invasion of 1780." *The Bulletin of the Fort Ticonderoga Museum* 13, no. 6 (1980): 398–407.

Chipman, Daniel. *Memoir of Col. Seth Warner.* Albany, N.Y.: Joel Munsell, 1848.

"Colonel Warren's Regiment in the Servis of the United States of America," 3d August, 1777. New-York Historical Society Collections.

Commager, Henry Steele, and Richard B. Morris, eds. *The Spirit of 'Seventy-Six: The Story of the American Revolution as Told by Participants.* New York: Harper & Row, 1958.

Crockett, Walter Hill. *Vermont, The Green Mountain State.* 2 vols. New York: The Century History Company, 1921.

Cubbison, Douglas R. *The American Northern Theater in 1776: The Ruin and Reconstruction of the Continental Force.* Jefferson, N.C.: McFarland, 2010.

———. *Burgoyne and the Saratoga Campaign, His Papers.* Norman: University of Oklahoma Press, 2012.

Davies, K. G., ed. *Documents of the American Revolution, 1770–1783.* Vol. 14 of the *Colonial Office Series.* Dublin: Irish University Press, 1976.

Dawson, Henry B. *Battles of the United States by Sea and Land*, Vol. 1 of *The War of the Revolution*. New York: Johnson, Fry, and Company, 1858.

De Puy, Henry. *Ethan Allen and the Green-Mountain Heroes of '76*. Boston: Horace Wentworth, 1853.

Digby, William. *The British Invasion from the North: The Campaigns of Generals Carleton and Burgoyne, from Canada, 1776–1777, with the Journal of Lieut. William Digby, of the 53d, or Shropshire Regiment of Foot*. Albany, N.Y.: J. Munsell's Sons, 1887.

Donath, David Allen. "Jacob Bayley Ascendant: Settlement, Speculation, Politics and Revolution in the Upper Connecticut River Valley." MA thesis, University of Vermont, 1978.

Duffy, John J., and H. Nicholas Muller III. *Inventing Ethan Allen*. Hanover, N.H.: University Press of New England, 2014.

Duffy, John, with Ralph H. Orth, J. Kevin Graffagnino, and Michael Bellesiles, eds. *Ethan Allen and His Kin: Correspondence, 1772–1819*, Vols. 1 and 2. Hanover, N.H.: University Press of New England, 1998.

Farnsworth, Harold, and Robert Rodgers. *New Haven in Vermont, 1761–1983*. New Haven, Vt.: Town of New Haven, Vt., 1984.

Ferling, John. *Almost a Miracle, the American Victory in the War of Independence*. New York: Oxford University Press, 2007.

Fisher, Carleton Edward, and Sue Gray Fisher. *Soldiers, Sailors, and Patriots of the Revolutionary War—Vermont*. Camden, Me.: Picton Press, 1992.

Fletcher, Ebenezer. *Narrative of the Captivity and Sufferings of Mr. Ebenezer Fletcher . . . Who Was Wounded at Hubbardston, in the Year 1777, and Taken Prisoner by the British*. Chicago: Newberry Library, Special Collections.

Fortescue, J. W. *A History of the British Army, 1763–1793*. Vol. 3. London: Macmillan and Co., 1911.

Foster, Herbert D., with Thomas W. Streeter. "Stark's Independent Command at Bennington." *Proceedings of the New York State Historical Association* 5 (1905): 24–95.

Fox, Dixon Ryan. *Yankees and Yorkers.* New York: New York University Press, 1940.

Gilchrist, Helen Ives. *Fort Ticonderoga in History.* Ticonderoga, N.Y.: Fort Ticonderoga Museum, 1935.

Graffagnino, J. Kevin. " 'Twenty Thousand Muskets!!!': Ira Allen and the Olive Branch Affair, 1796–1800." *The William and Mary Quarterly* 48, July 1991, 409–31.

Graffagnino, J. Kevin, Samuel B. Hand, and Gene Sessions, eds. *Vermont Voices: 1609 Through the 1990s, a Documentary History of the Green Mountain State.* Montpelier, Vt.: Vermont Historical Society, 1999.

Graffagnino, J. Kevin, and H. Nicholas Muller, eds. *The Quotable Ethan Allen.* Montpelier, Vt.: Vermont Historical Society, 2005.

Graves, Robert. *Sergeant Lamb's America.* New York: 1940.

Graydon, Alexander. *Memoirs of His Own Time, with Reminiscences of the Men and Events of the Revolution.* Edited by John Stockton Littell. Philadelphia: Lindsay & Blakiston, 1846.

Hadden, Lieutenant James M. *Hadden's Journal and Orderly Books, A Journal Kept in Canada and Upon Burgoyne's Campaign in 1776 and 1777.* Albany, N.Y.: J. Munsell's Sons, 1884.

Haldimand, Frederick. Unpublished papers and correspondence. (MSS Add 21661–21892.) British Library, London. Also, the Newberry Library, Chicago.

Hall, Benjamin H. *History of Eastern Vermont.* New York: Appleton & Co, 1858.

Hall, Henry. "Castleton Fort." *Proceedings of the Vermont Historical Society* 2, no. 4 (1931): 194–206.

Hall, Hiland. *The History of Vermont, from Its Discovery to Its Admission into the Union in 1791.* Albany, N.Y.: Joel Munsell, 1868.

Bibliography

Hamilton, Alexander. *The Works of Alexander Hamilton.* Vol. 2. New York: Charles Francis & Company, 1850.

Harvey, Robert. *A Few Bloody Noses: The American Revolutionary War.* London: Constable & Robinson, 2001 and 2004.

Hill, Alfred Hoyt. *The Campaign of Princeton, 1776–1777.* Princeton: Princeton University Press, 1948.

Hoyt, Edward A. Hoyt, and Ronald F. Kingsley. "The Pawlet Expedition, September 1777." *Vermont History* 25, no. 2 (2007): 69–100.

Jones, Charles Henry. *History of the Campaign for the Conquest of Canada in 1776.* Philadelphia: Porter & Coates, 1882.

Keegan, John. *Fields of Battle: The Wars for North America.* New York: Alfred A. Knopf, 1996.

Ketchum, Richard M. *Saratoga, Turning Point of America's Revolutionary War.* New York: Henry Holt, 1997.

Lamb, Roger. *A British Soldier's Story: Roger Lamb's Narrative of the American Revolution.* Edited and annotated by Don N. Hagist. Baraboo, Wisc.: Ballindalloch Press, 2004.

McIlwraith, Jean N. *The Makers of Canada: Sir Frederick Haldimand.* Toronto: Morang & Co., 1910.

Madison, James. *The Papers of James Madison.* Vol. 8. Chicago: University of Chicago Press, 1973.

Massie, Robert K. *Catherine the Great: Portrait of a Woman.* New York: Random House, 2011.

Melish, Joanne Pope. *Disowning Slavery: Gradual Emancipation and "Race" in New England.* Ithaca, N.Y.: Cornell University Press, 1998.

Moore, Frank. *Diary of the American Revolution from Newspapers and Original Documents,* Vols. 1 and 2, New York: Charles Scribner, 1860.

Narratives of the Revolution in New York, A Collection of Articles from the New-York Historical Society Quarterly. New York: New-York Historical Society, 1975.

Bibliography

The National Archives of Britain, Kew: Miscellaneous colonial documents.

Nelson, James L. *Benedict Arnold's Navy: The Ragtag Fleet That Lost the Battle of Lake Champlain but Won the American Revolution.* Camden, Me.: International Marine/McGraw Hill, 2006.

The Newberry Library, Chicago: Miscellaneous Revolutionary War documents in Special Collections.

New York in the Revolution. Albany, N.Y.: Office of Secretary of State Comptroller, 1904. New-York Historical Society Collections.

Nye, Mary Greene. "Loyalists and Their Property." *Proceedings of the Vermont Historical Society* 10, no. 1 (1942).

Mary Greene Nye Index. Vermont State Archives, Middlesex, Vt.

O'Callaghan, E. B., ed. *Orderly Book of Lieut. Gen. John Burgoyne, from His Entry into the State of New York Until His Surrender at Saratoga,* 16th Oct., 1777. Albany, N.Y.: J. Munsell, 1860, facsimile printed by University Microfilms International, Ann Arbor, 1981.

Pearson, Michael. *Those Damned Rebels: The American Revolution as Seen Through British Eyes.* Boston: Da Capo, 1972.

Pemberton, Ian C. B. "Justus Sherwood, Vermont Loyalist, 1747–1798." PhD thesis, University of Western Ontario, 1972.

Pettengill, Ray W., trans. *Letters from America, 1776–1779, Being Letters of Brunswick, Hessian and Waldeck Officers with the British Armies During the Revolution.* Boston: Houghton Mifflin Company, 1924.

The Province of Ontario. Vol. 17 of *Canada and the Provinces.* Toronto, 1914.

Records of Council of Safety. Vermont State Archives, Middlesex, Vt.

Rhodehamel, John, ed. *The American Revolution: Writings from the War of Independence.* New York: Library of America, 2001.

Roberts, James A., comptroller. *New York in the Revolution as Colony and State.* Second edition. Albany, N.Y.: New York (State) Comptroller's Office, 1898.

Roberts, Kenneth, ed. *March to Quebec, Journals of the Members of Arnold's Expedition.* New York: Doubleday, Doran, 1938.

Sabine, Lorenzo. *Biographical Sketches of Loyalists of the American Revolution.* 2 vols. Boston: Little, Brown, 1864.

Sabine, Lorenzo. *The American Loyalists, or Biographical Sketches of Adherents to the British Crown in the War of the Revolution.* Boston: Little, Brown, 1847.

Saffell, W. T. R. *Records of the Revolutionary War.* Baltimore: Charles C. Saffell, 1894; reprinted by the Genealogical Publishing Company, Baltimore, 1969.

Shalhope, Robert E. *Bennington and the Green Mountain Boys.* Baltimore: Johns Hopkins University Press, 1996.

Sheer, George F. and Hugh Rankin. *Rebels and Redcoats.* New York: World, 1957.

Sherman, Michael, Gene Sessions, and P. Jeffrey Potash. *Freedom and Unity: A History of Vermont.* Barre: Vermont Historical Society, 2004.

Shy, John. *A People Numerous and Armed: Reflections on the Military Struggle for American Independence.* Ann Arbor: University of Michigan Press, 1990.

Spring, Matthew H. *With Zeal and Bayonets Only: The British Army on Campaign in North America, 1775–1783.* Norman: University of Oklahoma Press, 2008.

Smith, Richard B. *Ethan Allen and the Capture of Fort Ticonderoga.* Charleston, S.C.: History Press, 2010.

———. *The Revolutionary War in Bennington County: A History and Guide.* Charleston, S.C.: History Press, 2008.

Smith, William Henry, ed. *The Saint Clair Papers: The Life and Public Services of Arthur St. Clair.* Vol. 1. Cincinnati: Robert Clarke & Co, 1882.

Stark, Caleb. *Memoir and Official Correspondence of Gen. John Stark.* Concord, N.H.: G. Parker Lyon, 1860.

Stephenson, Michael. *Patriot Battles: How the War of Independence Was Fought.* New York: Harper Perennial, 2007.

Henry Stevens Papers (Series A-006). Vermont State Archives, Middlesex, Vt.

Stilwell, Lewis. *Migration from Vermont,* Vol. 5 of *Growth of Vermont.* Montpelier Vt.: Vermont Historical Society, 1948.

Stone, William L. *The Campaign of Lieut. Gen. John Burgoyne and the Expedition of Lieut. Col Barry St. Leger.* Albany, N.Y.: Joel Munsell, 1877.

Talman, James J., ed. *Loyalist Narratives from Upper Canada,* Toronto: Champlain Society, 1946.

Teachout, Peter R. " 'Trustees and Servants': Government Accountability in Early Vermont." *Vermont Law Review* 31, no. 4 (2007): 866–905.

Thacher, James, M.D. *Military Journal During the American Revolutionary War from 1775 to 1783.* Boston: Richardson and Lord, 1823.

Thompson, Charles Miner. *Independent Vermont.* Boston: Houghton Mifflin, 1942.

Thompson, Zadock. *Thompson's Vermont: Natural, Civil and Statistical History.* Printed for the author by C. Goodrich, Burlington, Vt., 1842.

Trevelyan, George Otto. *The American Revolution: A Condensation into One Volume of the Original Six-Volume Work.* Edited, arranged, and with an introduction and notes by Richard B. Morris. New York: David McKay, 1964.

———. *The American Revolution.* 4 vols. New York and London: Longman's Green & Co.; reprinted 1926–29.

Valentine, Alan. *Lord George Germain.* London: Oxford University Press, 1962.

Vandewater, Frederic F. *The Reluctant Republic: Vermont, 1724–1791.* New York: John Day, 1941.

Bibliography

Vermont Historical Society Collections, Vol. 1. Montpelier, Vt.: Vermont Historical Society, 1870.

Vermont Historical Society Collections, Vol. 2. Montpelier, Vt.: Vermont Historical Society, 1871

Centennial Anniversary of the Independence of the State of Vermont and the Battle of Bennington, August 15 and 16, 1877. Rutland, Vt.: Tuttle & Co., 1879.

von Eelking, Max. *The German Allied Troops in the North American War of Independence, 1776–1783.* Translated and abridged by J. G. Rosengarten. Baltimore: Genealogical Publishing Company, 1969.

Wallace, W. Stewart. *The United Empire Loyalists: A Chronicle of the Great Migration.* Toronto, 1914; reprinted, Memphis: General Books, 2010.

Wardner, Henry Steele. "The Haldimand Negotiations." *Proceedings of the Vermont Historical Society* 2, no. 1 (1931).

Washington, George. *The Writings of George Washington.* Vols. 22–23. Washington, D.C.: Government Printing Office, 1937.

Washington, Ida H., and Paul H. Washington. *Carleton's Raid.* Weybridge, Vt.: Cherry Tree Books, 1977.

Watt, Gavin K. *The Burning of the Valleys: Daring Raids from Canada Against the New York Frontier in the Fall of 1780.* Toronto: Dundurn, 1997.

———. *A Dirty, Trifling Piece of Business.* Vol. 1 of *The Revolutionary War as Waged from Canada.* Toronto: Dundurn, 2009.

Wilbur, James Benjamin. *Ira Allen, Founder of Vermont, 1751–1814.* 2 vols. Boston: Houghton Mifflin, 1928.

Wilbur, Lafayette. *Early History of Vermont.* 2 vols. Jericho, Vt: Roscoe Printing House, 1899 and 1900.

Willcox, William B., ed. *The American Rebellion, Sir Henry Clinton's Narrative of His Campaign, 1775–1782, with an Appendix of Original Documents.* New Haven: Yale University Press, 1954.

Williams, John A., ed. *The Public Papers of Governor Thomas Chittenden. State Papers of Vermont.* Vol. 17. Montpelier: Published by
the Vermont Secretary of State, 1969.

Williams, Samuel. *Natural and Civil History of Vermont.* Walpole,
N.H.: Printed by Isaiah Thomas and David Carlisle, June, 1794.

————. *The Natural and Civil History of Vermont, Vol. 1. The Second
Edition, Corrected and Much Enlarged.* Burlington, Vt., 1809.

Williamson, Chilton. *Vermont in Quandary: 1763–1825.* Montpelier,
Vt.: Vermont Historical Society, 1949.

Wrong, George M. *Washington and His Comrades in Arms.* Vol. 12 of
The Chronicles of America Series. New Haven: Yale University
Press, 1921.

-NOTES-

Reporting on wars and revolutions across multiple time zones, as I did as a foreign correspondent, seems less fraught than covering it across centuries past since the American Revolution. I began with primary sources heavily weighted toward the earliest books I could find, starting with a history of Vermont, dated 1794, which I acquired at an auction. More than a score of other books I consulted were published in the nineteenth century and, whatever their flaws, did not lend themselves to traditional footnotes. I checked historical events against popular contemporary accounts, notably in Frank Moore's two-volume *Diary of the American Revolution*, published in 1860. I also relied upon the extensive archives of Dartmouth College and the rare books collection in its Rauner Library. I visited the Vermont Historical Society in Barre, Vermont, and the Newberry Library in Chicago and made two trips to the British Library in London to view the original manuscripts compiled in the Vermont Historical Society's bound Collections of the Haldimand Papers in 1871. I approached this as an investigative journalist as well as a scholar, with a reverence for the facts as they happened and were recorded at the time.

Chapter One: A Land Rush North

For accuracy and context of quotations, I referred whenever possible to John Duffy with Ralph H. Orth, J. Kevin Graffagnino, and Michael Bellesiles, eds., *Ethan Allen and His Kin: Correspondence, 1772–1819* (Hanover, N.H., 1998).

For the origins of the New Hampshire Grants, see Samuel Williams, *The Natural and Civil History of Vermont* (Walpole, N.H., 1794); Hiland Hall, *The History of Vermont, from Its Discovery to Its Admission into the Union in 1791* (Albany, N.Y., 1868); Benjamin H. Hall, *History of Eastern Vermont* (New York, 1858); and Lewis Stilwell, *Migration from Vermont*, Vol. 5 of the Vermont Historical Society's series *Growth of Vermont* (Montpelier, 1948).

Stilwell remarked upon the youthfulness of the early pioneers who came, largely from Connecticut, to settle the New Hampshire Grants. Even as late as 1800, two thirds of Vermont's population had not passed their twenty-sixth birthday. "The proportion of young folks, when settlement began, must have been younger," he concluded.

The "New Light" evangelism motivating settlers to separate from the established Congregational church is discussed in Zadock Thompson, *Thompson's Vermont: Natural, Civil and Statistical History* (Burlington, 1842); and Robert E. Shalhope, *Bennington and the Green Mountain Boys* (Baltimore, 1996).

For further details on Governor Benning Wentworth, see Walter Hill Crockett, *Vermont, The Green Mountain State*, Vol. 1 (New York, 1921). Crockett also describes the primitive homesteads in the New Hampshire Grants.

For the early life of the Allens, see Duffy et al., eds., *Ethan Allen and His Kin*; James Benjamin Wilbur, *Ira Allen, Founder of Vermont, 1751–1814*, Vols. 1 and 2 (Boston, 1928); and Lafayette Wilbur, *Early History of Vermont*, Vols. 1 and 2 (Jericho, Vt., 1899 and 1900), Chapters 29–30.

The anecdote about seventeen-year-old Ethan standing on his father's grave is recounted in Michael A. Bellesiles, *Revolutionary Outlaws: Ethan Allen and the Struggle for Independence on the Early American Frontier* (Charlottesville, Va., 1993).

As noted in a footnote in Duffy et al., eds., *Ethan Allen and His Kin*, a rare description of Ethan Allen with his cousin Remember

Baker appeared in a notice in the *Courant* newspaper, dated April 27, 1773, offering a $100 reward after they evaded arrest for blasphemy in Salisbury, Connecticut: "Baker is about 5 feet 9 or 10 inches high, pretty well sett, something freckled in his face. Said Allen is near 6 feet high, firm built, goes something stooping, dark hair; each of said fellows being arm'd with sword and pistol, and are notorious for blasphemous expressions in conversation, and ridiculing everything sacred."

For the origins of the Green Mountain Boys and their rebellion against New York, see Charles Miner Thompson, *Independent Vermont* (Boston, 1942); Duffy et al., eds., *Ethan Allen and His Kin*; and Zadock Thompson, *Thompson's Vermont*. "It was about this time that the settlers of the New Hampshire Grants began to be called Green Mountain Boys," Zadock Thompson wrote. "The name was first applied to the military but was soon extended to the settlers in general."

For Cadwallader Colden's order that settlers in the New Hampshire Grants should pay New York a confirmation fee, see *Vermont Historical Society Collections*, Vol. 1 (Montpelier, Vt., 1870), 150ff. (This series is hereafter referred to as *VHS Collections*.)

For the early interactions of "those turbulent sons of freedom," Ethan Allen, Seth Warner and Justus Sherwood, see the above, and also Daniel Chipman, *Memoir of Col. Seth Warner* (Albany, 1848). Sherwood's circumstances are identified in Ian C. B Pemberton's PhD thesis, "Justus Sherwood, Vermont Loyalist, 1747–1798" (University of Western Ontario, 1972), and in James J. Talman, ed., *Loyalist Narratives from Upper Canada* (Toronto, 1946).

Justus Sherwood's support of Seth Warner in retrieving Remember Baker's musket was later erased from Vermont history because of Sherwood's Loyalist convictions. For subsequent accounts of the incident that identify Sherwood only as a "friend," see Zadock Thompson, *Thompson's Vermont*.

Ira Allen's 1798 book *The Natural and Political History of the State of Vermont*, as it appears in *VHS Collections* 1: 319–499, covers his narrative recounted here. James Benjamin Wilbur's *Ira Allen* expands upon the same narrative in more depth.

Chapter Two: Seizing Fort Ticonderoga

For details of the Westminster Massacre, see Benjamin H. Hall, *History of Eastern Vermont*, as well as Hiland Hall, *History of Vermont*. Contemporary news reports feature in Frank Moore, *Diary of the American Revolution from Newspapers and Original Documents*, Vol. 1 (New York, 1860).

Philip Skene's failed attempt to set up his own royal colony with Ethan Allen's support was discussed in Hiland Hall, *The History of Vermont* and was mentioned by Ira Allen in his own autobiography. Moore's *Diary of the American Revolution* attributes a slightly different account of Skene's downfall to the *Virginia Gazette* in April 1775.

Ethan Allen's capture of Ticonderoga was considered significant enough by 1858 for inclusion in Henry P. Dawson's encyclopedic *Battles of the United States by Sea and Land*, Vol. 1, *The War of the Revolution* (New York, 1858). The basic narrative, with documents, appears on pages 30–39.

Ethan's best publicist was his brother Ira, who, in his autobiography, written twenty-four years after the capture of Fort Ticonderoga, quoted his brother Ethan as informing its British commander that he had captured Ticonderoga "in the name of the Great Jehovah and the Continental Congress," a claim conspicuously absent from contemporary accounts but revived in 1868 in Hiland Hall, *The History of Vermont*.

In a single rambling, unpunctuated sentence, on May 10, 1775, Ethan Allen reported to the committee of correspondence in Albany, New York, how he had taken Fort Ticonderoga and asked for five hundred men immediately. He was turned down. The episode is recounted in Duffy et al., eds, *Ethan Allen and His Kin*, Vol. 1.

Note that early accounts of the origins of the New Hampshire Grants, up to the seizure of Fort Ticonderoga, tend to overlap in part because Vermont's early historians were not shy about lifting from each other.

For a more recent account, see Helen Ives Gilchrist, *Fort Ticonderoga in History* (Ticonderoga, N.Y., 1935). In this context, it is worth noting that Fort Ticonderoga was originally built by the French, who named it Carillon. On July 8, 1758, the British assaulted the log breastworks with 15,000 regulars and American provincials but failed to dislodge 3,500 French and Canadian defenders. Ethan Allen's cousin Remember Baker was cited for heroism as a ranger in the failed assault, the bloodiest day of combat on the American continent until the Civil War battle at Antietam in September 1862.

On August 3, 1775, Ethan Allen complained to John Trumbull about his humiliating rejection by "the old farmers" for command of the regiment of Green Mountain Boys in favor of his less flamboyant cousin Seth Warner. The historian Hiland Hall remarked that they were "both distinguished leaders but they were different men, and fitted to occupy different positions," confirming that Warner's selection to head the regiment found general approval across the New Hampshire Grants. See *VHS Collections* 1: 9–10.

As is noted in Duffy et al., eds, *Ethan Allen and His Kin*, Vol. 1, money quickly spent by the American army invading Quebec included $1,000 paid to bribe the Caughnawaga Mohawks to remain neutral.

The expeditions to Canada are documented in Dawson, *Battles of the United States by Sea and Land*. Dawson notes the arrival of Seth Warner with 170 Green Mountain Boys on September 16, 1775, to join General Richard Montgomery after an inept performance by other American units.

Muster rolls listing Seth Warner's Green Mountain Boys as an additional Continental regiment are included in *New York in the Rev-*

olution as Colony and State (Albany, N.Y, 1898) by James A. Roberts, comptroller.

Chapter Three: Congress Invades Canada

The misbegotten American invasion of Canada is described by a dozen participants in Kenneth Roberts, ed., *March to Quebec: Journals of the Members of Arnold's Expedition* (New York, 1938). Roberts's 1930 novel *Arundel* drew heavily from the journals.

History of the Campaign for the Conquest of Canada in 1776 by Charles Henry Jones (Philadelphia, 1882) follows the tribulations of the retreating American army following its defeat at Quebec City on New Year's Eve 1775, including the ravages of smallpox and the tensions that erupted into a shootout between Massachusetts and Pennsylvania troops at Fort Ticonderoga.

For a British military perspective on this and other Revolutionary War campaigns, see J. W. Fortescue, *A History of the British Army*, Vol. 3 (London, 1911). Other analyses of the Canadian campaign include Chapter 15 in Crockett's *Vermont: The Green Mountain State*, Vol. 1. Ira Allen, who saw action in the campaign, described "this disastrous retreat" in his own *Natural and Political History of the State of Vermont* in 1798.

Ethan Allen's failure to join Montgomery as promised is discussed in Duffy et al., eds., *Ethan Allen and His Kin*, and in Dawson, *Battles of the United States by Sea and Land*.

Hiland Hall, in his *History of Vermont*, wrote that Ethan Allen's rush to add to his laurels won at Fort Ticonderoga caused him to attack Montreal without considering the chances or consequences of failure.

The gallows at Tyburn in what is now London's Hyde Park are identified in Ethan Allen's popular *A Narrative of the Captivity of Ethan Allen* (Walpole, N.H., 1807), and in Duffy et al., eds., and *Ethan Allen and His Kin*.

Chapter Four: This Thievish, Pockey Army

A Narrative of the Captivity of Ethan Allen, Allen's account of his capture in Montreal in September 1775 and ensuing thirty-two months
of captivity, includes Allen's account of being transported to England,
Ireland, and back to Canada before being deposited on parole in New
York City, and finally freed in May 1878. Originally published in 1779,
the bestseller appeared in at least twenty editions from 1779 to 1930. I
consulted the 1807 edition published in Walpole, New Hampshire; a
reprint of the limited 1930 edition issued by Fort Ticonderoga in 1930;
and the 2000 reprint annotated by Stephen Carl Arch.

Despite obvious prejudices—Ethan refuses to give his rival Benedict Arnold any credit in the seizure of Fort Ticonderoga—Allen
provides coherent and convincing details of his captivity. Other biog-
raphies have relied upon those details. Michael Bellesiles, a foremost
biographer of Ethan Allen, described the *Narrative* as "an intensely
personal document" that Ethan used "as a sort of therapy to banish his
depression and promote his self-esteem."

An account of Ethan Allen's mistreatment and slim prospects for
release in New York appeared in the *Freeman's Journal* on December 3,
1776. It's worth noting that General William Howe would not deign
to discuss Ethan Allen's treatment with George Washington, whom
the British treated as a civilian because his general's rank was not conferred by the king. Washington, in turn, ignored the letters addressed
to "Mr. Washington," on grounds that they were irrelevant to his official duties.

For details on Benjamin Whitcomb's shooting of Brigadier Gordon and Whitcomb's subsequent promotion, see Lieutenant James M.
Hadden, *Hadden's Journal and Orderly Books, A Journal Kept in Canada
and Upon Burgoyne's Campaign in 1776 and 1777* (Albany, N.Y., 1884).

General David Wooster's career is capsuled in Dawson's *Battles
of the United States by Sea and Land.* After returning from Canada,

Wooster was fatally wounded at age sixty-seven near Danbury, Connecticut, on May 17, 1777.

Chapter Five: A Green Mountain Boy Serves His King

The naval battles at Valcour Island in Lake Champlain on October 11 and 12, 1775, are documented in Dawson, *Battles of the United States by Sea and Land*, and in Jones, *History of the Campaign for the Conquest of Canada in 1776*, the latter of which confirmed Benedict Arnold as an authentic American hero. The best-told account is *Benedict Arnold's Navy: The Ragtag Fleet That Lost the Battle of Lake Champlain but Won the American Revolution*, by James L. Nelson (Camden, Me., 2006). Douglas R. Cubbison also puts the naval battles in the larger context of the failed American campaign with *The American Northern Theater in 1776: The Ruin and Reconstruction of the Continental Force* (Jefferson, N.C., 2010). And *Chronicles of Lake Champlain: Journeys in War and Peace*, by Russell P. Bellico (Fleischmanns, N.Y., 1999), explores the lake's strategic and practical significance for both sides.

The fratricidal excesses of the American Revolution, and George Washington's hatred of Loyalists, were documented by the British historian Henry Belcher in *The First American Civil War* (London, 1911), which includes this nuanced dedication: "This fragment of history is respectfully offered to the memory of the unknown men on either hand who in this civil contest perished amidst the neglect or obloquy of their fellow-citizens, the Americans, plundered, maltreated, and starved, the British, flouted as the scum of the earth."

Justus Sherwood's stubborn refusal to recant his support for the Crown was shared by thousands of other Americans, as many as one third of whom remained loyal to Britain. Lorenzo Sabine reckoned that at least 25,000 Loyalists took up arms. See Sabine's two-volume *Biographical Sketches of Loyalists of the American Revolution* (Boston, 1864). Another book, *Loyalist Narratives from Upper Canada*, edited by

James J. Talman, includes a brief but significant memoir from Justus Sherwood, summarizing his mistreatment, war service, and financial losses incurred in defense of the Crown; this memoir informs the outline of my book.

In *The United Empire Loyalists: A Chronicle of the Great Migration* (Toronto, 1914), W. Stewart Wallace explained: "The Tory who refused to take the oath of allegiance became in fact an outlaw. He did not have in the courts of law even the rights of a foreigner.... He might be assaulted, insulted, blackmailed or slandered, yet the law granted him no redress."

The dungeon to which Justus Sherwood had been sentenced before his escape was described as "a bottomless pit" by *Rivington's Gazette*, a Tory newspaper in New York City, as is documented in Moore, *Diary of the American Revolution*, Vol. 2.

Lord Germain's controversial career is examined in Alan Valentine's meticulous biography *Lord George Germain* (London, 1962). Valentine reminds us that "what Lord George Germain thought in London in 1777 was based on events already outdated in America."

For information on the Brunswickers and other German units hired to fight in Burgoyne's invasion, see Max von Eelking, *The German Allied Troops in the North American War of Independence, 1776–1783*, originally published in German in 1863; I read the version translated and abridged by J. G. Rosengarten (Baltimore, 1969). Many German soldiers, according to Eelking, opted to remain in America after the war with the consent of their officers. Ray W. Pettengill, trans., *Letters from America, 1776–1779* (Boston, 1924), offers the voices of Brunswickers serving from Castleton to Bennington and Saratoga.

Chapter Six: Burgoyne Bogs Down in Vermont

Details of Vermont's role in opposing Burgoyne's invasion are published in the *VHS Collections* 1: 163–249. For the British perspective, see William A. Stone, *The Campaign of Lieut. Gen. John Burgoyne and the Expedition of Lieut. Col. Barry St. Leger* (Albany, 1877). I also drew on E. B. O'Callaghan, ed., *Orderly Book of Lieut. Gen. John Burgoyne, from His Entry into the State of New York Until His Surrender at Saratoga, 16th Oct., 1777* (Albany, N.Y., 1860); I relied on the facsimile printed in Ann Arbor in 1981.

For General St. Clair's decision to evacuate Fort Ticonderoga and the ensuing chain of events, see William Henry Smith, ed., *The Saint Clair Papers: The Life and Public Services of Arthur St. Clair*, Vol 1 (Cincinnati, 1882). A heavily anecdotal account of the Burgoyne campaign appears in Stone, *The Campaign of Lieut. Gen. John Burgoyne.*

Further details are available in Ira Allen's *The Natural and Political History of the State of Vermont* and in James Benjamin Wilbur's *Ira Allen.*

The *Pennsylvania Evening Post* (July 17, 1777) quoted an officer in St. Clair's retreat from Ticonderoga as protesting that "we are told our country calls us either knaves or cowards; I conceive that they ought to be grateful to our general for had we stayed we would very certainly been taken, and then no troops would have stayed between the enemy and the country."

Another narrative of the retreat, *Military Journal During the American Revolutionary War from 1775 to 1783*, by then surgeon's mate James Thacher, was published in Boston in 1823. Thacher is also valuable for his medical observations, from the ravages of smallpox to trauma surgeries on the casualties of battle.

However, the phases of the moon in July 1777 (calculated by the Astronomical Applications Department of the U.S. Naval Observatory) casts doubt on the account, by Thacher and others, of a romantic evacuation by moonlight. Pitch-darkness helped the American army get away.

For the British soldier's perspective, see William Digby, *The British Invasion from the North: The Campaigns of Generals Carleton and*

Burgoyne, from Canada, 1776–1777, with the Journal of Lieut. William Digby, of the 53d, or Shropshire Regiment of Foot (Albany, N.Y., 1887). In notes that appear in this volume, James Phinney Baxter wrote, "What made it the more embarrassing to the British government was the opposition of its people to the war. The principle for which the colonists had taken arms was a popular one," prompting some officers in England to resign their commissions, refusing to serve in a war against their own countrymen. And while "unusual bounties were offered, enlistments proceeded so slowly that the King found it necessary to look across the channel for aid," such as from the German princely states of Hesse and Braunschweig.

Don H. Hagist, ed. and annotator, *A British Soldier's Story: Roger Lamb's Narrative of the American Revolution* (Baraboo, Wisc., 2004), includes Lamb's account of retreat from Fort Ticonderoga and battle of Hubbardton. *Sergeant Lamb's America*, by the novelist Robert Graves (New York, 1940), is based on the journal of Sergeant Lamb with scrupulous attention to historical facts and is thus helpful in re-creating the conditions of a soldier's life on General Burgoyne's campaign.

Burgoyne's dismissive treatment of Loyalist rangers like Justus Sherwood was not unusual, according to W. Stewart Wallace, who writes, in *The United Empire Loyalists*, "The truth is that the British officers did not think much more highly of the Loyalists than they did of the rebels. For both they had the Briton's contempt for the colonial, and the professional soldier's contempt for the armed civilian."

The battle at Hubbardton has not gotten the attention that it deserves. George Otto Trevelyan, in *The American Revolution* (New York and London; reprinted in 1926–29), compared the intensity of the Hubbardton battle, on a smaller scale, to the fury of Britain's battle at Waterloo in 1814. "The Germans pushed for a share in the glory and they arrived in time to obtain it," Burgoyne conceded, grudgingly, to Lord Germain after the battle of Hubbardton, according to Dawson's *Battles of the United States by Sea and Land*.

See Chipman, *Life of Col. Seth Warner* for an account of the battles into which Warner led the Green Mountain Boys.

Ebenezer Fletcher's narrative of his captivity and escape is recounted in a manuscript, dated 1813, courtesy of the Newberry Library. Updated editions revealed that Fletcher became a millworker and trunk maker, married twice, fathered six sons and six daughters, sang in his church choir, and lived seventy years.

Chapter Seven: The Most Active and Most Rebellious Race

A Memoir and Official Correspondence of General John Stark as compiled by his son, Major Caleb Clark, and published in Concord, New Hampshire, in 1860, relates in detail Stark's colorful career, culminating in his victory in the battle near Bennington in 1777 and his subsequent command of the army's Northern Department.

A popular account of the battle of Bennington was published in the *New-York Journal* on September 22, 1777.

Dysentery and malignant sore throat in 1777, contracted among combatants on both sides, are noted among epidemic diseases listed by Zadock Thompson in *Thompson's Vermont*.

The scalping of Jane McCrea is discussed in Appendix no. 4 of Stone's *Campaign of Lieut. Gen. John Burgoyne*. McCrea's slaying was to New Yorkers what the battle of Lexington was for New England in contributing to Burgoyne's defeat, Stone wrote, noting that the martyrdom also became "a rallying cry among the Green Mountains of Vermont." The American neoclassical painter John Vanderlyn was inspired in 1804 to depict McCrea's demise at the hands of two brutal warriors.

Biographical details about the "fighting parson" Rev. Thomas Allen appear in an appendix to John Stark's autobiography. Allen graduated from Harvard in 1762, "being ranked among the first classical scholars of that time." He also joined the first militiamen overrunning Justus Sherwood's riverside redoubt in the battle of Bennington. He appears in Stark's and St. Clair's memoirs, among others.

See Stone's accounts of the clumsiness of the horseless Brunswick dragoons and Baum's failure to take along lightly armed rangers. Stone concluded that Baum was duped into letting the Americans infiltrate his ranks, mistaking them for Tory volunteers.

Chapter Eight: Victory at Bennington

For the best accounts of the battle of Bennington, see Stark's memoir and Chipman, *The Life of Col. Seth Warner*. Dawson's *Battles of the United States by Sea and Land* devotes a chapter to documenting the sequence of events at Bennington. Zadock Thompson's *Thompson's Vermont* includes an overview. The actual battle was fought in New York state, just across the Vermont line, and more details can be found in Herbert D. Foster's "Stark's Independent Command at Bennington," written with the collaboration of Thomas W. Streeter and published in the *Proceedings of the New York State Historical Association* 5 (1905): 24–95. For the perspective of various historians and politicians, see the collaboratively authored booklet *Centennial Anniversary of the Independence of the State of Vermont and the Battle of Bennington, August 15 and 16, 1877* (Rutland, Vt., 1879).

A letter at the National Archives of Britain posits how the Brunswickers replaced their heavy losses at Bennington and Saratoga. On April 20, 1779, Major General William Faucitt wrote Lord (Viscount) Weymouth: "The Brunswick recruits are chiefly deserters from the Prussian and Austrian Armies, and, upon the whole, made a pretty good appearance."

The liveliest account of John Brown's raid behind Burgoyne's lines was written by Edward A. Hoyt and Ronald F. Kingsley and published in the journal *Vermont History* 25, no. 2 (2007): 69–100. Titled "The Pawlet Expedition, September 1777," the article estimated that the American raiders severing Burgoyne's communications and supply chain exceeded two thousand militiamen, Continentals, and rangers, including between ten and twenty black troops and one Indian volunteer.

Ebenezer Allen's letter emancipating the slave Dinah Mattis and her baby, Nancy, was officially recorded in Bennington, Vermont, and appears in the *VHS Collections* 1: 249. Though Dinah and her infant were soon lost to history, a legal copy survives in Bennington. Vermont, claimed to become the first state to prohibit slavery by constitutional provision. In theory, if not in practice, no slave was lawfully owned in Vermont, because, as Judge Theophilus Harrington ruled, "no one could ever produce a bill of sale from God Almighty."

Arrangements for Sarah Sherwood's reunification with her husband, Justus, are recorded in *The State of Vermont, Records of Council of Safety, 1775–1779*, 1: 192.

Chapter Nine: Ethan Allen Sails Free

In Alexander Graydon's *Memoir of His Own Time, with Reminiscences of the Men and Events of the Revolution* (Philadelphia, 1846) he described his fellow parolee Ethan Allen as "a man of generosity and honor." Graydon's book is also valuable for its depiction of a Continental officer's life and losses in the cause of the American Revolution.

Ethan Allen's narrative may come closest to the truth when he documented the extensive abuse of American prisoners of war confined in appalling conditions in New York City.

Sir William Howe's mistress, Elizabeth Lloyd Loring was described as "a flashing blond" in *The Campaign of Princeton, 1776–1777* by Alfred Hoyt Bill (Princeton, 1948). In 1778, the Lorings fled to England, where Joshua died bankrupt in 1789. At Howe's behest, Elizabeth enjoyed an official living allowance for forty-two years, until her death in 1831.

See Ethan Allen's *Narrative* for his self-serving account of being exchanged for a Scottish lieutenant colonel in Elizabeth, New Jersey, and his subsequent interview by George Washington at Valley Forge, Pennsylvania.

The petty "cow war" between Vermont and New York is covered in Benjamin H. Hall, *History of Eastern Vermont.*

Chapter Ten: Conniving with the Enemy

Secret negotiations between Ethan and Ira Allen, in Vermont, and Canada's governor general Frederick Haldimand, from January 11, 1779, to March 25, 1783, are revealed in detail by a trove of documents, constituting the Haldimand Papers, *VHS Collections*, Vol. 2 (Montpelier, Vt., 1871). The original manuscripts are available in the British Library in London, which I visited in 2007 and 2009. (See BM21835, BM21836, BM21838, BM21839, and BM21842.) Perhaps most pertinent is BM21840, containing Justus Sherwood's neat journal of his secret negotiations with Ethan Allen and his frustrations with the "inherent deceit" of the Allens. On a related note, BM21187 covers letters from Justus Sherwood and George Smyth to Frederick Haldimand, 1777–1784.

BM21838 covers letters from Justus Sherwood and George Smyth on the prisoner exchange.

BM21839 includes letters from Robert Mathews and Frederick Haldimand to Justus Sherwood and George Smyth, 1780–1783.

BM21840 covers letters from Justus Sherwood in the Secret Service, 1780–1781.

BM21842 covers other secret intelligence.

An original letter at the Newberry Library, dated November 9, 1780, from Frederick Haldimand in Quebec warned Major Christopher Carleton that Justus Sherwood was "at great risk" and should be withdrawn as soon as possible. Haldimand revealed that George Washington had also proposed a prisoner exchange that could be frustrated if he learned of the talks with Vermont. Washington also expressed misgivings that a cease-fire "with so extensive a part of the frontier" would "deprive us, in a great measure, of intelligence, or subject us to mistakes."

Chapter Eleven: Green Mountain Boys Disbanded

See Appendix no. 1 of Stone's *Campaign of Lieut. Gen. John Burgoyne* for an anecdotal account of Seth Warner's narrow escape from an ambush at Bloody Pond by changing horses.

George Washington's curt letter of November 12, 1780, informing Seth Warner that his Green Mountain Regiment would be disbanded, was drafted by his aide Tench Tilghman. See *The Writings of George Washington* (Washington, D.C., 1937).

For Ira Allen's talks with Justus Sherwood at Ile aux Noix, see James Benjamin Wilbur, *Ira Allen.*

Pemberton's "Justus Sherwood" portrays Sherwood's side of his negotiations with Ira Allen, mentioning how Sherwood was "disappointed" that Ira Allen had brought no instructions with him. More on this episode can be found in *VHS Collections*, 2:111ff.

Skepticism about Ethan and Ira Allen's true motives was also expressed by Henry Steele Wardner in a speech in 1931, as documented in *Proceedings of the Vermont Historical Society* 2, no 1 (1931).

The Horatio Nelson vignette appears in Jean N. McIlwraith, *The Makers of Canada: Sir Frederick Haldimand* (Toronto, 1910). Its credibility is supported by Nelson's request for a pilot in Quebec City that summer.

Chapter Twelve: Spy Base on the Lake

Sherwood's spy activities at his Loyal Block House on Lake Champlain are covered in *VHS Collections*, vol. 2., and Pemberton's "Justus Sherwood."

Information about Jacob Bayley, Ethan Allen's nemesis in the

Connecticut Upper Valley, appears in David Allen Donath's master's thesis, "Jacob Bayley Ascendant: Settlement, Speculation, Politics and Revolution in the Upper Connecticut River Valley" (1978). A colloquial biography of Bayley also appears in Stark's *Memoir*.

According to Pemberton's "Justus Sherwood," Sherwood and George Smyth also devised a plan to seize the Continental scout Major Ben Whitcomb, but were told not to proceed while Carleton was in communication with Congress.

For Joseph Fay's entry into prisoner exchange talks, see *VHS Collections* 2: 159. Sherwood confided his suspicions to Haldimand that Fay brought nothing new.

General Washington's request, dated June 25, 1781, that John Stark mobilize Green Mountain Boys and their kin to replace the departing Continentals appears in *VHS Collections* 2: 139. Stark's pledge to enlist "those turbulent sons of freedom" follows on page 145. The incident is also noted in Stark, *Memoir*, and in Hiland Hall's *History of Vermont*. Stark's unsuccessful request for a $5,000 loan, which Washington denied, and the bankruptcy of the Continental Army's Northern Department are recounted in Stark's *Memoir*; Washington's secret plan for the expedition against Cornwallis in Yorktown is mentioned in an editor's note on page 212.

Chapter Thirteen: A Fake Invasion Canceled

Haldimand's domestic problems in Canada are covered in *VHS Collections* 2: 151–52. The volume also covers Sherwood's reaction to Joseph Fay's private letter to Haldimand (pages 158–9); Sherwood's critical assessment (149); and Haldimand's restriction of his communications with the Allens concerning Vermont (161–63).

Ethan and Ira Allen's secret negotiations with Frederick Haldimand and Justus Sherwood are discussed in Chilton Williamson, *Vermont in Quandary: 1763–1825* (Montpelier, Vt., 1949).

For the scuttled British invasion of Vermont in October 1781, see Ira Allen's *The Natural and Political History of the State of Vermont* and Charles Miner Thompson, *Independent Vermont*. A draft of Haldimand's proposed proclamation appears in *VHS Collections* 2: 141.

Chittenden's letter to George Washington reminding him of Vermont's sacrifices appears in Hiland Hall's *History of Vermont*, Appendix no. 10. Washington's letters to Chittenden appear in *The Writings of George Washington* 23: 419–20, as well as in *VHS Collections* 2: 228.

For an essential British overview of the loss of Vermont, see William B. Willcox, ed., *The American Rebellion: Sir Henry Clinton's Narrative of his Campaigns, 1775–1782, with an Appendix of Original Documents* (New Haven, 1954). Clinton's conclusion that "Vermont would have probably joined us" appears on page 292.

Justus Sherwood's decision to give up on Vermont and pioneer in Ontario is tracked in *VHS Collections*, vol. 2, as well as in Pemberton's "Justus Sherwood."

For Sherwood's problems convincing defeated Loyalists to settle on the Ontario frontier, see *The Province of Ontario*, Vol. 17 of *Canada and the Provinces* (Toronto, 1914).

Chapter Fourteen: A Bastard Joins the United States

Letters revealing James Madison's perspective on Vermont's future and its prospective relationship with the United States can be found in *The Papers of James Madison* (Chicago, 1973) and in *VHS Collections* 2: 242–3. "Alexander Hamilton was clearly the master-spirit in New York who brought about the settlement of the question in favor of Vermont. There was one bond of personal sympathy between the leading Vermonters and Hamilton, and that was dislike of Gov. [George] Clinton," wrote Nathaniel Chipman, a Vermont commissioner in negotiations with New York; the statement is documented in *VHS Collections* 2: 468–78n.

For more about Hamilton's perspective on Vermont's independence, see *The Works of Alexander Hamilton*, Vol. 2 (New York, 1850),
and Hiland Hall's *History of Vermont.*

See Michael Sherman, Gene Sessions, and P. Jeffrey Potash, *Freedom
and Unity: A History of Vermont* (Barre, Vt., 2004) for another perspective
on James Madison's objections. George Washington could not deliver on
his conditional promise to admit Vermont into the United States.

For negotiations on Vermont's entry as fourteenth state into the
United States, and details about the $30,000 in Spanish milled dollars
that Vermont had to pay New York claimants, see Hiland Hall's *History of Vermont*, 438–49 and Appendix no. 13 (506–11).

For Seth Warner's death in 1784 from paralysis and dementia, see
Chipman's *Memoir of Col. Seth Warner.* Other accounts include Appendix no. 1 in Hiland Hall's *History of Vermont.*

Dawson's *Battles of the United States by Sea and Land* erroneously
reported that the grateful state of Vermont "granted a valuable tract of
land" to Warner's widow and children. In fact, the rocky, swampy plot
was worthless for cultivation.

As is documented in Duffy et al., eds., *Ethan Allen and His Kin*,
Vol. 1, Ethan Allen's young new wife, Fanny Montresor, was also heiress to twenty thousand acres of Vermont land, confiscated from the
estate of her stepfather, Crean Brush.

In *Revolutionary Outlaws*, Bellesisles wrote that Ethan Allen
chose to be a Vermont patriot, rather than an American one, and "for
a decade the two were incompatible." For a persuasive refutation of
the myths surrounding Ethan Allen, see John J. Duffy and Nicholas
Muller III, *Inventing Ethan Allen* (Hanover, N.H., 2014).

Details on Crean Brush's suicide can be found in *History of Eastern Vermont* by Benjamin H. Hall, who also circulated a romantic but
highly improbable account of Ethan's courtship of Fanny.

Pemberton's "Justus Sherwood" covers Sherwood's new life in
Ontario and his death in 1798.

The information on Haldimand's regrets about his service to Britain comes from his private diary (B230), which can be found among his unpublished papers and correspondence in the British Library. After my two trips to the British Library, I retrieved this quote (page 159 of BM230) via the website of Canada's Brock University.

Ira Allen's tragic miscalculations leading to his downfall are highlighted by J. Kevin Graffagnino in his article " 'Twenty Thousand Muskets!!!': Ira Allen and the Olive Branch Affair, 1796–1800," in *The William and Mary Quarterly* 48 (July 1991): 409–31. Also see James Benjamin Wilbur, *Ira Allen.*

INDEX

Brownson, Gideon, 171, 203
Brush, Crean, 244
Bunker Hill, Battle of (1775), 33,
   116
Burgoyne, John, xii, 149, 152, 154,
   206
   American campaign and, 82,
      85–86, 87–88, 90, 92, 93–94,
      96, 97, 98, 102, 104, 105, 112–13,
      122, 123–27, 134, 136, 137, 143–
      44, 147, 163, 179, 191
   Bennington and, 134, 136, 137–
      40, 202
   Germain and, 82, 84, 85, 97,
      138–40, 147
   Jane McCrea murder and,
      117–20
   Loyalists and, 104, 117–18, 120,
      124, 125, 137–38, 145
   Native American forces and,
      117–21, 123, 125, 126, 128
   New Hampshire Grants and,
      112–13, 122, 123–27
   supply lines of, 88, 105, 122, 123,
      136, 140–41
   surrender of, 144, 146, 179
Burke, Edmund, 58, 86, 208–9
Burlington, Vt., 14
Butler, Samuel, 198

Calvinism, Calvinists, 1
Canada, xii, 16
   American Revolution and,
      14–15, 21, 27–28, 30–32, 33–53,
      61–66, 68, 72, 77, 84, 116, 122,

136, 141, 146–47, 162, 164, 165,
   169, 172, 179, 183, 187, 188–91,
   193, 195–96, 202, 206, 209, 215,
   216, 219
French and Indian War and, 3,
   22, 28, 48
Ira Allen plot on, 249–50
Loyalist exiles and, 145–46,
   229–30, 246–47
postwar period and, 225, 226–31
slavery in, 230
Washington's plan for seizure
   of, 235–36
Whitcomb's rangers and, 67–
   69, 71
Canada, Upper, 230, 236
Cape Fear, N.C., 59
Carleton, Christopher, 164–65,
   166, 174, 175, 176, 181
Carleton, Guy, 41, 42, 43, 47–49,
   50, 84–85, 164
   Germain and, 84, 147
   Lake Champlain battle and,
      71–74, 84
   Sherwood and, 76, 80
Castleton, Vt., 98, 105, 113, 126, 173
catamounts, 1–2
Catherine II "the Great,"
   Empress of Russia, 85
Chambly, Canada, 43, 63, 64, 68
Champlain, Lake, 2, 3, 7, 12, 13, 14,
   20, 21, 27, 29, 34, 48, 52, 67, 172,
   174, 175, 249
   American flotilla destroyed on,
      97, 98

ABOUT THE AUTHOR

Christopher S. Wren, foreign correspondent, reporter, and editor for *The New York Times* for nearly three decades, headed its news bureaus in Moscow, Cairo, Beijing, Ottawa, and Johannesburg. He served in the U.S. Army as a Green Beret paratrooper. He has covered conflicts in Vietnam, the Middle East, the Balkans, and Africa. Wren is a visiting professor in Dartmouth's Master of Arts in Liberal Studies Program.

A
SURVEY
OF
LAKE CHAMPLAIN,
including
LAKE GEORGE, CROWN POINT AND S.ʳ JOHN.

Surveyed by Order of

HIS EXCELLENCY MAJOR-GENERAL S.ʳ JEFFERY AMHERST,

Knight of the most Honᵇˡᵉ Order of the Bath.

Commander in Chief of His Majesty's Forces in North America,

(now LORD AMHERST)

BY

WILLIAM BRASSIER, DRAUGHTSMAN.

1762.

British Miles.

| 5 | 10 | 15 | 20 | 25 | 30 |

Places whose Latitude has been Observed.

Crown Point 43.° 50.ᵐ 7.ˢ } Vide Topog. Desc. p. 8.ᵈ
More Point   45. 0. 0.

OBSERVATIONS.

Lake Champlain to which the Dutch formerly gave the name of Corlaer, is called by the Indians Caniad eri-Guarunte signifying The Mouth or Door of the Country. It lies in a Deep Narrow Chasm of the Land, bounded up to the Waters Edge with Steep Mountains on the Western Shore, which continue thus to bound it as far as Cumberland Bay: the Ranges of the Mountains then trench off North West, and the Shore is Low, and in many parts Swampy. Many Streams, some of which at times Issue an Abundance of Waters, fall into this Lake on the West Side, but they cannot be called Rivers: they are mere Cataracts and so barred with Rocks and Sand there is no entrance to them.

The Eastern Shores are formed by a Low Swampy Tract of Land: the Mountains keep off at the distance of about 12 Miles. There are some Considerable Streams which fall into the Lake on this Side. Otter Creek is the Largest. The Soundings of the Lake are very deep in general; in many Places 60, 70 and 80, and in some parts 100 Fathoms.

* Vide Topographical Description
by Govᵣ. Pownall. p. 18.